Kevin McAleer - **ERROL FLYNN**

Kevin McAleer

ERROL FLYNN
AN EPIC LIFE

Palm**Art**Press
Berlin

Bibliografische Information der Deutschen Nationalbibliothek
Die Deutsche Nationalbibliothek verzeichnet diese Publikation in der Deutschen
Nationalbibliografie; detaillierte bibliografische Daten sind
im Internet über http://www.dnb.de abrufbar.

ISBN: 978-3-96258-005-6

© PalmArtPress
Publisher: Catharine J. Nicely
Pfalzburger Str. 69
10719 Berlin, Germany

www.palmartpress.com

Printed in Germany

This book is dedicated to

Britta Gansebohm

and to the memory of

Chris Moore

TABLE OF CONTENTS

FOREWORD

Kevin McAleer, already an accomplished novelist and chronicler of life in and around two great cities, his native Los Angeles and his adopted home of Berlin, has lit upon the magnificent idea of telling in humorous verse the story of the most Byronic figure in the pantheon of Hollywood movie stars—and not just any verse but Lord Byron's own chosen form, the exacting *ottava rima* stanza. How Errol Flynn himself would have delighted in it: the starring role in a verse epic, of course, but more than this, the *mock*-epic effect of giving the status of a true classic hero to the faux hero, the screen hero, that he was. It would so have appealed to Flynn's sense of humor: the wry title of his autobiography *My Wicked, Wicked Ways* says it all. He was certainly more a byword—a catchword, indeed, bequeathing the world the phrase "in like Flynn"—for seduction than acting chops. You could say he was a make-believe Byron (who himself was largely make-believe) but McAleer gives us the genuine substance of the man. Flynn's sailing adventures and his courage and physical prowess were real; famously, he did most all his own film stunts. Like many of his movie star contemporaries, the John Waynes, Robert Mitchums and James Stewarts, Flynn was not a swashbuckler only on the screen. The fakery of the movies spurred them on to prove their manhood by taking real risks. Sadly, Flynn's son Sean both inherited and observed this, and it led to his tragic death as a war photographer in Vietnam.

Flynn certainly burned the candle at both ends, drank hard and partied hard in true Hollywood style, womanized relentlessly, became a caricature of himself, knew heartbreak, and died young: a subject fit not only for a droll satirical kind of epic but a subject fit for empathy and re-consideration. I find it hard to overestimate the cunning of McAleer's decision to give Flynn a Byronic costume, not only in the charisma Flynn shared with his Lordship but in Byron's own verse panache. McAleer's wit and verbal deftness are the vessel on which his glorious project is launched and they swell the sails of his splendid, hilarious and touching book. It's a heartfelt tribute not only to Flynn but to Byron himself and all the fearless ones who have seized the stage of life and demanded the spotlight.

My own earliest days were spent in Hollywood as a child of its golden age. My parents Rex Harrison and Lilli Palmer, both of them movie stars, gave me a glimpse of the glamorous figures whose flame, like Flynn's, burned all too hot and brief: Tyrone Power, who wherever he went would sing, "Enjoy yourself, enjoy yourself, it's later than you think"— all too prophetically alas—and who drove me round the English lanes in his sportscar one memorable afternoon; Gary Cooper, with whom as a young boy I flew the English Channel—it was a commercial flight, but rendered indelible by sitting next to him, courtesy of Coop's affection for my mother. Other titans of the silver screen patted me fondly on the head, long before I could understand what their very presence meant to filmgoers across the globe

I grew up awed by them but also content to live a less clamorous life; I fled, aged eleven, into scribbling my first novel, and have only ever peeped out from that dear jungle to watch my parents' successors and Flynn's, too, in admiration. What a fine and deserving subject for a loving ballad Flynn is! Happily, he has found in Kevin McAleer the perfect bard to immortalize his Homeric daring, his women and his woes, McAleer whose erudition is a consummate match for his own Angeleno roots (his novel *Surferboy* is greatly to be recommended) and constituting ideal equipment for the heroic comedy of his subject's life. Here is the essence of Hollywood: the aspirations, the endless romantic opportunities, the pitfalls, the pratfalls and redemptions, and the surprising smarts belonging to so many of the seeming clotheshorses of the movies. Many were brilliant in their own right—musicians, writers, art collectors—as we often learn only after their death. In *Errol Flynn: An Epic Life* they bestride the stage again. And we too, we are all in McAleer's book—we the audience who made and continue to make Hollywood what it is, a platform for giant shadows, supernatural figures—men born of women, just like us, yet projecting themselves as the forces of nature we all long to be. Flynn lived our dreams, and it is superbly fitting that his enterprise should be sung and given enduring voice in McAleer's adept and witty verse.

Carey Harrison

PREFACE

Taking Byron's *Don Juan* stanza and using it to tell Errol Flynn's story seemed a natural. The *ottava rima* has a long mock-epic history, starting with Boccaccio, and seemed to lend itself to Flynn, whose life alternated high-romantic episodes with those of a more fatuous nature—"fatuous" the term Flynn himself used in describing his own quite conscious approach to living. In the early stages of *Don Juan*, Byron wrote his publisher John Murray: "You are too earnest and eager about a work never intended to be serious. Do you suppose that I could have any intention but to giggle and make giggle?—a playful satire, with as little poetry as could be helped, was what I meant." Moreover the racy content, waggish style, sardonic attitude, narrative vigor and unsparing candor of Flynn's autobiography *My Wicked, Wicked Ways* are strikingly similar to Byron's masterpiece; and since Flynn was not just the embodiment of Byronic romanticism but one of the twentieth century's great Don Juans, having played the role to ironic and world-weary perfection in a Hollywood film, it seemed only fitting to use Byron's rollicking *ottava rima* stanza to recount the life of this sexual buccaneer.

Flynn himself admired Byron's verse, and to mention a number of their shared traits: there was the aristocratic insouciance, the capriciousness, restlessness, self-imposed exile from their respective homelands, lavish way of life, their dandyism, haughty tempers, startling physical beauty, brooding and rebellious natures, philosophical skepticism and atheism, their countless women (at whose hands they were not infrequent victims), their preference for boyish-figured females, the antipathy toward their mothers, their fear of domesticity, their love of male companionship, their view of themselves as both insiders and outsiders, their comfort in all strata of society and particularly with those persons on its margins, their love of conversation and laughter, their infectious gaiety, their affinity to water and skill as swimmers, their competence as boxers, their keeping of menageries, their cultivation of an "image," their impatience with sentimentality and cant, their dread of boredom, their taste for the exotic, their chronic indebtedness, and not least their rare charm and artistic talent.

Another shared trait was their self-styled wickedness. One could apply Samuel Taylor Coleridge's remark about Byron to Flynn—that he was someone who "from morbid and restless vanity, pretended to be ten times more wicked than he was." In fact both could be not only kindly men but were fervent champions of the underdog. Upon Flynn's return to the United States from Cuba in 1959, after having been with Castro's insurgents when they took Havana, Errol's amanuensis, Earl Conrad, who understood Flynn as well as anyone, greeted him by extending a hand and saying, "Lord Byron," as if he were George Gordon back from Greece, and Flynn's face "blossomed into a wide smile."

Early on I noticed that whenever I mentioned that certain preoccupation of mine—Errol Flynn—people would smile, and not in a gratuitous or indulgent way—they'd give you a real smile, filled with fondness and an almost childlike joy. Yes, as a matter of fact, they would "blossom" into a smile. Try that with whatever other actors from Hollywood's golden era and you may get all kinds of reactions, ranging from mock-swooning to fawning-reverential, but you won't consistently be gifted with that bright smile.

This is a work intended for those who smile, inwardly or outwardly, when the name Errol Flynn is mentioned—meaning practically everyone.

NOTE TO READERS

I have added extensive endnotes to flesh out various matters broached in the poem but would recommend that you keep from reading most of these notes until having finished the work as a whole, i.e. reading them selectively, so as not to halt the flow of the stanzas, the notes being of a more scholarly nature, thus not so much supplementary as parallel to Flynn's story as related in the poem, which is largely of a piece.

There's only one slight difference between
Me and my epic brethren gone before,
And here the advantage is my own, I ween;
(Not that I have not several merits more,
But this will more peculiarly be seen)
They so embellish, that 'tis quite a bore
Their labyrinth of fables to thread through,
Whereas this story's actually true.

Don Juan, canto I, stanza 202

BOOK ONE

TASMANIAN DEVIL

CANTO I

Boss Boy, Carry On!

(1909-1929)

. . . Tall, handsome, slender, but well knit; he seem'd
Active, though not so sprightly as a page;
And every body but his mother deem'd
Him almost man; but she flew in a rage,
And bit her lips (for else she might have scream'd),
If any said so, for to be precocious
Was in her eyes a thing the most atrocious.

Don Juan, canto I, stanza 54

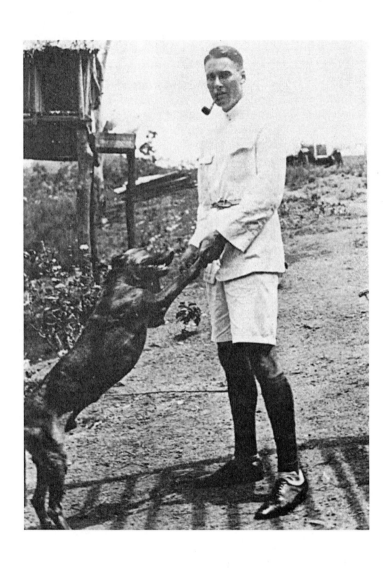

Errol Flynn as a Cadet Patrol Officer in New Guinea, 1927

CANTO I

1   They said he was Irish and it's quite true
That his dad's parents hailed from Erin;
And yet Errol Leslie Thomson Flynn, to
Give his full name (later nicknamed "The Baron")
Came from the land of the didgeridoo,
Which is why he was ready and rarin',
Irreverent, jocular, tough and saucy,
Since that's your birthright when born an Aussie.

2   O Tasmania! That land so striking!
Of lush rainforests yet temperate climate,
Rugged coastlines that make for great hiking,
This or that peak which bids you to climb it,
And other things that'd be to your liking;
And though I've not been to this land sublime, it
Is not fear of flying or that I'm frugal,
It's just much simpler going online with Google.

3   Born was our wee Tasmanian hellion
To a descendant of Midshipman Young,
Part of the ill-famed *Bounty* rebellion,
In the Flynn household a sword being hung,
Looted from Bligh by this middy rapscallion,
Serving now as a memento to gung
Ho times—and so it's no wonder that Errol
Had a pronounced taste for mayhem and peril.

4   A zesty beauty was Marelle Flynn née
Young, with a flair for the histrionic,
She loved song and dance and at a soirée
Her mirth was infectious as the plague bubonic;
A woman whose charms are never passé,
She might have sprung from a poem Byronic,
This lovely and fetching belle of the ball,
Like Scarlett O'Hara with an Aussie drawl.

21

ERROL FLYNN

5   But Errol, for his part, found her much less
Winsome than stern, more harsh than amusing;
And once when caught peeking up a girl's dress,
He got a verbal and physical bruising
From Marelle which caused him so much distress
That in his mind it spawned a confusing
Of Mom with the visual yield of his stunt,
He later in life calling her "The Cunt."

6   Quite a byname to assign your madre,
But it's the indelicate truth, I fear,
And making things all that much more tawdry,
Errol would say it *avec plaisir,*
Flat out enjoying this shocking bawdry.
Though Marelle was kin to a mutineer,
Her touted lineage could never belie
The fact that for Flynn *she* was Captain Bligh.

7   But while his highly strung mother he spurned,
Flynn's learned dad was an inspiration.
The man's taxonomic powers discerned
Myriad forms of fish and cetacean,
In point of fact leaving no stone unturned
In search of all manner of rare crustacean,
This prof of marine biology
From whom Errol gleaned his ecology.

8   Flynn junior would often accompany
His father to probe aqua incognita,
At age of five once hauling from the sea
An arthropod of the class Pycnogonida,
Which, showing Dad, he pronounced flawlessly
(Nearly as tough as *Bhagavadgita*)
And in later years Theo Flynn would insist
His boy had the stuff of a fine scientist.

9   So too thought Errol—he'd shrewdly observed
     When ducks consumed pieces of fatty meat
     It wasn't long in their stomachs preserved
     'Fore making a rearward exit *tout de suite,*
     So on them he played a trick undeserved,
     String tied to some pork he had a duck eat
     It and reprised this act seriatim
     Until achieving his desideratum

10   Of half a dozen quacking malcontents
     Linked bill-to-tail on the length of greased string,
     Something you'd witness beneath circus tents,
     Which got our youthful prankster to thinking:
     You know, a smart chap could make a few pence.
     So our little Tasmanian Ringling
     Sold tickets so that his playmates could gape
     At his quite naughty if ingenious jape.

11   In fairness to Mom, Errol was a handful;
     Added to that, Dad was often away
     Researching and teaching, his own life cram-full
     Of tasks and acceding the day-to-day
     Care of their son to Marelle, she manful
     In exercising that good old mainstay
     Of stamping a lesson on a boy's mind
     By leaving him with a blistered behind.

12   One wonders just how this mother-son battle
     Shaped Errol's view of the opposite sex.
     It can't be that it played no role at all,
     And leastwise one very strongly suspects
     It later made Errol quick to skedaddle
     From all females who might unduly vex—
     But on the other hand, I'm like that too
     And don't think of Mother as some strident shrew.

ERROL FLYNN

13   If I'd a mom, though, who got on my case
At drop of a hat and threw nasty fits,
Making me feel like a lousy disgrace
Owing solely to my animal spirits,
I would resent this and pick up the pace
Of my misconduct to give her more nits
To pick—and then if she opted to spank,
I too might call her a blankety-blank.

14   And since it would seem that Errol also
Suffered a degree of benign neglect
At hands of not only father Theo
(Pursuing his life of the intellect)
But Mom (when the two weren't going toe to toe)
It would be reasonable to expect
That Errol should seek to get their attention
If only by earning dishonorable mention.

15   Because at these times it was Marelle who
Was always the first one to come unglued
Whereas Theodore was more inclined to
Turn a blind eye to his son's turpitude,
Assuming a more equanimous view,
In the long run I can only conclude
That for the two there was no R&R
Because they were so very similar.

16   Not only her essential character
—Cheeky, headstrong, animated, carefree—
But her main interests would be a factor
In Errol's progress, who by age of three
Was swimming and then of course the impact her
Theatrical gift had (this not to be
Confused with her gift for *theatrics*) and sharing
With Errol her signal love of seafaring.

17   To convey this passion his mother told
      Errol of Midshipman Young, and she made
      Sometime allusion to those other bold
      Forebears who'd engaged in the human trade
      Of "blackbirding" in which natives were sold
      To Queensland sugar plantations where they'd
      Be subject to very unsavory
      Conditions that smacked of chattel slavery.

18   And she was daughter of a sea captain
      Who but of course had some yarns of his own
      About stirring deeds of staunch sailormen
      Whom Errol's fancy would nobly enthrone
      As heirs to such mariners as Magellan
      And Sir Francis Drake and Ponce de Leon—
      All part of a mother-son symbiosis
      Where love-hate found its apotheosis.

19   Theodore's career was going places now,
      It soon developing that one of these
      Places was England—and so bidding ciao
      To his beloved Antipodes
      (Both his home soil and diametric frau)
      He took his boy with him on the high seas
      Along with five duck-billed platypuses
      For scientific research purposes.

20   They'd never seen such critters in England,
      Platypuses being quite timorous,
      Also confined to their Aussie homeland,
      And hardly what you'd call omnivorous,
      So needed to be fed a special brand
      Of grub were they to remain vigorous
      On the forty-day steamer voyage that
      Took them far from their natural habitat.

21   "Special" was the food but not exactly
Beef wellington or lobster thermidor
(Or even canned noodles by Chef Boyardee);
Instead Errol's sensible dad Theodore
Purveyed the Lutheran delicacy,
Which platypuses would seem to adore
(But at which mere thought my poor stomach squirms)
He serving the creatures a diet of worms.

22   Young Flynn shared my view, and so making port
In Durban, South Africa, he sought fare
That promised to be of a tastier sort,
Finding some tadpoles he managed to snare
And in a can to the steamer transport,
Feeding the duck-bills this tidbit so rare,
For once not some kind of mischievous prank,
But two were soon floating feet up in the tank.

23   Professor Flynn had a panic attack,
Errol now gauging the situation:
He knew that it would be rash to hold back
The awkward polliwog information
Because his father would *really* blow his stack
When he cut up the beasts and speculation
Gave way to evidence that his own son
Was more than likely the culpable one.

24   When Washington chopped down the cherry tree,
His father asking him who had done it,
George answered truthfully it had been he.
Errol's confession, though, wasn't to profit
A precocious sense of integrity,
Or in abiding by some moral tenet,
Or just because a lie was mendacious,
But since it wouldn't have been efficacious.

25   Theo was not at all pleased, but still no
     Whipping ensued (that was Marelle's department),
     The other duck-bills surviving the slow
     Boat to England in the baggage compartment
     And British savants exclaiming: "Good show!"
     Mother then came and Flynn had to depart, sent
     Off to a very elite boarding school
     Located somewhere outside of Kabul.

26   Not really—though it might have been for all
     He'd see of his parents in the next two years;
     The school was in England but gone AWOL
     Was Marelle to Paris, where it appears
     She didn't exactly don a prayer shawl
     But kicked up her heels while shedding no tears
     That her own marriage was (briefly) asunder,
     Theo returning to the Land Down Under.

27   Flynn's school was bad but school breaks were the worst
     As classmates all left for their homes en masse
     And Errol left stranded in this accursed
     Exile from mater and paterfamilias,
     His heart becoming now very well-versed
     In the sore burdens of loneness, alas,
     For even if Paris wasn't remote,
     Mom seemed to always be missing the boat.

28   These were the years that helped make Errol tough.
     On first arriving at the English school
     He'd proven he wasn't some piece of fluff
     By answering other boys' ridicule
     Of his accent with some pretty rough stuff
     That served as a very effective gag rule
     By showing that if you stepped on his toes
     He'd make you pay with a bloody nose.

ERROL FLYNN

29   Flynn was two years in this prep school limbo,
Away from home and the Hobart sea breeze:
Envision him now, his long arms akimbo,
In defiant pose, as brash as you please,
No easy mark, no pushover him, bo',
This scrappy "cobber" who scoffed at high teas,
And if you think my words have a false ring
Then step right on up and take your best swing!

30   Flynn was also fond of playing hooky—
So was expelled from this institution,
And so his parents to a new one took he
(Please forgive me the rhymster locution,
But thus crumbles the poetic cookie)
Flynn, though, resisting any diminution
Of his aversion to authority
And views of the moral majority,

31   For with his impulse to run through the world,
He couldn't be bothered by things like "rules,"
Which only stymied a life unfurled,
Were only adhered to by witless fools,
Not by guys in whom the life-force swirled,
With appetites equal to Pantagruel's,
Meaning Flynn bit off more than he could chew
And so was expelled from this second place too.

32   Errol was shipped back to Australia
To be enrolled in another swank school
Where he styled his old English regalia,
Hardly disposed his wardrobe to retool,
Being *now* smitten by Anglophilia,
Sporting striped pants and a black coat and cruel
Eton collar and a smug attitude
Toward boys showing scholarly aptitude.

33   Errol was first and foremost an athlete,
     Being quite good at a number of sports,
     Rarely if ever sustaining defeat
     With racket in hand on the tennis courts,
     And as a boxer he was no deadbeat,
     Sparring with hardnosed Australian cohorts—
     But after a year he was sent on his way,
     Another black eye to his résumé.

34   Even his athletic exploits could not
     Save Errol from his pronounced love of pranks,
     Great fun at the time but which only got
     Him shunted from the honored schoolboy ranks—
     This last lark ("last" since finally he was *caught*)
     Was ice cream dropped on the heads of staid wanks
     At an official Hobart High School function
     And the headmaster, with no compunction,

35   Banishing him from the gala event.
     Errol refused, though, to just sit and pout,
     Now seeking reprisal against this gent
     And opportunity to further flout
     Decorum and give his deviltry vent
     By that same evening then venturing out
     To vandalize the man's automobile,
     Smearing jam on its seats and the steering wheel.

36   Next stop was Sydney where Flynn was enrolled
     In another top school on the basis
     Of Theo's good name, worth its weight in gold—
     And once more it was off to the races!
     With Flynn you weren't going to break the mold!
     He falling from *this* academy's graces
     By having been caught in a state of undress,
     Aptly, with daughter of the school's laundress.

37   But there was a gold rush in New Guinea—
That's where he'd go—to strike it rich!
Escaping his present ignominy
While scratching that stubborn wanderlust itch
Which had been born of one tale too many,
Courtesy of mom, that yarn-spinning bitch!
This was one place, though, she wouldn't follow
Her restive, contentious and self-willed Apollo.

38   In 1545, New Guinea's name
Was spawned when the Spaniard Yñigo Ortiz
De Retez happened upon the selfsame
Island and, he having sailed the Seven Seas,
Saw some resemblance between the untame
Natives of this place (they were devotees
Of headhunting and cannibalism
And the religion of animism)

39   And those on the west coast of Africa;
Which was like someone, say, from New Guinea
Reaching Virginia and then Corsica
And dubbing this latter place "New Virginny,"
The folks there the same white exotica—
And wouldn't we then all brand him a ninny?
Yñigo Ortiz was the same kind of schmuck,
But the name he'd christened the island with stuck.

40   Let's jump ahead to 1828
—No need for a lengthy chronology—
When Holland the isle did first penetrate,
Which caused (now a tricky tropology:)
European nations to salivate
And grab a piece of the pie, sans apology,
All making to get their share of dessert in
Selflessly bearing the White Man's Burden.

41   In 1905, Great Britain transferred
Rule of its New Guinea territory
To her Australian cousins who secured
German-held parts through spoliatory
Action in World War I, administered
Them after within the category
Of an official League of Nations mandate
And ousted Japan when it tried to infiltrate.

42   In the years following World War II,
The state of Australia still continued
To govern by dint of the tried and true
Mandate system but this term now eschewed
For one untainted and brand spanking new,
Which it was hoped wouldn't be construed
As sequel to the colonial whip—
It ruling New Guinea as a "trusteeship."

43   And seeing as we've taken things this far,
Let us not now our recital disband:
The Australians finally said *au revoir*
To their own eastern half of the island
In 1975 (Dutch power
Having been relinquished upon demand
In the western half some years earlier
As grabby Indonesia grew surlier),

44   Granting self-rule to what they now call
Papua New Guinea, which didn't kill
Off all the adjunct royal folderol,
Retaining the queen of their own free will!
Though not so really bizarre after all,
Since that land from which Papua split still
Had and still *has* Queen Liz as monarch—
Which calls for another exclamation mark!

45   What else on New Guinea that you should know?
Here are more facts for your edification,
Then we'll be getting right on with the show:
As for the fauna and vegetation,
It commands an abundant overflow,
With such biodiversification
That it can give you the heebie-jeebies—
Witness 200 thousand insect species.

46   And its landscape is equally diverse,
With craggy mountains and rainforests dense
And swampland and glaciers (that were the curse
Of British explorers who lacked all sense,
Trying this rugged terrain to traverse)
And still to this day, as a consequence,
The infrastructure falls terribly short,
With planes often being the sole transport.

47   This primitive setting also plays host
To numerous active volcanoes and
Of quakes and tsunamis it too can boast,
And so pretty much of a no man's land
—At best a glorified trading post—
Which Errol came to discover firsthand
When he arrived in 1927
To try his luck in this freebooter's heaven.

48   On the ship over Flynn hadn't been idle,
Befriending one of the passengers who
Was able to help our hero sidle
Into an appointment, quite impromptu,
As a Cadet Patrol Officer—a title
That had cachet for a young buckaroo
Fresh off the boat and a high-school dropout,
Lacking in means but also lacking self-doubt.

49   Flynn met the Government Secretary
Who asked if Errol knew sanitation
(Alleviating unsalutary
Conditions of the native population
Was—with their duties constabulary—
Intrinsic to a Cadet's vocation)
Errol replying: "Why of course everything!"
And moments later he was in full swing.

50   Errol declaimed his infinite knowledge
Of water and tropic bacteria,
—As if he'd studied the stuff in college
With a stint of fieldwork in Nigeria—
Disgorging all he'd been able to dredge
From his father's books (it'd surely weary ya
To list it all here) and got the position
Based on this erudite disquisition.

51   Flynn's principal job was to roam around
With native escort and eradicate
Conditions that formed a disease breeding ground
While also attempting to educate
Backward locals in the basics of sound
Health and hygiene—having to remonstrate
That pigs shouldn't live right under their huts
And help them make soap from their coconuts.

52   Picture Flynn now all accoutered in white,
With natty cane and in suave pith helmet,
Tall and official, his carriage upright
While scouting the village, this dapper Cadet,
Aiding those primitives to see the light,
His handsome visage and fine silhouette
Leaving no doubt a very long-lasting
Impression that's straight out of Central Casting.

53 He *looked* the part, which Flynn would discover
  Was half the battle in playing a role,
  Both in his life and as a big-screen lover,
  For Plato was right: each man in his soul
  Loves the ideal—our gaze seeks to hover
  About someone graced with an aureole,
  Somebody who can incarnate our dreams,
  Even if he is not all that he seems.

54 This certain role was of short duration,
  Cadets being District Officers in training
  And their appointment a career way-station
  To emerging one of the isle's reigning
  Commissioners—and so qualification
  For a young man with hopes of obtaining
  The cherished post of nascent magistrate
  Was having your high school diploma, mate.

55 Flynn knew his post as Cadet would be brief,
  It also pending the verification
  Of his school record, a record which we've
  Noted was rife with insubordination—
  Not helped by the fact that his bid to deceive
  Showed a great lack of appreciation
  For the Government Secretary who
  Was sure to be grieved by Flynn's dipsy-doo.

56 Errol Flynn saw the writing on the wall,
  So made the most of his limited time,
  Wowing the locals with his Australian crawl
  In swimming meets and displaying sublime
  Technique in swatting that fuzzy white ball
  In tournaments (careful not to begrime
  Those spruce tennis whites!) as well as to make
  Friends he could use when exposed as a fake.

57   When the Cadets finally gave him the boot,
Flynn's dream of gold had been long put aside—
To the goldfields was a perilous route,
Certain native tribes not yet pacified,
And you required plenty tackle and loot
And couldn't just waltz in all starry-eyed,
For although tales of strikes proliferated,
They'd also been greatly exaggerated.

58   One day a visit to a bar Flynn paid
And met a guy with a copra plantation.
"Know much about copra?" the man essayed,
Errol replying in indignation:
"Do I know copra? It's my stock-in-trade!
Was raised on the stuff! What an imputation!"
He carried on yakking for some time more—
When it came to coconuts *he* knew the score!

59   As for his government office, why hell,
He'd left that, resigned, he couldn't handle
Their brutalization of the natives: "I tell
You, old sport, it was an all-fired scandal!
So for Christian reasons I bid farewell,
The game was simply not worth the candle."[1]
This struck a chord with the copra nabob
Who offered compassionate Errol a job.

60   Flynn grabbed his hand and informed the tycoon
He had him a first-rate copra man and
—Though quite some ways from this stellar saloon—
He'd do him the favor of taking command
Of his plantation and native platoon;
And thus having very nicely deadpanned
His way to the post, Errol made posthaste
To the town library, no time to waste.

ERROL FLYNN

61   But it yielded scant information
     (Except how to crack open coconuts)
     On how to run a copra plantation.
     Flynn was now frantic and felt like a putz
     For getting into this situation,
     So to a friend he then spilled his guts,
     A Briton by the name of Basil Hoare
     Who'd been a naval captain in the war.

62   Hoare now skippered a schooner sailing with
     A New Guinea crew. "Nothing to it, just grab
     The Boss Boy," he said with his wonted pith,
     Very buttoned-down, didn't like to blab,
     That British reticence being no myth,
     In contrast to Flynn with his gift of gab,
     Who asked if he might not elaborate
     On what the term "Boss Boy" should designate.

63   "Every plantation," Basil did explain,
     "Has a Boss Boy with greater knowledge of
     Copra than you'll ever hope to obtain.
     Just tell the Boss Boy, when push comes to shove:
     Boss Boy carry on!—while sure to sustain
     The strong impression that you, as his guv,
     Have a firm hand on that ol' masterswitch,
     And the plantation'll run without a hitch."

64   Errol took ship for New Ireland and Kavieng,[2]
     From there made a one-day journey to
     The copra plantation with its work gang,
     Bunking in a cabin with ocean view
     And full of old mildewed books—Errol sprang
     Upon these volumes, a dream come true,
     Now able to while away the lonely hour
     In his little beachfront ivory tower.

65   Flynn called the Boss Boy and told him to haul
      The work crew up for general inspection,
      The Boss Boy confiding to Flynn that all
      His natives were a bristly collection
      Of tough kanakas he hoped wouldn't maul
      Each other to death, a broad cross-section
      Of two rival tribes and sworn enemies
      Not vaunted to observe the niceties.

66   They gathered before Errol's bungalow
      In all their loin-clothed muscularity—
      But "noble" savages à la Rousseau?
      Kind gentle souls 'neath the barbarity?
      Harmless back-to-nature types like Thoreau?
      The sole thing that Flynn knew with any clarity
      Was he was sole white man for fifty miles
      And these natives likely not Anglophiles.

67   In surveying them he calmed the panic
      That seized him by leaning nonchalantly
      On his walking stick—oh so Britannic!—
      And after chitchatting insouciantly
      With the Boss Boy, he gripped his talismanic
      Cane and again scrutizined these scantily
      Clad fellows, breathed in deeply, and with élan
      Pronounced that magic phrase: "Boss Boy—*carry on*!"

68   The Boss Boy gave orders to the whole crew,
      Which then marched off in every direction—
      And each morning this scene played out anew,
      The workforce flocking for its inspection,
      And following Errol's swaggering review,
      Walking stick in hand, he'd bark to perfection:
      "All right, Boss Boy, carry on!"—and then
      Go swimming—and next day do it again.

ERROL FLYNN

69   Flynn swam and the coconuts multiplied;
Then later he began venturing out
With trusty cane that rarely left his side
And pistol on hip as he strutted about,
Now and then making appearance astride
His horse in order to leave little doubt
As to in fact who was running the show
And calling the shots *ex officio.*

70   But carry on, Boss Boy. Apart from the odd
Armed intervention to break up the fights
Among his work crew, a one-man riot squad,
And apply first-aid, Errol spent his nights
With those mildewed books on the shelf and gnawed
On German syntax and savored the delights
Of the French subjunctive—all this the reading
Matter with which the young Flynn was feeding

71   His sudden hunger for the written word.
Along with the books there were German and French
Dictionaries, which was not his preferred
Way to learn languages; still he could drench
Himself in prose with his gray matter stirred
By lust for learning and desire to wrench
From books all the knowledge he'd scorned in school
And prove to *himself* he was nobody's fool.

72   But while ingesting this literary lore,
Errol was feeling the lure of the sea—
Becoming restless, he craved a bit more
Freedom of movement; and so because he
Still had the Boss Boy minding the store,
Flynn thought that fish-dynamiting would be
His ticket, he informing the government
His workers were needing a food supplement,

73   Since they were laid up with beriberi—
      This of course a complete fabrication,
      True reason being that he wished to ferry
      Copra from all the outlying plantation
      Isles to the New Guinea center (very
      Gainful this trade) and the operation
      Needed a schooner that Flynn wished to buy
      Jointly with another Australian guy.

74   To come into possession of it, though,
      And cover his portion of the expense,
      He needed money and to get the dough
      He needed fish and for fish a license,
      Which he finagled through his tale of woe
      And via assistance of well-placed friends—
      Then Errol, this hurdle nicely overcome,
      Started blowing marine life to kingdom come.

75   But there was a rival challenger who
      Was muscling in on Flynn's action—a shark
      Responding to all of the blasts as if you
      Had just rung the dinner bell—and this Monarch
      Of the Food Chain, this Blackguard of the Blue,
      Was targeting Flynn as an easy mark;
      So Errol consulted a local fisherman
      Who pledged to shorten the glutton's lifespan.

76   He showed Errol how to take a live fish
      And fasten it to a dynamite stick
      With extra-long fuse, a succulent dish
      For our greedy fiend—it splashed like a brick
      When Flynn tossed the thing, the shark not sluggish
      In gulping a charge to kill Moby Dick,
      But taking scant notice and keeping right on
      Scooping up fish, not at all put upon.

ERROL FLYNN

77   Then his pace altered—he made a quick spurt—
The fuse in the innards of this marauder
Searing his guts and beginning to hurt.
Errol could trace his course through the water
By smoke that escaped from his mouth . . . red alert!
Things are now getting quite a bit hotter,
The trail of smoke heading right Errol's way,
A threatening Vesuvius to his Pompeii.

78   Owing to the extra-long fuse, the beast
Had infinite leisure to lollygag,
Adding more fish to his moveable feast,
An abundance of time to zig and zag
(But getting bad heartburn to say the least)
Then just as if it were a slapstick gag
(Though I doubt highly that anyone laughed)
He swam 'neath the boat and blew a hole in the craft.

79   If that weren't enough, then all of the other
Sharks in the neighborhood, smelling the blood,
Made for the boat to devour big brother,
And ate him up fast, this explosive stud
(Even descending upon one another—
In shark feeding frenzies, no one's your bud),
Flynn doubly ruing this choice of venue
Since he's the next item on the menu . . .

80   And right here the anecdote pulls up short,
Errol Flynn's memoir discloses no more.
Did the boat founder or limp back to port?
He captain her in or swim fast for shore?
And if this latter then how did he thwart
Those ravenous sharks? Our hero forbore
To give an ending, just making a joke
How after the brigand went up in smoke,

81   Whenever Flynn fished then *he* was the sole
Shark to gobble the profits—which can make
You wonder, because it's so slick, if the whole
Story is true or an outlandish fake.
To keep embellishments under control
Was sometimes for Errol no piece of cake
Whenever his tales to New Guinea trekked,
A land where his fancy could rove unchecked.

82   It is no accident that all those years spent
Out in New Guinea form a major chunk
Of Errol's memoir and serve as content
For his two novels;[3] some of *Wicked* is bunk—
Though not a whole lot, maybe five percent,
And if you're not some eremitic monk,
How many people can say that nineteen
Of twenty statements they make are pristine?

83   Errol Flynn's stories are suspiciously smooth;
But when author John Hammond Moore went out
To New Guinea years later to gain the truth
And speak with old-timers and traipse about
Exploring Errol's itinerant youth,
He found that those stories which one might doubt—
The "fishier" of these tales—indeed were
Grounded in facts and no gross imposture.

84   Moore discovered that most of the events
In Errol's autobiography were
No unalloyed lies but true in the sense
That they'd either happened to our raconteur,
Or absent the hard and fast evidence,
To someone he knew; if not simon-pure,
And often with magnifications rife,
Flynn's tales were the product of real lived life.

85   Be that as it may, let's dawdle no more:
      Errol's alleged fish-dynamiting spree
      Earned enough cash to help buy that longed-for
      Boat with his friend, which they dubbed the *Maski*
      And in Papuan translates "Screw it" or
      "Screw you" if displeased with your addressee—
      So, still neglecting the copra plantation,
      Errol undertook the crop's transportation.

86   They plied the north coast in search of business;
      Planters weren't selling, though, because the price
      Of copra was low, so to make a success
      Of their venture (or to be more precise,
      So the financiers wouldn't repossess
      Their boat) they opted for live merchandise—
      Passengers—and with the finance company
      Acting as agents and handling the money.

87   It was one thing to sail along the coast,
      Leaving your kanakas to handle this,
      That and the other, but Flynn couldn't boast
      Navigation skills; it would be hit-and-miss,
      So much was certain, were Errol to host
      An open-sea cruise; but he could then kiss
      The *Maski* goodbye if he didn't, for now
      He needed to exhibit this very know-how.

88   They lined up some passengers to Rabaul,[4]
      Flynn rushing off to Kavieng with his ship
      And native crew, not throwing in the towel
      In spite of the fact that this certain trip
      Caused our colt skipper to inwardly howl:
      Soon as he took the schooner from its slip,
      He'd be unmoored in a twofold sense,
      Trusting solely to luck and to Providence.

89   Pray tell, how from point to point does one steer
On the wide ocean? How to sail at night
From port to port? And how to keep clear
Of treacherous uncharted reefs that might
Rip out your hull from the front to the rear?
Baffled and with no assuagement in sight,
Flynn ran for help to that same Basil Hoare
Who had advised him so sagely before.

90   Errol explained his vexing conundrum,
Asking of Basil just what he should do,
And Hoare admonished him not to be glum
But just employ their old method anew,
"Though don't go and summon the Boss Boy, chum,
This time call the bosun, he'll see you through—
Say: *Bosun carry on!*" But since Hoare knew ships,
Flynn asked if he hadn't some *technical* tips.

91   Basil Hoare banished the thought—navigation
Wasn't learned overnight—just the bosun call
And stow any needless cogitation!
Flynn had his doubts, but Kavieng to Rabaul
Required no tremendous demonstration
Of seamanship (not some long drawn-out haul);
So taking on board a family of five,
He crossed his fingers that they'd safely arrive.

92   He stood near the helm, a few feet away
From the bosun, stretched out his arm, the palm
Of his hand poised knife-like, pointing the way
Across the sea, Flynn the picture of calm,
Like he did this sort of thing every day,
And then commanded, with no evident qualm:
"Carry on bosun!"—then the ship's sails stirred
While Errol kept trying to look self-assured.

ERROL FLYNN

93   Trips to Rabaul as a rule took ten days;
However, they drifted about for fourteen,[5]
All things considered pretty fast, leastways
Seeing as the bosun was just as green
As Flynn and that there were further delays
Due to the gales, causing them to careen
Like sailors three sheets to the wind on shore leave,
Though shore seemed something they'd never achieve.

94   As the crew idled, soaking up the clime,
Scrubbing down the deck with their coconut
Husks and otherwise just killing time
Trolling for fish, the husband was all but
Fit to be tied—"A despicable crime!"
He snarled at Flynn. "An outrage, a clearcut
Instance of imperiling lives! And when
We get to Rabaul you'll be thrown in the pen!"

95   On making Rabaul the husband went straight
To higher-ups to report this barge as
Captained by a fake. Errol fails to state
In *Wicked* how he weathered the charges
Proffered against him by his human freight;
But it would seem that the brass showed largesse,
Since Flynn—though still shaky in navigation—
Soon had the *Maski* back in operation.

96   But then he was fired from his copra job
(Boss Boy or no, he'd been too long away)
So Flynn placed on hold his life as a gob
Selling his share of the *Maski* to pay
For this and that mining thingamabob
And eight sturdy natives so they might convey
Fifty-pound loads of produce, chiefly rice,
Together with prime trading merchandise.

97   The New Guinea natives were vital to
The mining of gold—without black muscle
It would have largely remained *in situ,*
The ground tree-covered, so you had to tussle
With stubborn earth that was laced through and through
By tangled root networks, as well as hustle
Varied supplies over territory
Both thick with jungle and undulatory.

98   Once arrived, Flynn staked a decent-sized plot
Some hundred yards square then registered it
And started to dig. Was it the right spot?
Would *this* be the labor to turn a profit,
He finally able to play the bigshot?
Two or three fellows had already hit
Quite sizeable veins, there was gold, no lie,
Though hopefully they hadn't bled it dry.

99   But it emerged that Flynn's hunt for gold
Was doomed because he was so amateurly
Equipped for the task, with the mountain cold
Ravaging his men who held up poorly
At high altitude, Flynn opting to fold
Up operations and cut losses early,
For once in his life Errol now *can't* do
(He'll try again, though, in the third canto).

100   Yet there was always black gold to be had
(And we're not talking here about crude oil),
Flynn thinking that it might not be a bad
Move to ditch prospecting and employ all
His energies (and an energetic lad
He was as we know) to creatural spoil
As a slave trader in the family tradition
(So likely he had a predisposition).

ERROL FLYNN

101   Years on, in Hollywood, Flynn liked to shock
People by posing as something of a swine
In telling them of his days working ad hoc
As a brute "slaver," not kindling benign
Images, though still a bit of a crock
Since it implies a guy way out of line—
But a "recruiter," the better term, meant
You were licensed by the Australian government.

102   You went to the District Office and drew
Up the work-contract; and then the native
Recruits underwent a physical to
Check their fitness (the administrative
Minimum for chest expansion, thank you,
Was thirty-one inches); and regulative
As well was the interventionist state
In terms of wages and what recruits ate.

103   No outlaw stuff this recruiting business
(Though Flynn might have wished it to have been so,
For any time he'd a chance to *transgress*
It made him happy) albeit there's no
Doubt that should somebody wish to impress
The world with their rectitude then they'll forego
A career—not "slaving"—but one in which you'd
Sell men into indentured servitude.

104   Of his slaving days Errol tells the story
Of once outfitting a jungle party
So as to launch an exploratory
Mission for specimens hale and hearty
To work plantations and gold to quarry;
Then three days after they'd made their start he
And his boys were ambuscaded—a hail
Of arrows and spears waylaying their trail.

105 One of them suffered a lance in the gut,
A second one took a shaft in the neck;
The other boys fled while Errol stayed put,
Leaping behind a tree, trying to check
The raiders with his revolver (his foot
Taking a long poisoned arrow, the fleck
Of scar to be borne by him all of his days),
Squeezing off bullets and one of which slays

106 A native who falls squealing like a pig.
That drives them off. Coming round from his shock,
Flynn grabs his knapsack, not caring a fig
For his hurt foot and not stopping to gawk
At his dead victim, and hobbles right quick
Down the clay hillside, he racing the clock,
And for his five other boys greatly fearing,
Finding them huddled though in the next clearing.

107 At dusk the garramut drums began sounding,
Warning the jungle that there was a white
Killer at large; and from the surrounding
Trees issued ominous voices, so flight
Seemed ill-advised; and also compounding
Their discomfiture was that when the night
Fell, so too did the rain with a tropical
Madness that verged on the misanthropical.

108 They'd nothing to eat, were high up and cold,
Errol's foot hurt and he feared infection
And his malaria had taken ahold
Of him that same day (its resurrection
Happening from time to time, and all told,
In Errol Flynn's present state of abjection,
Couldn't have picked a *worse* time) and so he
Was sweating and freezing simultaneously.

ERROL FLYNN

109   No shuteye of course was to be had, not
With those infernal tom-toms hammering.
It was the kind of relentless onslaught
To make the coolest of chaps start yammering.
And no doubt done with malice aforethought
Since this type of relentless clamoring
Was hardly dissimilar to the Chinese
Water Torture which breaks you by degrees.

110   Then the drums stopped, on the following day,
No telling why, still and all a reprieve.
Were the natives spooked by the guns? Were they
Just rendered happy by what they could thieve
From the packs? In any event, no dismay
Was Flynn's at their halt, so he took his leave
And scurried like mad back to the seacoast,
No recruits in tow, but alive and not toast.[6]

111   He shipped to Kavieng and there caught a "nail
In the hoof" (Aussie slang for gonorrhea)
And such a virulent form even jail
Was looking good now—or Chad or Korea—
Anywhere but New Guinea! So Errol made sail
Straight back to Sydney with the idea
Of receiving treatment, which is just as well,
As this canto's gone on for quite a spell.

CANTO II

Flynnanigans

(1929-1932)

One of the two, according to your choice,
Woman or wine, you'll have to undergo;
Both maladies are taxes on our joys:
But which to choose, I really hardly know;
And if I had to give a casting voice,
For both sides I could many reasons show,
And then decide, without great wrong to either,
It were much better to have both than neither.

Don Juan, canto IV, stanza 25

Somewhere on the eastern coast of Australia with *Sirocco*
crew members Charlie Burt (far left) and Trelawny Adams, 1930

CANTO II

1   Whom among us does not experience
Homecomings with mixed emotion? You see
Kith and kin, quite true, yet ambivalence
Will often arise from the fact that we
Once more discern those adverse inducements
That brought us to pack up our bags and flee
In the first place and make a beeline for
Some distant land—and preferably offshore.

2   The high point of a homecoming's always
That joy-filled reunion with the loved ones;
But following all the huggy displays,
When things would seem to be going great guns,
Then sets in the invidious malaise,
A restiveness that accosts native sons
When arriving in their former backyard,
Since they've the feeling that they're going *backward.*

3   Flynn's ambivalence was surely greater
Than most, with little to show for his two
Years adrift; though a real operator,
He'd failed in making his fortune (you
Will recall that his basic motivator
To dare New Guinea was wealth to accrue)
And 'stead of gold funding a life of ease,
He'd only brought back a social disease.

4   Then there was the further complication
That Errol was broke, not even for food,
So he began cadging alimentation
At a Sydney pub where there rendezvoused
The New Guinea crowd, and information
Being conveyed that in the interlude
There was a company interested in
A gold claim belonging to Errol Flynn.

ERROL FLYNN

5   The claim was worthless with respect to gold,
But it lay between two parcels of land
The company sought to develop. Flynn sold
His claim that same day for a cool two grand,
Then partied, and next day, lo and behold
(Having drunk and caroused to beat the band)
He woke to find that—replacing his plot—
He was proprietor now of a yacht.

6   Though his finances were a fiasco
Just the week before, Errol paid cash-pounds
For a sailboat with the name *Sirocco*
(Pretty hard to rhyme because it confounds
You to dredge up much beyond "Morocco";
Yet fitting, since here the sirocco abounds)
And paid off his debts, at least the great bulk,
And then pondered what to do with his hulk.

7   All the above is Errol Flynn's version—
There never having been any gold claim
Nor lucky windfall—and his aversion
To the straight truth of just how the yacht came
To be his was a distaste for reversion
To facts unheroic, and even lame,
As to the purchase, since yielding the scratch
Was Marelle (to paraphrase Errol) the Snatch.[7]

8   Maybe done out of generosity?
Or glad Errol wished to follow in the wake
Of her sailor-clan? But if you ask me,
More than birthright or kindness were at stake:
She just preferred him back in New Guinea—
Which is just where Captain Flynn planned to take
Sirocco, a long three-thousand mile trip
And rigorous test of sound seamanship.

9   But why this voyage? Why *not* this voyage!
    The call of adventure was reason enough,
    Yet another rite of manly passage
    But one that Errol couldn't simply bluff
    His way through now, his mates an assemblage
    Of untaught greenhorns exceedingly rough
    Around the edges in terms of sailing—
    Though doubtless capable, if needed, of bailing.

10   Including Flynn they were a four-man crew:
    Charlie Burt, a vagabond from the Isle
    Of Man; and Trelawny Adams, Brit through
    And through, from Cambridge, with his diffident style;
    And Rex Long-Innes, Sydney socialite who
    Was son of a high-court judge—and a trial
    It'd surely be for this untried formation
    Whose spunk should elicit our admiration:

11   This was a *harbor* yacht, not one designed
    For the open ocean, a mere thirty-eight
    Feet with a fairly deep draft, not the kind
    Of boat to wander about through the Great
    Barrier Reef; and this also combined
    With the fact none of them could navigate,
    And Rex Long-Innes first having to learn
    That front was the "bow" and back was the "stern."

12   Flynn set the trip down for posterity
    In novel form with his prose work *Beam Ends,*
    A yarn that he spins with dexterity
    And gusto and wit; and it recommends
    Itself in terms of the plot's verity
    Because it hews closely to real events,
    With just a few exceptions here and there
    Added for the sake of dramatic flair.

ERROL FLYNN

13   Flynn wrote the book in 1936
With the sea voyage still fresh in his mind,[8]
By which point he was at work making flicks;
And Errol's novel reads just like the kind
Of action-packed, fast-paced adventure pics
Whose leading roles he was being assigned:
Earl of Essex, Robin Hood, Captain Blood,
Playing always the jaunty resourceful stud.

14   Jaunty as well was his technicolor quill
In writing *Beam Ends*, a title he picked
To indicate sailing with more guts than skill
(Perhaps applying to this here *Gedicht*)
And Flynn's maiden novel gives us a thrill
A minute, he forbearing to inflict
On we the readers that journey's doldrums—
So as a result, right along it hums.

15   Let's take a page out of Errol's own book
And get underway! And also we might,
So long as we're at it, take a brief look
At what Flynn himself just happened to write
About how they Sydney Harbor forsook:
"When at last we sailed" it was "dead of night,
Unsung and without farewells"—which is fine,
But unmentioned here: it was clandestine.

16   They owed a fellow named Lars Halvorsen
Forty-five pounds for some alterations
To the *Sirocco*; but Flynn and his men
Couldn't fulfill their cash obligations,
So they decided to scamper off when
Evening did fall, and recriminations
Were not forthcoming, Lars rang no alarm,
He being in dutch to that lethal Flynn charm.

17   But soon they hit trouble. Passing through Sydney
Heads the bateau was thrashed by conflicting
Currents and swells, giving the third degree
To the small craft while also inflicting
Widespread flood-damage to the boat's galley
And simultaneously afflicting
The crew, to a man, with bad seasickness,
Which must have set a record for quickness.

18   When finally they made Port Stephens the ship
Had taken on two feet of water. They spent
The next couple days in trying to whip
Things back into shape, while Long-Innes went
Out on a sortie to the village—his trip
Cut short, he returning with the lament
That the fisherfolk, those no-count rotters,
Had a "deplorable lack of daughters."

19   They didn't long in Port Stephens tarry,
Now hoisting their anchor to make a run
Straight for Coff's Harbour, which had a very
Tricky entrance, not a barrel of fun,
The harbor itself meager sanctuary—
Though halfway to Brisbane, great distance won,
They'd be at Coff's, so they kept on sailing,
Favorable winds and weather prevailing.

20   But then the heavens grew inauspicious
And dark clouds from the southern quarter reeled
Them in and *Sirocco* caught in a vicious
Storm that struck swiftly and refused to yield
For three straight days and notably pernicious
Because, as mentioned, the "port" was no shield
To fend off Poseidon's unholy wrath,
So for the boys it was one prolonged bath.

ERROL FLYNN

21   Then the weather broke, and on a bright day
They left Coff's Harbour and scooted along,
A fair wind blowing, now hoping to weigh
Anchor in Brisbane, the boat going strong
When its unruly engine went astray—
A rasp, rattle, BANG—and so their headlong
Progress impaired, their mobility nixed,
Thus to Ballina to get the thing fixed.

22   Ballina was on the Richmond River,
To gain it you crossed a perilous bar,
But Errol's intrepid little sliver
Of boat performed like a bona fide star,
Crossing all seven breakers to deliver
Her gritty crew safe and sound to the far
Side and the calm water of the Richmond,
Relieved they'd made it—and just a bit stunned.

23   On docking they caught holy hell from the pilot
Whose blackball flag they had brashly ignored,
So Flynn asked the pilot aboard for a shot
Or two of whiskey and peace was restored;
But this didn't translate as *requiscat*
In pace since that same night they explored
The local taverns, raising cain, till they met
Up with a cop—who then joined their quintet.

24   Because he was sole policeman in town,
Errol and his crew now had a free pass,
Having such fun they resolved now to clown
Around in the place and lift high the glass
For the next two weeks—though the next showdown
With that less *festal* bar was at least as
Much of a factor in their choice to dwell
For a longer stretch before bidding farewell . . .

25   When finally they made fast to a yacht mooring
      In Brisbane, they'd taken four weeks instead
      Of one from Sydney—not reassuring
      In a narrative sense since full speed ahead
      Is what I desired, with no detouring,
      At canto's inception, but my wish outsped
      The snail's pace of the stalwart *Sirocco,*
      Slowed by our aggregate-detail cargo.

26   And so because seeing as how all told
      The voyage, which was slated for six weeks,
      Lasted six *months*, I'm going to make bold
      To speed our tempo, which also bespeaks
      My hope that I'll finish this poem before old
      Age is upon me and my headbone creaks.
      (And insofar I'm not greatly miffed he,
      Flynn, bless his heart, only lived to fifty.)

27   Arriving in Brisbane it was much the same:
      Drinking and gambling, wenching, carousing
      (How's that for pith—I daresay I'll tame
      My verbiage yet) and when the roughhousing
      Was over they returned to a sailing frame
      Of mind by setting aside their browsing
      Of taverns and girls when they decamped on
      Up the coast to lay siege to Rockhampton.

28   The city was in a festival mood,
      Letting rip now with its annual fling,
      The whole place for days on end getting stewed,
      And here where Flynn entered the boxing ring
      To fight Bud Riley, one menacing dude,
      Whose handler J. Sharman was offering
      The tidy sum of five Australian pounds
      To any brave man who could stay three rounds.

29   The *Sirocco* was always short of loot,
So Rex nudged Errol and spoke for the crew
In opining that Riley, the big galoot,
Wasn't so tough, Flynn would break him in two;
Nonetheless Errol remained irresolute,
Not savoring the thought of this set-to;
Challenge reprised, though, and still no taker,
Errol stepped forward—he wasn't some Quaker!

30   And he proceeded to get a lacing—
But stayed the three rounds; though whether they were
All of three *minutes*, which takes some pacing,
Errol doesn't mention; but de rigueur
Or not, there's certainly no disgracing
Yourself when you go up against a slugger
Billed as "Heavyweight Champ of the Western
Districts," as Flynn did with feigned unconcern

31   And mix it up with the man for however
Much time, because a single Queensbury
Round can oftentimes seem like forever
—Just keeping your gloved fists up over three
Minutes is hardly a flimsy endeavor—
And Flynn whipped so bad that for two days he,
By his own account, couldn't even eat.
(And beaten shitless could he even excrete?)

32   But after the general riotousness
Of Rockhampton's fair there then ensued days
And weeks of comparative quietness,
The *Sirocco* drifting among the maze
Of coral islands that Nature's largesse
Has granted the world to fund hideaways
From the madding crowd—the Great Barrier Reef,
Where souls can obtain some repose and relief.

33   They came upon isles that rose from the sea,
Green pyramids fringed by sands gleaming white,
And through clear water they quite readily
Distinguish the hues of the reef shining bright,
Submerged coral gardens beautifully
Opalescent with the play of sunlight;
And further out is the long booming line
Of cottony breakers, their foaming brine

34   Forming the Barrier Reef's outer wall
And making a placid pool for our crew
Who take the plunge joyfully one and all
Into cool waters of deep turquoise blue,
Swimming about and probing the atoll
With diving goggles for a fish-eye's view
Of teeming life-forms that flourish below,
A world all its own each rocky grotto;

35   Lying then nude on the deck in the sun
And dining on coconut milk and fish,
And 'fore all their hides get too overdone
The sun starts to set, commencing to squish
Into the horizon, its quotidian
Duty accomplished, and no one could wish
A splashier exit, this showy confection
Of vivid color, supernal reflection

36   Of the reef's glory, and wed with the sound
Of tiny waves softly lapping the strand
And which the fast sinking sun has now drowned
In deep copper hues; and then there's the land
Breeze gently wafting and the whole scene crowned
By a tropic moon that comes to supplant
The gold-glowing orb—and taking to their cots,
Sweet slumber descends on our argonauts.

ERROL FLYNN

37   Then on to Cooktown and through Cook's Passage,
That tiny gap in the Barrier Reef
Leading to the Coral Sea, the voyage
From there being neither easy nor brief,
Errol's crew having to summon raw courage
—Pushing back thoughts that they might come to grief—
At their first sight of that "great blue expanse"
Stretching "to nothingness in the distance."

38   This here crossing was a grimmer rendition
Of the first leg of their trip from Sydney
To Brisbane, the parlous Coral Sea dishin'
Out waves that banged the boat mercilessly,
And the crew stumped as to their position
(Except it was lousy admittedly)
Since they were no longer hugging the coast
And their plotting talents still not the utmost.

39   Salvation then came on the fourth day at sea
When they espied land off the starboard rail,
Not at all certain this shore was New Guinea,
But they just wanted to slip the harsh gale,
So they dropped anchor off of a sandy
Cove dotted with palms—and in fact their sail
Was done—New Guinea!—they'd finished their trip,
So in their honor I'll skip a last quip.

40   What now? For the time being Errol would stay
On in New Guinea, he not yet sated;
Also it might yet afford him a way
To make his fortune; and captivated
Was Flynn by all that green country which lay
A bit more inland and irrigated
By the Laloki, a prime location
For what would be his tobacco plantation.

41   Errol had a native workforce erect
A stately house out of palm and bamboo
By the Laloki River, a perfect
Retreat from the world, his own Xanadu,
Where he'd be able to resurrect
His soul from the backbreaking work to do—
Arising each day at the crack of dawn
To duly decree: "Boss Boy carry on!"

42   And then of course there was Tuperselai,
Flynn buying her from Boss Boy Allaman,
Whose daughter she was, alluring yet shy,
Graced with that satiny Melanesian
Skin of lustrous mahogany and high
Breasts and black locks—so it stands to reason
That Errol should fork over cash and two pigs
And make her mistress of his jungle digs.

43   Though she was sluggish in coming around,
Errol was kindly and patient and sweet,
All of which helped getting things off the ground,
She first responding by washing his feet,
And later his back, then his hands, and she wound
Up in his arms, her surrender complete,
By the soft-aired Laloki, whereupon
The rest was simple—*Boss Girl carry on!*

44   And there was also mental stimulation
At hand with reading matter aplenty
Lining the shelves of this habitation.
Errol was now all of two-and-twenty,
And it was not merely cultivation
Of tobacco on which Errol was intent, he
Also desired to cultivate his mind,
Alert and agile but still unrefined.

ERROL FLYNN

45   By light of a hurricane lamp (attracting
Every damn bug in the jungle, also
The jungle fauna—rather distracting
Those lizards up there on the ceiling, you know;
And likewise proving somewhat exacting
Were crablike spiders who were not the foe
Of insects—and consequently your friend—
But errant *birds* at the receiving end

46   Of outsize webs of fishing-line thickness)—
By light of the storm lantern Errol would sit
Imbibing not liquor but nothing less
Than great literary spirits—to wit:
Plato, Aristotle, Marcus Aurelius;
The Russian novelists with their glum writ;
Assorted Frenchmen like Edmond Rostand,
Hugo, Balzac and Guy Maupassant;

47   Stevenson, Maeterlinck, Marx, Weininger
And Wells and Prescott—pretty much, in short,
Whatever he could lay his hands on there
Or otherwise get his father to export,
Or Sydney Library, by sea or air.
And when a parcel of books came he'd sort
Through, nay *fondle*, all those volumes as one
His fingers through a girl's lovely hair might run.

48   For Errol these books were alive and vital
And cued him to certain manners and speech,
Neo-romantic Rostand his idol—
And one might suppose that theatrical peach
Cyrano de Bergerac and its title
Figure would have had quite a lot to teach
Young Errol who was much drawn to panache, a
Word that first cracked English via that smash play.

49   The youthful Errol's own systematic
Reading and study of humankind's lot
Inculcated in him the Socratic
Truth that the unexamined life was not
Worth living—and all this with a pragmatic
Function in that it allowed him (somewhat)
To sift and unpack all the Chinese boxes
Of his mind with its clashing paradoxes.

50   And so because Flynn was given to think,
He had the parallel impulse to write,
Composing his thoughts through the spilling of ink,
And this assuming the form of seven tight
Feature pieces in a far from rinky-dink
Paper with a readership far from slight:
The famed and illustrious *Sydney Bulletin*—
Though his byline didn't read "Errol Flynn."

51   Errol went by the pen name "Laloki,"
Which to my mind is a handle exquisite,
Though some might find it just a tad hokey
Or sentimental—but nonetheless is it
Not better than, say, "Okefenokee"?
In Flynn's reports he offers explicit
Account of how natives killed turtles (by fire—
Just hack off their heads and they will respire

52   Through the cut windpipe, their heart still beating)
Or how the Goiaribari treat
Their women (like dirt, and end up eating
Them in some instances—bon appétit!)
All of this making for lively reading,
And not one syllable that you'd delete,
So clean was the prose, the *Bulletin's* stringer
Proving a very adept word-slinger.

ERROL FLYNN

53   Perhaps the start of a writing career?
      His tobacco, meantime, had been undercut
      By the Australian government's clear
      Stand on New Guinea crops trying to butt
      Into the home market and interfere
      With local output—and now because shut
      Out of the Aussie market (and grittin'
      His teeth) Errol shipped his leaf to Great Britain.

54   But it brought only a very cheap sale
      On London's market, Errol's curing process
      Turning out faulty, so he chose to bail
      On New Guinea for a while and assess
      His next stratagem. (Also hitting the trail
      Since his finances were in a fine mess,
      All those to whom Errol Flynn was in debt
      Not in the mood to forgive and forget.)

55   The date was August 1932
      When Errol finally returned to Sydney
      With no fair notion of what he might do,
      All of his days spent lazing by the sea,
      Swimming and sunning and pitching the woo
      To the beach cuties, our man's repartee
      A mixture of cocky self-deprecation
      And real worldly sophistication.

56   Lounging and laughing and flashing his smile,
      And ready to pounce on his sundry prey,
      A toothsome saltwater crocodile
      Snapping up morsels all the livelong day,
      That prey including not just the nubile
      Sheilas (already a solid mainstay
      Of Errol's diet) but also whatever
      Tips might issue in a quick-cash endeavor.

57   Lolling about in the warm Bondi sand,
    Strutting on down to the water to swim,
    Muscles well-toned, skin beautifully tanned,
    Shoulders impossibly broad and waist slim,
    That touch of hauteur and air of command
    Which his fine bearing imparted to him
    —That is, while making all the girls *lovesick*—
    Errol was spotted by a guy named Warwick.

58   John Warwick was the casting director
    For a picture entitled *In the Wake*
    of the Bounty, Warwick seeking an actor
    To play the first mate: spying Errol's beefcake
    Figure he thought now here was his Fletcher
    Christian in the flesh—how's *that* for a break!
    Warwick was eager to take on board
    A man who'd grown up swinging Captain Bligh's sword!

59   And playing Flynn's relative Edward Young
    Would be this very same Warwick—also
    An actor of sorts—and so the unsung
    Errol saw suddenly, ex nihilo,
    His future collide with his own far-flung
    Ancestral past; or in other words, though
    He'd luck to have talent (and to be plucky)
    His greater talent was *being* damn lucky.

60   He said "I'll try anything once" when they
    Pitched him the role, and the performance he gave
    In his first picture, if no Olivier,
    Portrayed a Fletcher determined and brave;
    And Flynn's physique coupled with his matinée-
    Idol good looks and fine speaking-voice save
    The part from high camp—if not the blond wig,
    Which they should have tossed in the *Bounty*'s brig.

ERROL FLYNN

61   Clark Gable, Brando, Mel Gibson and Flynn—
The great leading men of their day, all tried
Their hand at playing what is a shoo-in
For cinema's one great unqualified
Tragic hero: torn between compassion
And duty, torn between fealty and pride,
He's our filmic Hamlet, if you ask me,
With a sea of troubles *and* troubles at sea.

62   The film itself, though, was no giant hit,
Half-documentary and half-feature
While trying to perform a temporal split
Between the past (the *Bounty* tale, to be sure)
And present (showing offspring of the bandit
Crew on Pitcairn) and this hybrid creature,
With its static scenes and jumbled screenplay,
Was never released in the U.S.A.

63   But was Flynn bitten by the acting bug?
It appears so, yes, though since it would be
Long months till the public could view his mug
Larger than life on the silver screen, he
Had the feeling they'd promptly pulled the plug
On his film career. A scarce quantity
Errol remained and no more offers came
His way much less instant fortune and fame.

64   Tobacco planter to published writer
To movie actor within just a year!
And 'fore that, you name it, Errol had tried 'er,
From skipper to slaver to overseer,
From gold-prospector to fish-dynamiter,
Ever the fellow to play it by ear,
With gifts so varied that Errol well could—
But still no closer to a real livelihood.

65   Errol was anxious about his future—
New Guinea, he feared, was just a dead end.
He'd gone there partly seeking adventure,
Essentially though so as to ascend
In the world and that brass ring to capture.
And although *Wake of the Bounty* might portend
Greater things to come, Flynn had seen his share
Of portents prove out to be castles in the air.

66   He also harbored ambitions to rise
In society and to that end had
Gained a fiancée—did I not apprise
You of this turn of events? Well, the sad
Fact is that Flynn had been rather unwise
And something of a precipitate lad
In swearing his love to Naomi Dibbs,
This one of his more unfortunate fibs.

67   For Errol this woman signified *class*
Because she was part of the upper crust,
He for his part handling her like cut glass,
Containing somehow his powerful lust,
Never unsheathing his manly cutlass,
Never betraying Naomi Dibb's trust
That theirs was a love "on a higher plane"—
But leaving his lower parts in acute pain.

68   They'd been "engaged" now for almost three years,
But what in fact would it mean to *marry*?
Love, joy and laughter? Blood, sweat and tears?
His parents' union had made him wary
Of marriage, bearing out all his worst fears,
And his own life now presently very
Unsettled and riddled with question marks—
At which point he met a certain "Madge Parkes."

ERROL FLYNN

69   This likely wasn't the lady's true name,
       Flynn changed it in *Wicked*—you'll soon see why—
       And did I say "lady?" Try one gorgeous dame!
       The kind of woman to make a rabbi
       Drop-kick his Talmud and loudly declaim
       The *Kama Sutra*, or a fierce Samurai
       Bust both his swords right over his knee
       And go off on a sake-drinking spree.

70   Statuesque she was, sporting auburn hair,
       With heavenly or, if you like, hell
       Of a figure while also wafting an air
       Of tact and breeding; and in a nutshell,
       She was charming, witty and had savoir faire
       Along with a touch of the Jezebel—
       A scarlet woman, as it were, you see,
       Our siren married and now pushing forty.

71   Urbane, well-traveled, spirited and gay,
       She enjoyed swimming, also liked to dance,
       Was stylish without being *recherché,*
       The kind of female who perforce enchants;
       And what I guess I'm trying to convey
       Is that Errol's first hot and heavy romance,
       His first "real woman," indeed was no other
       Than the doppelgänger of his mother.

72   And she was wealthy. In nights dining out,
       And after drinks at a ritzy dance place,
       Never was there the shadow of a doubt
       Who'd treat and she did it with faultless grace,
       Not in the business of trying to flout
       The unspoken rules, she leaving no trace
       Of just how the bill had been settled since they'd
       Walk out of somewhere and it'd simply be paid.

73   And Madge adored sex—adoring it so,
That Flynn was a rapid convert to the school
Of thought which holds that the gynic libido
Emerges more active and does not cool
When middle age looms with the big 4-0.
(However as Flynn himself aged—and here you'll
No doubt smile wryly—his special delight
Was girls *decades* shy of their sexual height.)

74   Sex was her thing and she Flynn's training ground,
Her own needs so great that the constitution
Of our phallic star, later so renowned,
Was undergoing a dissolution;
And one night after another hard round,
Feeling like he could use a transfusion,
Flynn arose feebly from Madge's mattress,
Relieved to escape her scorching caress.

75   She lay there sleeping, a vision, a dream,
Her arms outspread with her beautiful hair
Spread on the pillow, and a thing supreme
Her figure with thighs designed to ensnare,
Fulsome hips (yet not too broad in the beam)
Tight waist and her breasts—good Lord what a pair!
He took all this in and then Errol's gaze
Began *another* vision to appraise.

76   Spread over the dresser there gleamed manifold
Jewels in colors and sizes assorted,
A number of rings and others with gold
Or silver chains. He'd often escorted
Madge out with these rocks, but now to behold
All of those gems together here hoarded
Brought home to Flynn just how much she was worth
While calling to mind his own fiscal dearth.

ERROL FLYNN

77   To Errol it seemed that in their affair
Madge Parkes was getting the far better deal.
She took him to places with long stemware,
All places that had a strong snob-appeal,
He'd had his fill though of fine Camembert
And even for sex now had lost his zeal
Because far from paradisiacal,
Her needs had grown nymphomaniacal.

78   His gaze drifted from the dressing-room table,
Away from the lustrous and dazzling jewels
And back to those legs to rival Grable
And bust to incite Pavlovian drools
And curvaceous hips both willing and able
And face over which men had once fought duels—
On Madge his eyes lingered for a short while,
Wrestling with his conscience—her or the pile?

79   It was clear there were no prospects for Flynn
In Parkes. Errol still had big albeit
Somewhat vague plans for his future, which in
So far as he was able to see it,
Wasn't in Oz, he by no means sanguine,
So there remained little choice but to flee it—
And since Madge was getting constantly laid,
Flynn felt he ought to be consonantly paid.

80   In other words, it didn't take long
For Errol to choose a firm course of action:
He knew emphatically that it was wrong,
Far the most dastardly malefaction
He'd yet committed, but the urge still strong,
So in his state of near stupefaction
He started dressing—oh so stealthily—
Then snatched up the jewels as his rightful stud fee.

81   He raced downstairs like the place was on fire
And hurried through the streets but didn't run
(Running a sure thief-identifier)
And back at his lodgings he took his hard-won
But ill-gotten gains and placed them entire
(He'd scooped up plenty but hardly a ton)
Into the hollow of a shaving-brush
(Pretty darn crafty in view of his rush).

82   A number of inches was the shaving
Brush's handle at whose end was a crown
That when unscrewed now disclosed a lifesaving
—At least Errol *hoped*, in case of shakedown—
Hollow interior made for a thing
To constrict blood vessels and thus shutting down
The bleeding if you contracted a nick,
Namely an old-fashioned "shaving stick."

83   Flynn placed the jewels in the hollow section,
The broken-off end of the stick on top,
And then screwed the crown back on, a deception
Liable to outsmart your basic dumb cop
From whom any thoroughgoing inspection
Of Flynn's belongings would certainly stop
Short of reducing his toiletry articles
Into their sundry component particles.

84   Flynn had to get out of town right away,
So caught a boat that was leaving Sydney.
He'd safely boarded, they all set to weigh
Anchor and sail from the harbor, when he
Saw bulking large in his stateroom doorway
Two plainclothes cops who had come round to see
Just what they might be able to uncover
On the person of our light-fingered lover.

ERROL FLYNN

85   First place they looked was the heels of his shoes,
    Guessing that they might be hollow, then checked
    His shoulder padding, another old ruse,
    And the whole time Errol sought to affect
    A derisive mien, putting to good use
    His inborn and nurtured lack of respect
    For law enforcement—but his open sneer
    Also intended to mask his great fear . . .

86   "Are you shitheels finished? Why don't you take
    One leg and you take the other and shake me,
    I might just have them up my arse"—thus spake
    Flynn, they responding: "Say, that would not be
    Such a bad idea." No, a grave *mistake*
    It would be, said Flynn, then promised that he
    Would shove through a porthole the first of them
    Who assayed this foolhardy stratagem.

87   "Come and touch me, one of you yellow-livered
    Sons-of-bitches!" It was not as if these
    Hardened Australian plainclothesmen shivered
    In their boots at his words and got knock-knees,
    But Errol seemed like the sort who delivered
    Fully on his threats, not a boy to sneeze
    At by any means, so they let it ride
    And by way of answer intensified

88   Their search of his baggage—and then Errol for
    His part *did* sneeze at them by simulating
    A great big ACHOO summoned with a roar
    When one of them started investigating
    The tricked shaving brush, which you might deplore
    As juvenile stuff effectuating
    The precise opposite of its design,
    But the cop was clearly no Albert Einstein,

CANTO II

89   Failing to penetrate Errol's schoolboy
     Attempt to distract him from the very
     Thing he was holding. (The transparent ploy
     Can also derail an adversary
     Who may *anticipate* that you'll employ
     Cunning—just witness that cautionary
     Tale where doing the overt is better,
     Edgar Allan Poe's *The Purloined Letter*.)⁹

90   Whether or not Errol's sneezing and bating
     Tactics really served to draw attention
     Away from the search and thus extricating
     Him from his fix, they show a dimension
     Of his own temperament, so fluctuating,
     That was a constant and hence bears mention:
     Equipped with a heart uncommonly stout,
     Flynn was an ace at *brazening things out.*

91   With the two cops now having left empty-
     Handed and the vessel full underway,
     Errol unscrews the shaving brush and he
     Prises the gemstones, one by one, away
     From their settings and flings these into the sea
     Via the convenient porthole, the day
     Having now ceded to night of pitch black—
     All hail our prudent kleptomaniac!

92   Returning the jewels to their hiding place,
     Flynn leaves his cabin to take some fresh air,
     Getting the wind and the spray in his face
     As he leans over the railing, a rare
     Sense of elation now come to replace
     That of impending mischance, the big scare
     He'd gotten now making way for a feeling
     Akin to pride in his double-dealing.

ERROL FLYNN

93 He'd gotten away with it! Though guilt he had,
The guilt made it that more delectable.
He'd done a thing irrefutably bad,
Not to say highly disrespectable,
Something that made him a first-rate cad,
But now with the deed undetectable
And he himself pretty much off the hook,
Flynn felt just swell about being a crook.

94 But Errol's present exhilaration
Was not exclusively owing to his
Narrow escape from incarceration
And his sexually taxing miss
But that *other* form of ruination
Going by the misnomer "wedded bliss"
With his fiancée Naomi Dibbs,
Entailing both in-laws and baby cribs.

95 Also, as mentioned, Flynn felt that to make
His fortune he'd have to forsake Down Under
And head Up Top; and icing on the cake
Was that his newly acquired plunder
Gave him a very substantial grubstake,
Buying him time to effect a wonder
In this or that project or endeavor
In China or India or wherever.

96 But not in Australia—that much he knew.
In stealing the jewels, Errol hadn't planned
To bid a definitive farewell to
His shack job, intended, and native land;
But through his thievery, out of the blue,
Errol had managed to force his own hand,
His subconscious impulses, as a group,
Now consummated in one fell swoop.

97   And I believe there was yet another
Subliminal urge to his larceny:
Because Madge was so like Errol's mother,
The not at all latent misogyny
Fostered by "The Cunt" found in Errol's lover
A target and ergo the sheer *villainy*
Of Flynn's transgression, which had victimized
A generous woman he otherwise prized.

98   But let's leave Flynn now, leaning on the rail,
Looking out over the expanse of sea,
Trying to make out whatever detail
He can on the far distant shore since he
Will not be returning again—though braille
Is needed to pierce the obscurity,
The mainland now fading wholly from sight
As Errol sails blindly into the night.[10]

CANTO III

A Heroic Inheritance

(1932-1934)

. . . Pray tell me, can you make fast,
After due search, your faith to any question?
Look back o'er ages, ere unto the stake fast
You bind yourself, and call some mode the best one.
Nothing more true than not to trust your senses;
And yet what are your other evidences?

Don Juan, canto XIV, stanza 2

Flynn and woman identified as "Sakai" aboard the SS *D'Artagnan*,
Saigon 1933, photographed by Hermann F. Erben

CANTO III

1   They say that a man never goes so far
As when he doesn't know where he's going,
And this would equally apply to our
Wayward rascal because he is blowing
Town to get under the legal radar—
And in a few months, long before Boeing
747s, Flynn will have gone
Halfway round the world, fast fleeing the Dawn.

2   He traveled a route that was easterly,
Not straight to Hollywood, only in case
That's what you're thinking. I daresay that he
Will be leading us all a merry chase
And that we'll have quite a ways to journey
—Doing so, though, at a murderous pace—
Before we see ERROL FLYNN up in lights
And putting fresh snap into period-piece tights.

3   The luscious dessert will be along nigh,
That oh so sweet movie-icon payoff;
But first we're obliged to fortify
Ourselves with the hearty beef stroganoff
Of Flynn's early years, which will underlie
And nourish our real understanding of
The later Flynn and his certain actions
As one of the world's great star attractions.

4   When you read bios of Flynn or get hold
Of one of the film documentaries,
They interview all the bright stars of old
And other Hollywood luminaries
For sage insights into our hero bold,
All of them stretching their vocabularies
To the breaking point in attempting to draw
A cogent verbal portrait, blah blah blah.

5   But after all those fine words have been spilled
And stories told of this escapader,
His character still has not been distilled,
And then our qualified commentator
Will say so tacitly (however skilled
His rundown has been) sooner or later
By stating (pensively rubbing his chin):
But I never knew the real Errol Flynn.

6   They always surmised there was something more to
Him which they'd failed to discern and withstood
All their best efforts in guessing the "true"
Self within Errol, for these Hollywood
Types could have had little if any clue
As to Flynn's venturesome young adulthood—
Those years when his daring, nerve and raw guts
Were forged in the land of the garramuts.

7   In fact when Errol arrived on the scene,
The Warners public-relations department
Took varied measures to quarantine
Flynn's fans from his past and misrepresent
Him as so Irish he bled emerald-green—
His *genuine* past the one you'd invent,
So wild that no one would buy it, and cuz
Who even knew where Tasmania was?[11]

8   For likely the first time in history
(For all I know maybe even the last)
Press agents had no compensatory
Work to perform on an actor's dull past
But took Errol's spicy cacciatore
("Stroganoff," in truth, was kind of half-assed)
Of a résumé and toned it way down—
Quite a feat midst the hoo-ha of Tinseltown.

9   But we're not there yet, not by a long shot,
So let us return to pre-Hollywood Flynn
Where we'd left him having slipped a tight spot
And heading for . . . that, dear reader, again,
Is the burning question, but we'll stay hot
On Errol Flynn's trail just like Rin Tin Tin,
Not losing his scent: the law he can slip
But we'll tail him clear down to Sunset Strip.

10   On the ship from Sydney, Flynn got as far
As Brisbane and once more he was flat broke
(He keeping the jewels as a reservoir)
But rather than starting to swim breaststroke,
And due to the fact of having no car,
Errol just started to walk, the poor bloke,
Across Queensland, later hopping a freight,
And working his way to the north of the state.[12]

11   From here Errol managed to catch a boat
Out of Australia straight for New Guinea,
The other side of that Coral Sea moat,
Where Errol felt that he wouldn't have any
Trouble to lose himself in the remote
And pathless isle, a country where many
Opportunities would surely emerge
To give his assets a much needed surge.

12   And Errol's luck held! It is a long story,
But very soon he was the half-owner of
A gold claim he'd won in a lottery,
An Edie Creek plot, so a cut above
The rest, and it also happened to be
Next to a claim where the bright yellow stuff
Unearthed there might well have paid a king's ransom
Together with that of his queen—and then some.

ERROL FLYNN

13   Flynn became head of the operation,
The cash for the project provided by
His moneyed partner, and this allocation
Permitting Flynn to put in a supply
Of all he would need to stay the duration
And this time give it that old college try,
Digging and sluicing to his heart's desire,
Not folding camp early like four years prior.

14   Flynn found some natives for sale and bought 'em
And then back at Salamaua took care
Of the requisite procedure and brought 'em
Out to the local District Office where
Each was indentured as Flynn's factotum
For the next two years. Then they packed up their
Various stuff and marched off single file
Through the thick jungle, mile upon mile,

15   Up and down all those mountains precipitous
While warding off all the venomous snakes
As well as mosquitoes ubiquitous,
Just like the leeches, while beset by aches
Produced by this trail circuitous;
And then every morning pulling up stakes,
Not altogether fit as a fiddle,
The garramuts dwindling their sleep to little.

16   Arriving at Edie Creek they at once bent
To their hard labor, eviscerating
The earth in keen quest of its gold content,
Slashing and gashing and mutilating
The soil with an avaricious intent,
This effort hugely exhilarating,
All rising at six and digging till night,
Then hitting the sack and out like a light.

CANTO III

17   They dug and they sluiced and they sluiced and dug,
       Deeper and deeper into the hillside,
       Flynn's lust for wealth acting just like a drug,
       His fervor this time not to be denied!
       No doubt about it, he'd caught the gold bug,
       A virus whose impact was magnified
       By fact of there being no end of prospectors
       Digging like crazy in their own sectors.

18   Errol had high hopes, as indicated,
       Because adjacent his own claim was one
       With a rich vein that had generated
       Wealth for its owners and would likely run
       Directly under the demarcated
       Boundary dividing the claims—a ton
       Of gold was his if he clung to his dream
       And kept a close watch for that telltale gleam.

19   And one day they did spy that auric glint—
       A trace of color, a bit of paydirt
       To lift their spirits, providing a hint
       Of far greater things, which made them exert
       Themselves to the full in their final sprint
       To the finish line when the ground would spurt
       Gold just like crude from a Texas derrick
       (Indeed they were waxing somewhat chimeric).

20   The trickle of gold, though, remained a trickle;
       Somehow the vein of the neighboring plot
       Pulled up just short of Flynn's claim—O fickle
       Fate!—the whole windfall worth diddly-squat!—
       That is to say, at least for all practical
       Purposes since in the end all Flynn got
       Was fifty ounces or so of gold dust,
       A painful back and deep sense of disgust.

ERROL FLYNN

21   In aggregate time Errol Flynn had spent
      Over four years in New Guinea; he'd never
      Wanted to exceed *five* years, so that meant
      He'd be compelled to very soon sever
      His bond with that isle which had helped to cement
      His basic character of a clever
      And resourceful chap who landed on his feet—
      And who, if called for, was a skillful cheat.

22   He couldn't cheat fate, though, which dictated
      He leave the South Seas. It was little use
      To sell off his claim—its worth now negated,
      Everyone knew it; but he could produce
      Money by selling his boys, who rated
      A good twenty pounds per head for Flynn whose
      Contract transferred to a copra planter,
      At which point he was all set to meander.

23   He first arranged shipment, through Barclay's Bank,
      Of his gold dust out to England where it
      Would be when Errol strolled down the gangplank.
      To beat the exchange he then bought illicit
      Diamonds in a deal into which he sank
      A few hundred pounds and didn't omit
      To insure these rocks against loss or theft,
      There being so few honest people left . . .

24   And so many untrusting creditors!
      Errol, it would seem, *owed* hundreds of pounds
      To diverse parties, and with solicitors
      Now getting into the picture and—zounds!—
      Even New Guinea District Officers.
      Errol felt just like a fox with the hounds
      And knew that if his creditors suspected
      That he'd skip out before they collected,

25 They would alert the Burns Philip Agency,
  A shipping concern which regulated
  All steamer service, said delinquency
  Leaving said traveler's trip terminated
  Till reinstatement of his solvency;
  And so Errol slyly propagated
  The tale of another recruiting trip,
  And when they weren't looking he boarded his ship.

26 The name of the steamer upon which he
  Booked passage was the SS *Friderun*,
  Out of Salamaua and stopping briefly
  In Rabaul (where Errol had first begun
  His intrepid New Guinea odyssey)
  And whence the ship sailed now on its sea-run,
  Forever Flynn leaving this wild setting
  Of his young manhood—but never forgetting.

27 And now as the *Friderun* leaves its port,
  Flynn gazes across the expansive bay
  To the three jungly volcanoes athwart
  Rabaul called the "Mother and Daughters," they
  As green and verdant as ever and the sort
  Of sight for which tourists good money pay—
  But Errol just gives them a final look,
  Sans sentiment, he now closing the book.

28 But where was Flynn going—that is, as opposed
  To simply *away*? Well, this time he'd more
  Than a rough notion, in fact he proposed
  To sail for Britain to become an actor,
  And this idea first having imposed
  Itself on Flynn's mindscape when his director
  In *Wake of the Bounty* offered the thought
  That it'd not hurt to give England a shot.

ERROL FLYNN

29   That's where he'd get the experience
And requisite formal training to make
A go of the thespian art; and good sense
Also decreed that if he wished to take
A whack at Hollywood (and all evidence
Indicates strongly he did) his big break,
No matter how hard he might persevere,
Wouldn't come in the southern hemisphere.

30   And persistence wasn't Errol's strong suit.
No doubt he could rise to the occasion
But wasn't one to sustain a pursuit
If it made for too much aggravation;
Not that the fellow wasn't resolute,
But life was a game, in his estimation,
And he a restless player who was out
To win, to be sure, but if not: next bout.

31   The jungle had more than done its own part
In priming Errol for acting: it taught
Him the audacious if delicate art
Of donning facades; it namely begot
A knowledge in him of how to outsmart
Folks by assuming personae you're not—
The front that he brought to his New Guinea tasks
Imparted the priceless lesson of *masks.*

32   Now safely aboard the *Friderun,* he
Has ditched his creditors and any cops
(Flynn would always love islands where the sea
Furnished quick escapes) and first of his stops
Will be to China, and more precisely
Hong Kong—at two weeks, not the shortest of hops—
Giving us time, though, in getting to know
One other traveler the ship has in tow.

33   Dr. Hermann F. Erben was his name,
An expert in tropical maladies
And like Errol Flynn adept at the game
Of high adventure; and albeit these
Two would have little contact when it came
To real meetings, and despite the unease
That he would visit on Flynn—nay the *strife*—
Flynn called him "the great influence in my life."

34   Erben was born in 1897,
November 15th, of which I make mention,
Exact day and month, that is, thank heaven,
Not due to any anal retention
Regarding dates but just because Kevin
McAleer himself—this no invention—
Has the same birthday, which gives me a chill,
You welcome to make of it what you will.

35   Apropos anal retention and such,
Doc Erben hailed from Vienna, Freud's city,
And shared two more things with him inasmuch
As he attended the university
Medical school and was not at all Dutch
(As good friend Errol, and more's the pity,
Styled him in *Wicked*) but rather a Jew,
The fact of which Flynn was careful to eschew.[13]

36   After years living in the USA,
In 1930 Doc Erben acquired
Citizenship—and then anchors aweigh!
All through the 1930s Erben hired
On as ship's doctor with a wide array
Of vessels so he might pursue his desired
Lifestyle of remaining in the traces
While sating his craving for faraway places.

ERROL FLYNN

37   His keen wanderlust would be the root cause
Of problems for him in 1940
When U.S. naturalization laws
Caught up with Erben: it was found that he
Had been in violation of the clause
That you live five years continuously
In the U.S. before the submission
Of your American citizenship petition.

38   Flynn came to Erben's defense, even taking
Up his case with the nation's First Lady,
Eleanor Roosevelt, and thus staking
His own reputation on the shady
Hermann F. Erben—and no mistaking
Flynn's endorsement: though people weren't swayed, he
Labeled the charges against Erben smears,
According to statements for government ears.[14]

39   What drew Flynn to Erben? A man of science
And quite intelligent, needless to say,
Erben shared Errol's studied defiance
Of the insipid, the drab everyday,
As well as a thorough non-compliance
With accepted ways, refusing to obey
Convention and scorning society's
Moral injunctions and noble pieties.

40   This man, it seems, was able to endear
Himself to Errol and serve as a kind
Of older brother owing to the twelve-year
Gap in their ages, with Erben inclined
To mock everything that people revere
And impelled to stripping away the rind
Of all the world's pharisaical cant,
Affording Flynn's psyche a whole new slant.

CANTO III

41   "He showed me the complete irrelevance,"
Says Flynn in *Wicked*'s chapter three, *au fond*
Inscribed to Erben, "of the existence
We humans have while on earth," and beyond
This he ascertained "the unimportance
Of being earnest" and not to despond
When the Fates, those unfeeling taskmasters,
Strike hard, but "to laugh at the worst disasters."

42   All of this makes for—how shall I put it—
A certain tragi-comic attitude:
Life is meaningless, a bottomless pit,
And right from the start we're all of us screwed;
But don't go gnashing your teeth, just submit
And enjoy the *farce*, the ineptitude
Of Man and his Works, the apocalypse
Met with a gay smile gracing your lips.

43   It's life as Theater of the Absurd,
Or a black comedy à la *Candide*,
A world that is only to be endured
Through laughter because the gods pay no heed
To human grief, not even when incurred
By the pure and blameless—Leibniz's creed
Of this noxious world as being the best
Possible one in itself a fine jest.

44   Erben's perspective on life also seemed
Beholden to an aspect Viennese
That stemmed from Ernst Mach who not only deemed
Sensory input as the way to seize
The world's reality but he esteemed
Sensations—that is, neither abstruse theories
Nor "objective" materiality—
Themselves to be life's sole reality.[15]

45   In other language: there was no strict split
'Tween physical matter and human mind,
For our sensations didn't just transmit
The world to the self but in fact combined
In finally creating that self—to summate it:
You *were* sensations—and better defined:
You only existed through your *experience*
Of life since the "self" lacked any firm essence.

46   And since that world was a chance succession
Of diffuse stimuli—transitory
And ever in flux—one had the impression
Of a kind of hallucinatory
Cosmos where there was little concession
Made to whatever explanatory
Model of the wide-awake dreamer, all
The world being much too ephemeral.

47   The self was an unstable quantity
In a permutable world and hence no
Theory of life had the integrity
Of what one might term life itself—ergo:
Your life the sum total variety
Of all your sensations of it, inflow
Of sensory data the only thing
For catching reality on the wing.

48   That was Flynn's life: a quest for sensations
At once delightful and new and bizarre—
And not solely out of motivations
That were hedonistic but whose lodestar
Was curiosity, his explorations,
Like his mentor's, ranging from the boudoir
To the biosphere so as to increase
His store of what he called the "verities."

49   Take note of his use of the plural form:
    "Verities"—since Errol lacked a coherent
    Ontology by which he could warm
    His tormented soul, he no adherent
    Of a creed nor did his own thoughts conform
    To any doctrine or dogma but went
    Their own stubborn way—praiseworthy, you'd think,
    But it was one thing that caused him to drink.

50   With no belief system, when things got rough,
    To fall back on, he resorted to booze.
    In fact Errol took the theme by the scruff
    Of its neck in a journal entry whose
    Heading was "Faith." It is powerful stuff,
    Flynn here expressing the wish he might lose
    His own disbelief through some revelation
    And thereby quelling his "inward desolation."

51   In this one entry from 1953,
    Errol bewails his failure to withstand
    Materialistic fiddle-dee-dee,
    What he construes as "transitory and
    Ephemeral"—nettled by life's mystery,
    Errol desires to yet understand
    The wherefore of his existence and why
    Sound explanations are in short supply.

52   By this time Errol had taken to wearing
    A kind of monogram sewed on his suit,
    The jacket's handkerchief-pocket bearing
    A question mark, an eloquently mute
    Inquiry aimed at the world and airing
    Flynn's own disgruntlement in his pursuit
    Of life's ultimate and crowning answers,
    Like phantom Javanese shadow dancers.

ERROL FLYNN

53   Errol saw his life as a "picaresque
Painting" by Degas with its plenitude
Of "dancing girls, its theater, its burlesque";
Or one by Toulouse-Lautrec, an étude
In "high-colored panties"; or a grotesque
By some surrealist artist where you'd
"Have to peer hard to find meaning," the line
And color "a mosaic of insane design."

54   And if Errol's meeting Doc Erben was not
The *start* of this lifestyle, so much is true:
Erben delivered that consummate shot
In the arm needed so as to pursue
It in a purposeful manner and brought
Flynn into conflict with himself—he knew
The quest for sensations led nowhere fast
But that, as a native iconoclast,

55   Systematized thought went against his grain.
In fact one could say his later despair
Was among other main reasons the strain
Of trying to hold in his mind this pair
Of contradictory notions, his brain
Capacious enough but caught in the snare
Of seeking a modicum of transcendence
Based purely on empirical evidence.

56   But all this doubt and mental affliction
Would kick in only a decade later
When Errol had suffered the infliction
Of certain deep wounds . . . so back to our freighter,
The *Friderun*, which, per our depiction,
Had last been seen while crossing the equator
On its way to the free port of Hong Kong,
Where we'll arrive before too very long.

57   But a brief note on Flynn's itinerary
And escapades in the months to follow:
It will come as no extraordinary
Surprise to learn that we cannot swallow
His narrative whole, it being contrary
To Hermann Erben's who, though he did wallow
Oft in untruths, was true to the kernel
In terms of entries he made in his journal.

58   Fact of the matter is that Erben kept
A painstaking diary all of his days,
In principal part because his precept
Was to record his financial outlays—
Flynn himself noting that he was adept
At grubbing money—and I'd make the case
That there's no more careful record-keeper than
A dogged cheapskate with his logbook pen.[16]

59   If we go by Hermann Erben's account,
They didn't take part in Manila cockfights,
So we're compelled to also discount
Their dipping their roosters' beaks, as Errol writes,
In snake venom. And it doesn't amount
To all that much, the story he delights
In of a Macao temptress (on my honor:
She bears the moniker "Ting Ling O'Connor")

60   Who fleeced an infatuated Errol
Of cockfight winnings. And likely untrue
The tale in which he gazed down the barrel
Of a live pistol whose owner made spew
Lead at a Flynn sporting less apparel
Than he might have done when as if on cue
This spouse of the girl that Flynn was (choosing
With due discretion my verb:) *amusing*,

ERROL FLYNN

61   Burst into the steerage cabin that they
Were utilizing for their interlude—
Indeed I'll revise my judgment and say
That the anecdote should in fact be viewed
As patently *false* and the dead giveaway
Being that Doc Erben fails to allude
To this fray purportedly taking place
In his own cabin (loaned to Flynn for a space).

62   In his log there's indeed indication
That en route from Singapore to Ceylon
Errol was having a public flirtation
With a married woman, a liaison
Not without risk, but if an altercation
'Tween a riksha coolie and our Don Juan
Turns up in Doc's entry for Pondicherry,
Then why not one with a *shooting* adversary?

63   Flynn's version of the rickshaw episode
(It was an argument over the fare)
Has the malcontented coolie explode
With rage and draw his knife right then and there,
Albeit after Flynn sought to unload
His big Sunday punch, which just clobbered air,
Our nimble coolie then stabbing his belly,
Laying it open from here to New Delhi.

64   Errol apparently did have a scar
In later life that embellished his gut[17] —
But so too do I and my wound quite far
From being the consequence of a knife cut
Sustained in the Pondicherry grand bazaar;
And therefore Errol I'll have to rebut,
Citing Doc Erben's account, which is duly
Concise: "Flynn punches my rickshaw coolie."

65   Doc Erben's entries are so laconic
That there is not a whole lot to go on,
Not what you'd call a narrative tonic,
In point of fact they engender a yawn;
If we're to keep, then, our diachronic
Momentum—and because hither and yon
We've traveled already—then just call me wrong
About soon or *ever* reaching Hong Kong.[18]

66   From the subcontinent they voyaged west
To Africa, making port at Djibouti
In French Somaliland, not yet a nest
Of piracy and steep ransom the booty;
Had any raiders, though, tried to molest
Flynn's vessel it is with certitude he
Would've plunged headlong into the action—
Sole question being: Backing which faction?

67   They traveled up the Red Sea and then through
The Suez Canal, that majestic ditch
Sloshing with water of indigo blue
Relieving the arid wasteland and which
Seen from afar and a convoy in queue,
Strikes you at first as one almighty rich
Desert mirage: a great figment fleet
Of ships borne by shimmering waves of heat.

68   Having traversed the canal and the prow
Of Errol Flynn's steamship finally cleaving
Mediterranean waters, he now
Breathes in the bracing Occident, leaving
Behind the languorous East, at the bow
Of the *Compiègne*, his strapping chest heaving
With excitement as the ship attains speed
And puts space between it and Port Said.

ERROL FLYNN

69   A few days later they docked in Marseilles,
    Where Errol and Erben then disembarked
    And trod separate paths. It was a sad day,
    Asserted Errol who in *Wicked* remarked,
    "My heart was heavy," and Erben to convey
    Years later the same sentiment when he harked
    Back to that hour—so their versions agree
    In this final moment for once perfectly.

70   They'd spent two months amassing sensations,
    In line with Doc Erben's credo, and such
    Were largely thanks to the ministrations
    Of whores (past masters in the sense of touch)
    From a wide spectrum of Third World nations,
    Cementing their comradeship inasmuch
    As hunting for females has corresponding
    Effects on the hunters—known as male-bonding.[19]

71   Now in Marseilles the two bidding adieu,
    Uncertain if they'll ever meet again, a
    Thing rather doubtful with Flynn heading to
    London and Erben off for Vienna,
    Both of them going their separate ways through
    The big wide world—so let's get the Gehenna
    Out of this frog-eating land of the Gauls
    And head for England: Flynn's destiny calls!

72   Errol arrived at Waterloo Station
    With just two shillings, this scarcely enough
    For cab fare, and his planned destination
    The Berkeley Hotel, highfalutin stuff,
    What you would call an upscale operation,
    Errol this time proposing to bluff
    His way right into the place on the theory
    That when you look like a bum they're leery

73   Of you in the cheap flophouses—your odds
Are greatly improved at a first-rate address
Where the employees are hardly nimrods
But not *accustomed* to tramps in poor dress
Trying to perpetrate one of their frauds
By shoveling out a load of BS
About lost luggage, or some mountebank
Even claiming gold dust at Barclay's Bank—

74   Which is precisely what Errol Flynn did,
At probably London's swankiest inn,
With a performance largely unscripted
But so impressive that four-flusher Flynn
Was at once shown to the hotel's splendid
"Royal Suite" where the Prince of Transjordan,
In all his glory, had recently stayed—
More than Flynn bargained for, I'm afraid.

75   Keeping his cool he ordered a huge meal,
Gorged himself on it and signed for the thing,
Called Barclay's Bank to see what was the deal,
Learned that his gold would be some time clearing,
Then quickly wired an urgent appeal
To Theo Flynn for some hard cash to spring
Him from the Berkeley, pop wiring back sonny:
"IF YOU'RE AT THE BERKELEY WHY DO YOU
NEED MONEY?"

76   After a while the staff grew suspicious,
So Errol now turned in his second great
Act in 48 hours, a fictitious
Appendix-attack which put him prostrate,
Management proving very officious,
Bundling him off and then moving him straight
To a nursing home—not very conducive
In healing his woes, as most exclusive,

77 Which meant *expensive*. But still Lady Luck
 Was smiling on Flynn since a nursing home
 Of course has *nurses*, one falling lovestruck,
 This sort of thing a recurrent syndrome
 With girls encountering our young buck;
 So when he told all, her response was quite handsome,
 And since the door to Flynn's room had a lock,
 Her handsome response wasn't limited to talk.

78 So with their pre-assigned roles in reverse
 —Bedridden, as it were, the trained caregiver,
 Our patient now ministering to his nurse—
 She told him his secret was safe with her
 And that she wouldn't be at all averse
 To helping Flynn by applying the spur
 To her own dad, who was rich, on condition
 That Flynn keep playing attending physician.

79 The nurse was adorable, pretty, smiling,
 And an added bonus was the old-fashioned
 Florence Nightingale garb she was styling,
 All rousing in Errol Flynn an impassioned
 Reaction; that is, until this beguiling
 Damsel with all of her ready cash (and
 Personal readiness) thought they should marry—
 At which point Flynn chose no longer to tarry.

80 And in the meantime his gold dust had cleared,
 Worth almost two-thousand dollars, so he
 Escaped his financial dilemma and steered
 Himself to the theater district to see
 If work could be had; but just as he feared,
 London had very small use for would-be
 Actors in a far too-crowded profession,
 Especially now in the Great Depression.

81   Living off his gold and gems assorted,
Flynn finally joined with an agency
Which got him "extra" work that afforded
Additional padding for his CV;
Then some months later he was accorded
A place at the Northampton Repertory,
A short drive from London to the northwest,
Presenting his first real acting test.

82   He got the job by playing it clever:
Errol knew they would be able to gauge
His rawness since this his first time ever
Daubing on greasepaint and mounting a stage,
So he admitted to having never
In life trod the boards—although to assuage
Their doubts he said that they shouldn't wonder
That he'd been a big movie star Down Under.

83   Just looking at Flynn, you could believe it.
And he'd in fact had the principal role
In *Wake of the Bounty,* ace up his sleeve—it
Hadn't yet shown in England, on the whole
What might be deemed a blessèd reprieve—it
Also the case that Errol's was the sole
"Type" being sought by the Northampton Rep:
A sporty young male with plenty of pep.

84   Clearly Northampton was not the West End—
But also not what you'd call chopped liver,
A place G. B. Shaw liked to recommend,
Now and again hopping in his flivver
To catch a showing; and let's not pretend
That the Northampton failed to deliver
The goods when it came to both style and flair—
That the Rep was "provincial"—*au contraire*.

85   Its venue, for one, was designed for highbrows,
      Equipped with some six hundred red-plush seats,
      Having once served as an opera house,
      With orchestra pit that emitted bleats
      From an ensemble playing Johann Strauss
      Or excerpts from one of Tchaikovsky's suites
      Before a Rep drama got underway,
      And filling the gaps between acts of the play.

86   The Rep's director helped found Equity,[20]
      The set-designer was highly vaunted,
      The performers of top-notch quality,
      Execs gave the patrons what they wanted
      In terms of a tasteful facility,
      And therefore a grateful public responded,
      The Rep soon emerging one of the nation's
      Ranking theatrical organizations.

87   Not the West End but an excellent start—
      Flynn though was starting right near the bottom,
      In fact six feet under, because his first part
      In *The Thirteenth Chair*, this late in the autumn
      Of '33 (the type role that Bogart
      Would play early on before *he* shot 'em)
      Was a murder victim and thus sedentarier
      Even than the lifeless role of spear-carrier.

88   Yet this was one of those time-honored ways
      To train an actor—from the bottom-up—
      In a broad spectrum of roles and plays,
      Ibsen and Shaw in Northampton's lineup
      And Shakespeare with one of his old mainstays,
      Othello, here Errol able to sup
      At the Bard's table with such lines to utter
      As are served up to the First Senator.

CANTO III

89   In space of half a year Flynn appeared in
Twenty-two plays, working six days a week,
A theater crash-course that must have been
A fabulous boon to Errol's technique
And not to mention his self-discipline—
Each night performing, all while living cheek
By jowl and training with well-seasoned pros,
Assuming both lead roles and cameos.

90   Flynn's stage debut, later said a colleague,
He looked like "something out of a zoo,"
The poor fellow clearly out of his league,
His exits and entrances all askew,
His voice not projecting that much past the klieg
Lights let alone into the last few
Theater rows—and they had to lament
His albeit mild but *Aussie* accent.

91   Half a year later all of that had changed,
No Aussie discernible to the ear,
His voice even in a stage whisper ranged
To the back row and yet still light and clear
And not from its principle charm estranged
(That instrument we'd be privileged to hear
In his filmwork) and he moved with a grace
Which showed he had learned how to block and pace.

92   "The happiest days of my life were spent
At Northampton Rep," said Flynn, looking back
Some twenty years to a time when he went
From total unknown with a certain knack
To someone girded to mount an ascent
Of acting's Olympus and his bivouac
Eventually pitched right square on its summit,
A good dozen years before he'd fall from it.

93   When young and eager, though, and in the throes
       Of assimilating a novel craft,
       Knowing each day that your grasp of it grows,
       Learning all the ropes from fore to aft,
       The tricks of the trade and the strict no-go's,
       Your thirst for fresh insights never quite quaffed—
       Years later you might positively swear
       That things had largely been downhill from there.

94   We all attain "peaks" in our lives that may not
       Appear so then, for we're looking ahead
       To greater conquests; but when you have got
       A lifetime of context in which to embed
       Events of your past, you can have a soft spot
       Not for the steep pinnacles but instead
       The *climb* to attain those dramatic heights
       On which you'd so yearningly set your sights.

95   It's not the joy of just having a goal,
       Something toward which you may gratefully strive,
       Not just the feeling of your being "whole,"
       Senses atingle, completely alive;
       But it's that phrase I believe heart and soul:
       'Tis better to journey than to arrive—
       Meaning (so that there'll be no confusion)
       That on arrival there's oft disillusion.

96   We'll leave it there for right now since our hero
       Isn't that far yet; for the moment, in
       Learning to act, our budding De Niro
       Is acting just like he's in the pre-Lenten
       Carnival of Rio de Janeiro;
       That is, his modest wages aren't preventin'
       Errol from living it up in a style
       Distinct from the actorly rank and file.

CANTO III

97   Flynn was just earning a few pounds each week
But wore fancy clothes and drove a sportscar,
Kept up his tennis, had the harem of a sheik,
And let others pay for his drinks at the bar—
The life he was leading hardly unchic,
Like he was *practicing* being a star,
While also getting ample credit from
Town merchants who thought he'd a star-income.

98   He did, in a way, with all the loot he
Had salted away, the jewels and gold dust.
But he had learned that by acting snooty
He could spare assets he hoped would go bust
Later than sooner. And the great beauty
Of the whole thing was that nobody fussed
About what he *did* with the loans and so they
Got put aside for Flynn's planned getaway.

99   Being a young fellow in a hurry,
With no intention of sticking around
The Rep forever, he sought to scurry
Back to that actor's prescribed proving ground:
London—to see if he couldn't curry
Favor with the film industry, a sound
Plan since his looks and personality,
Great build and tremendous vitality,

100   Would make it easier to get ahead
In cinema than on the hidebound stage.
And although Northampton was no hotbed
For landing picture roles, still all the rage,
As elsewhere, were movies, knocking 'em dead
Day in and day out and making front page
Of the entertainment and other news,
Hyping the screen's leading-men and ingénues.

ERROL FLYNN

101   Hollywood had conquered this big blue sphere,
And Errol would always attempt to squeeze
A film in between his Shaw and Shakespeare,
Reveling in those magical movies
Whose stars could conjure a rare atmosphere
Of charm and romance—Claude Raines among these,
Kay Francis, too, and a vamp à la Theda
Bera whose name was "Lili Damita."

102   There in the dark at a late-night showing,
With just a few scattered seats occupied,
Red tips of random cigarettes glowing
And wisps of smoke that like specters abide
In the cone of light, Flynn sits there not knowing
That in a year he will take as his bride
The starlet Damita and gain top billing
In a film that'd make a box-office killing.

103   Not even Errol dared dream such a dream—
Although he'd high hopes, which meant in his case
That he had also a practical *scheme*
For going about securing his place
In Hollywood's sun—there was a thin beam
Of it piercing the fog which he would now chase
Straight down to London where were located
Studios that were Hollywood-operated.

104   This dispensation was in large part due
To the well-meaning Cinematograph Act
Of '27, this law designed to
Boost British films—which were getting shellacked
By the Hollywood stuff—insofar as it drew
Up a quota system which set exact
Percentages movie houses need meet
So British product could better compete.[21]

105   Then in a shrewd countermove, Hollywood
Just set up studios on British soil,
Not robbing locals of a livelihood,
Being staffed by Brits, yet there to despoil
The local market with films just not good,
Called "quota quickies," thus serving to foil
This law (conceived so the home trade might flourish)
By making "British film" look amateurish.

106   Native British companies also rushed
Out films in order to meet the quotas.
But it wasn't like exhibitors brushed
Aside the subpar product from Lotus
Land, largely since that product was pushed
On them by Hollywood reps whose modus
Operandi helped inveigle picky
British exhibitors to book a "quickie."

107   Exhibitors booked them because if they
Wanted the latest Garbo or Cooper
Then they had *better*—"block-booking" the way
That all those films which induced a stupor
Got screened at all, exhibitors to play
The role of de facto pooper-scooper
For flicks that often deserved their bad rap
As so-called C-movies ("C" standing for *crap*?).

108   The Hollywood studios also preyed
On top English actors, shipping them out
To the U.S. where they all gladly strayed
Because British film had been put to rout
By quota quickies and Hollywood's raid
Of them through the high-handed "talent scout"—
This here a case of the rich getting richer,
And years till Britain got back in the picture.[22]

ERROL FLYNN

109   All this formed the matrix that created
       A magnificent opportunity
       For Flynn because it facilitated
       Admittance to a movie community
       That was the planet's most celebrated
       While also affording immunity
       From Hollywood front-office politics, for
       Flynn's entry came through the English backdoor.

110   But first things first—you're no doubt curious
       As to how Flynn broke his Northampton ties
       (Even if the story might worry us):
       Errol had gradually come to despise
       A stage-manager whose injurious
       Tongue never ceased to scold and criticize,
       Errol stilling it for a change of pace
       By punching the badgerer down a staircase,

111   Which in itself might have been bad enough,
       But our stage-manager was a *female*;
       And what was worse, Errol didn't just cuff
       Some random woman but chose to assail
       The *producer's wife*—so out on his duff
       The very next day (and lucky that jail
       Didn't factor into the deal) was Flynn—
       Who for his part must have stifled a grin:

112   Unpunished had gone his misdemeanor
       While also negating his Rep contract,
       Freeing him to go in search of greener
       Pastures—and by dint of his being sacked
       Errol Flynn couldn't have made any cleaner
       Escape from those debts with which he'd been wracked,
       Since he'd no choice now *but* to hit the road
       To scare up some work and pay back what he owed

113   (He never did, of course, pay back the great
Bulk of his debts. And after Errol had
Grown rich and famous there then came a spate
Of bills sent to Warners by hopping mad
Lenders he'd managed to often frustrate,
All these sent glossies of Flynn who would add
Some words of his own, this kindhearted star:
"I'm willing to forget all this if you are.")[23]

114   Errol made straight for the Teddington section
Of London where the Warner Brothers ran
A studio. It seems that his selection
Of Warners was hardly catch-as-catch-can
But instead due to a prior connection
With them just right before Errol began
At the Rep, having made his movie debut
In England with a quickie: *I Adore You.*

115   It was a bit part and hardly bearing
Any mention at all (the picture now lost)
If not for the fact that it's the first pairing
Of Flynn and Warners (however low-cost)
And further proof of Errol's unerring
Gift for finding (whether sober or sauced)
Nifty shortcuts up to the next level,
As if he'd some kind of pact with the devil.

116   You sometimes wondered with Errol—the guy
Had fiendish good luck when young and it seemed
He'd struck a bargain with Satan (the high
Principal and interest later redeemed
Twofold in sorrow); and one can't deny
His devilish *good looks* alone might be deemed
Enough to give rise to suspicions that they
Derived from something very Dorian Gray.

117 The big difference being, I grant you, that
  Flynn's reckless lifestyle did indeed score
  The visage above his dandy's cravat
  With lines of experience, care and more;
  Though note that Errol's inner organs at
  His demise when he was but fifty bore
  Likeness to those of a grizzled old man,
  A shrouded portrait of his *true* lifespan.

118 True in the sense of the cumulative
  Life he'd compressed into just fifty years;
  And in the place of his own definitive
  Fictional double's it could be *Flynn's* ears
  For which the glib and manipulative
  Lord Henry (a man whom Dorian reveres)
  Intends, at book's start, his little sermon—
  And for Henry, Lord, please read Erben, Hermann:

119 "Be always searching for new sensations"
  Since "the true mystery of the world is
  The visible" which makes up its foundations,
  "Not the invisible"; do not seek your bliss
  In those "mean triumphs" or in aspirations
  For some nonexistent future happiness;
  "A new Hedonism . . . you might be its
  Visible symbol"—to quote some choice bits.[24]

120 And one might also even go so far
  To say that Errol *alone* embodied
  Gray's dual existence through his objet d'art
  In that Errol wasn't some two-faced fraud—he'd
  Never tried to maintain (not in his memoir
  Nor anywhere else) some slick facade—he'd
  Never been somebody you could "defrock":
  The fact is he loved being able to shock.

121   Errol assuredly personified
Dorian's double life (to which a lot
Is owed *Dr. Jekyll and Mr. Hyde*,
The allegory if not the strict plot),
The difference being that Errol kept tied
The psychological Gordian knot
Of high and low urges unreconciled,
So neatly cut by Stevenson and Wilde.

122   The moral discordance externalized
In both their stories to make manifest
Humankind's dual and even polarized
Nature was fought out in Errol's own breast,
Something that Errol himself recognized,
To which in *Wicked* he'd also attest:
"I know that there are two men inside me"—
Which on first reading rather mystified me.

123   It left me mystified because I thought:
"*Only* two men?" But Errol was trying
His best to explain his belief in what
He felt the principle underlying
Human existence—and I doubt our Scot
Or our Irishman would be denying
The essential truth of Errol's conviction
That life's a welter of contradiction.

124   Flynn understood this in the sense of mixed
Feelings, discrepant acts and divided
Allegiances—it's not that we're betwixt
And between so much as many-sided;
And Errol not so much a man bewitched
By life's lovely chaos as one guided
By rational thinking which was resistant
To life's being logically *in*consistent.

ERROL FLYNN

125   But I was giving the background story
       To Errol's big break: the film he'd been in,
       I Adore You, led not to *amore*
       On Warners part for this new fellow Flynn;
       But after Northampton Repertory,
       He thought to give Warners another spin
       In the emboldened belief that there might
       Be the prospect of love at second sight.

126   He managed to wangle an interview
       With Irving Asher the tyro director
       Of Warners-London; and whether it's true
       The chestnut that Asher's star-detector
       Was so astute he at once signed Flynn to
       A seven-year contract (I've cross-checked 'er
       And hold to the view that the chances are low),
       He put him in *Murder at Monte Carlo*.

127   This was a "quickie" just starting production;
       And whether true that he gave Flynn the *lead*
       At the outset or just used induction
       By first viewing film of the bit-part he'd
       Allotted to Flynn—regardless the construction
       You put on events—Errol did succeed
       In finally nabbing the film's starring role
       And making it onto the Warners payroll.

128   And it emerged that so greatly impressed
       Was Irving Asher with Flynn that he cabled
       Warners in Burbank that here was the "BEST
       PICTURE BET" yet and he also labeled
       Him as "IRISH" (which at last lays to rest
       How *that* myth grew) and then Errol's fabled
       Beauty was stressed by Asher who opined
       At cable's end: "GUARANTEE HE REAL FIND."

129   Asher recommended that Flynn be shipped
       Off to Hollywood immediately
       And sent Errol's film to Jack Warner who ripped
       It saying "she stinks" or alternately
       Never *bothered* to see it (although he then whipped
       Up a tale, later, in ultimately
       Claiming sole credit for discovering Flynn,
       Like picking a horse after seeing it win).

130   It just so happened that Jack Warner played
       No role at all in getting Flynn hired,
       But Asher (who earns every accolade)
       Went *under* Jack's head, as it were, and wired
       Head of production Hal Wallis to persuade
       Him to view Errol—and back Wallis fired:
       "WILL ABIDE BY SVENGALI ASHER'S JUDGMENT,
       SEND FLYNN OVER"—and so over he went.[25]

131   But what was it which made Irving Asher
       So certain that Errol would be a star?
       Seemingly Irving hadn't been as sure
       About him the first time around insofar,
       Hence unconvinced that he'd be a cynosure
       At the box office: Errol Flynn didn't jar
       Asher's attention in *I Adore You*,
       So why suddenly all the cry and hue?

132   Was it that he was just now looking for
       "British" types to export back to Warners
       And that Flynn's newly acquired top-drawer
       Accent was no longer a foreigner's,
       Namely an Aussie's, which it had been prior
       To England where he had filed its sharp corners?
       Or was it maybe that training he'd gained
       At the Rep which now his new standing explained?

133   Or, as one reads, was it under auspice
       Of Mrs. Asher who happened to see
       Flynn waiting in Irving's outer office
       And then told hubby to make sure that he
       Gave this Adonis a bit more of his
       Consideration than usually
       Reserved for unknowns in quest of a part—
       And thus giving Errol a big headstart?

134   Or instead was it that Flynn's acting job
       In *Murder at Monte Carlo* was so
       Damn charismatic that any poor slob
       Could see that this guy was destined to go
       Far in the business and maybe heartthrob
       Status as well in the offing? Well, though
       All the above may have been prime factors
       In another's rise, they weren't in this actor's.

135   Fateful for Flynn is that Asher now saw
       Him through other eyes—and I don't mean those
       Of his wife nor that of the camera
       (*Monte Carlo* didn't seem to disclose
       Great gifts, per sources, Flynn still pretty raw)[26]
       But through the schooled orbs of one who bestows
       The swashbuckling mantle on Errol Flynn thanks
       To a chance meeting: Mr. Douglas Fairbanks.

136   Douglas Jr. was debonair-apparent
       To Doug Fairbanks Sr., junior's namesake,
       His own immortal action-star parent,
       He of the film-stunts that threatened to break
       His neck, so bold and even aberrant
       They were, and guaranteed always to take
       Your breath away, his athletic prowess
       Unrivaled in its talent to wow us.

137   Doug Fairbanks Sr. was the cinematic
       Idol of every boy in the nation,
       A silent-film age in which to be static
       Was to be nothing, and their admiration
       Induced by means of his acrobatic
       Antics where the laws of gravitation
       Were waived as they are with high-flying birds,
       Doug's actions speaking far louder than words.

138   Doug Fairbanks Sr.! How quickly the minions
       Forget how you used to flip, twist and bound,
       The ether one of your prime dominions,
       Your mid-air feats all designed to confound
       Your plodding foemen—and although opinions
       May differ, I sense the villainous *ground*
       Was your preeminent adversary,
       To you as the cat is to the canary.

139   And when death managed in clipping your wings,
       They laid you to rest in a mausoleum
       Befitting popes, sultans, emperors, kings,
       And yours no less an imperium:
       The movie mecca, which to this day brings
       The world together through the medium
       Of film—the first time ever our planet
       Had any oneness—and Fairbanks began it.

140   Fairbanks began it not only by way
       Of his star allure and kinetic bounding,
       Pulling off stuff that was very *outré*,
       But extreme too in the sense of founding
       An institution whose aim was to pay
       Respect to movies as an "art"—astounding,
       The notion back then—and not only that,
       But movies as "science," our brash acrobat

141   Performing his greatest feat hitherto
With the Academy of Motion Picture
Arts & Sciences—and its big to-do
Now an annual television fixture
From Oslo to Lima to Katmandu:
The Oscar awards, that glitzy mixture
Of oversized egos, star power, and a
Shameless slice of Hollywood propaganda.[27]

142   As I was saying, Doug's tomb is a place
Becoming his fame, a last curtain call,
With its ornate double marble staircase,
Which one descends to a grassy sprawl
Cleaved by a long narrow pool which betrays
A likeness to that of the Taj Mahal
And leading up to a marble, column-backed
Altar, like from a Greek temple hijacked.[28]

143   Entombed here as well is Doug Jr., the son,
Who had been destined for many the same
Swashbuckling roles with which Sr. had won
The hearts of millions and worldly acclaim;
But Douglas Jr. would more or less shun
These roles and the whole movie-hero game,
With him later earning medals galore
As authentic hero in the Second World War.[29]

144   Doug Jr., a friend of Asher's, was touring
Teddington studios when he met Flynn,
This just before or maybe occurring
During *Monte Carlo*'s production—in
Whatever case, it left an enduring
Impact, Flynn getting so under Doug's skin
That in old age he recalled and alluded
To the magnetism this kid exuded.

145   Upon meeting Flynn, Doug was asked to see
    Some footage of him, and after viewing
    The boy in action he put in a plea
    For Errol as somebody worth pursuing—
    Perhaps not showing immense ability
    At this stage, since he was only debuting,
    But Flynn had "great looks, great charm" and gazelle-
    Like grace, he moving both "easily and well"—

146   This in a note to Asher—he meaning
    That the newcomer indeed had the stuff
    That dreams are made of, Doug Jr. gleaning
    An uncut diamond (that is, in the rough)
    Which he'd surmised but confirmed post-screening,
    Fairbanks now having seen more than enough
    To give Errol his complete approbation,
    This tantamount to a coronation,

147   A kind of tacit laying-on-of-hands,
    Anointing his own swashbuckler-successor,
    Since Fairbanks Jr. (our story expands)
    Was *looking* for one who might be possessor
    Of traits that in fact would meet those demands
    On him to mimic his predecessor—
    In sum: Doug was searching for someone who had
    The same verve and sparkle as dear old dad.

148   Doug said as much—so Asher the seer
    Was getting it straight from mouth of the horse,
    Flynn a "GUARANTEE" since the guaranteer
    (A man springing from the absolute source,
    His swashbuckling bloodline having no peer)
    Was able to handily reinforce
    Irv Asher's considered opinion that
    For this unique find you could go to bat.[30]

149   And Irving Asher would seem to have had
      A real liking for Flynn—decades later,
      In a filmed interview (no more a lad,
      Long a big Hollywood operator)
      One can discriminate more than a tad
      Of gleam in the eye of our elder narrator
      As he relates how both he and his wife
      Saw Flynn off for this new phase in his life:

150   As the ship departed Southampton they
      Waved bye to Errol who now was all set
      To overturn every last star cliché,
      Ashton's wife saying: "That fella I'll bet
      Will never go Hollywood"[31] —and then the gray-
      Haired Asher in quoting his wife is beset
      By mirthful laughter and with wicked glee
      Adds his own coda: "How wrong can you be!"

151   So there you have it: Errol Flynn's big break—
      And now the fundamental question is:
      Would Errol in fact have been able to snake
      Into the Hollywood feature-film biz
      Devoid of the given nexus? On the make
      He'd been, of course, but it wasn't in his
      Makeup to stick with things too very long
      Were they to go just a little bit wrong.

152   It wasn't that Errol lacked character,
      Which can be measured in all kinds of ways,
      But if you are a neophyte actor
      Stick-to-itiveness most certainly pays;
      In lieu of some Madge-like benefactor
      Assisting him through this initial phase,
      How long could Errol have suffered rejection,
      Staving off gloom and crippling dejection?

153   I wonder . . . I wonder not only because
Flynn was so antsy; but in contemplation
Of what makes for a patient soul it does
Appear to have a strong correlation
To the passion you bring to bear—and *was*
Flynn wholly committed to his new vocation?
A bit hard to say, once again, but my best
Guess is ambition mainly fueled his quest.

154   It was for writing that Errol Flynn's zeal
Was reserved. While learning his thespian trade
At the Rep, in fact, he wrote a great deal,
Penning a play called *Cold Rice* (the piece made
Fun of both womanhood and imperial
British India)[32] as well as a paid
Article for a Northampton gazette,
Serving to reveal young Errol's mind-set—

155   Though in no straightforward fashion, mind you,
Since notwithstanding the article's title
("Why I Became an Actor") small clue
Is given to this; instead we sidle
Into an account of what later grew
Into his novel *Showdown*: recital
Of an imagined cruise up the Sepik,
Which in Flynn's hands is nothing short of epic.[33]

156   Flynn's frame of mind is disclosed in the piece
Due to its being so emblematic
Of the relation between both of these
Acting and writing pursuits; schematic
Though it may sound, my own expertise
(As a keen writer who for pragmatic
Reasons must translate so that the cash flows)
Tells me Flynn acted to enable his prose.

157   And truth to tell, one needn't conjecture
      Since our boy frankly admitted as such
      In various published statements, the texture
      Of which is simply that writing was much
      More crucial to Errol than was the picture
      Business, and its psychological clutch
      So great that his films he'd have gladly foregone
      For one book post-mortem that would have lived on.

158   And from a passage in *Wicked* to cite:
      "I had chosen to be an actor, to make
      Big money, to become famous," despite
      There having been something vital at stake:
      "I had put by a deeper yearning to write";
      In fact it had all been one big mistake
      Since "nothing I dreamed of had matured"—
      And I'm inclined to take Flynn at his word.

159   More on this later—but the point here to
      Be made is that acting was never what might
      Be termed Flynn's "passion," at best *faute de mieux*,
      And one might even assert *faute de* **blight**
      Regarding his face and his form since you
      Can but truly love that for which you fight,
      And since you aren't able to author books
      By simply employing your handsome looks.

160   So had it not been for John Warwick's chance
      Sighting of Flynn whom he cast as top dog in
      Wake of the Bounty, which then caused to dance
      Visions of film glory in Flynn's noggin;
      And were it not for the fluke circumstance
      That U.S. films were presently hoggin'
      The British mart and Brits counterattacked
      By passing the Cinematograph Act;

CANTO III

161   And had it furthermore not been the case
That Hollywood foiled the counterattack
By then proceeding to put into place
Film studios under the union jack
And leaving John Bull with egg on his face
Since they continued to gaily ransack
The British market with quota-quickies
Which would seem to have served as a species

162   Of screen-test for those British actors who had
High Hollywood hopes; had not Asher been
Chums with the son of the Thief of Baghdad,
Son of that man among swashbuckling men,
Every action-hero's spiritual dad;
Had Asher's amigo not dropped by when
Flynn just happened to be hanging about
Teddington-London—I very much doubt

163   That he could have managed that critical
Hollywood leap so early in the game.
The causal chain would prove catalytical,
With history's foibles providing the frame,
For Errol's fast rise—an analytical
Mind isn't needed to recognize same
Nor to realize that a chafing fellow
Like Flynn (who enjoyed playing in *Othello*

164   But who'd much rather have been its author)
Wasn't too likely to stick around long
In a career hardly worth the bother
If your suspicion was pretty darn strong
That you were meant to pursue another
Trade and the one you were in was flat *wrong*
As it concerned your capping ambition,
Which for Flynn was the writerly condition,

ERROL FLYNN

165   And in the grand scheme of things might have been
Much better for him, and just goes to show
That certain big "breaks" end up breaking *men*.
So on that bright note, let's end this canto.
When we foregather and meet once again
Errol Flynn will be ensconced in El Pueblo
De Nuestra Señora la Reina de Los
Angeles—so until then adios.

BOOK TWO

HOLLYWOOD HOTSHOT

CANTO IV

Tiger Lil and Captain Blood

(1934-1937)

Alas! the love of women! it is known
To be a lovely and a fearful thing;
For all of theirs upon that die is thrown,
And if 'tis lost, life hath no more to bring
To them but mockeries of the past alone,
And their revenge is as the tiger's spring,
Deadly, and quick and crushing; yet, as real
Torture is theirs, what they inflict they feel.

Don Juan, canto II, stanza 199

Newlyweds Errol Flynn and Lili Damita outside their
Hollywood Hills home, 1935

CANTO IV

1   Be it ever so humble!—Errol you're in
    My part of the world, my old stomping grounds,
    And whomsoever I meet in Berlin,
    My current address, almost always astounds
    At the fact that this native Angelean
    Has chosen to live outside the bounds
    Of California where the world is edged
    In golden sunlight and joy is full-fledged.

2   "Wie schaffen Sie es denn hier in diesem
    kalten Deutschland zu leben?" diverse Krauts
    Are prone to query—and I will ease 'em
    Into my answer by expressing doubts
    As to whether LA'd really please 'em,
    Citing the traffic and crime thereabouts,
    The annual fires as well as earthquakes
    And a profusion of other headaches.

3   Then German women!—not the least reason
    Why this land still has a firm hold on me.
    And I know that I'm likely displeasin'
    Half of America in making free
    With the remark that were I to seize on
    A critical difference then it would be
    That U.S. women are full of affect—
    Such vile contraptions—while Germans are *echt*.

4   *Echt* means authentic, natural, real.
    When German women smile they do not bare
    Their fangs in a grimace and thus reveal
    Expensive dental work (even if their
    Teeth are quite sound) and they don't squawk and squeal
    In loud grating tones—their talk they don't share
    With every last soul in a three-mile radius,
    Because earsplitting is not what a lady is.

ERROL FLYNN

5   And U.S. women are both graceless and fat.
Here in Berlin's Bergmannstrasse where I
Have an apartment, my little ex-pat
Retreat up on the top floor where I try
To write far above the dull pitterpat
Of tourist feet coursing all up and down my
Fair lane—a must-see in every guidebook
But to me just tourist gobbledygook—

6   In this here thoroughfare where I reside,
Full of sightseers, there is a café
That I patronize and where I can bide
My time over lunch or *petit déjeuner*,
Or coffee or beer, and get a ringside
Seat for a pastime that feminists may
Label degrading and even debauching—
The sport of intercontinental girl-watching.

7   You sit there ogling this United Nations
Of parading women, the show in full swing,
Some you would love to give standing ovations
While others you'd like to consign to Sing Sing,
The tourists all having their conversations
So you can hear where they're from, and main thing
Emerging as you compare and contrast,
Is that U.S. girls (as a rule) are lard-assed.

8   Most German women, for their part, are not
Dumpy but tend to be somewhat tallish—
Willowy's the word—and yet they've still got
Breasts I wouldn't exactly term smallish,
Quite fulsome in fact; and to sweeten the pot
They have an overall physical polish
Comprising clean limbs and a fine molded face—
If not the master still a *masterly* race.

9   So as regards European women,
     Let us imagine we're actor colleagues
     Of Flynn's in Northampton but now with him in
     Hollywood, at Warners, the major leagues,
     We not yet *knowing* that he is swimmin'
     With the big fish, where the acting technique's
     Crude at best but where the land is sun-kissed
     And one can make money hand over fist;

10   And then one day in June 1935,
     Precisely a year after Errol Flynn sent
     Downstairs with a punch the producer's wife,
     We open the *Northampton Independent*
     And get an update on Errol's love life:
     In a pic captioned "Film Romance" a content
     Flynn is shown sampling *la dolce vita*
     In California with Lili Damita!

11   This French film actress who was right up there
     With Garbo and Dietrich (but with a bit more
     Sexual heat and enticement, *mon cher*)
     Was Errol's new Hollywood paramour;
     And a week later their ardent affair
     Issued in marriage, that deft guarantor—
     Predicted the *Independent*—of Flynn's
     Success, one of your more certain shoo-ins.

12   Nonsense. Laughable. The mere idea
     That marriage in some way might elevate
     Errol to the ranks of stardom, he a
     Callow beginner and distinct lightweight,
     This Aussie upstart, how could there be a
     Ghost of a chance Errol Flynn would go straight
     To the top thereby, how facile, how trite—
     And the *Independent* was perfectly right.

ERROL FLYNN

13   Let us backtrack: Flynn and Lili first met,
According to him, when sailing across
The northern Atlantic with the smart set,
Flynn Hollywood-bound, and the coup de grâce
Delivered by Lili, that brassy coquette,
Who'd been eyeing him but showed who was boss
In spurning Flynn when he asked for a dance,
Thus squelching a possible shipboard romance.

14   Nipped in the bud right before it could start!
With Flynn at Warners, though, week after week
Passing and he trying not to lose heart
(Just playing tennis to keep his physique
In trim while awaiting his first real part)[34]
Lili Damita, appearing *très chic*
In costume of white and plum-colored silk,
And topped by beret, this time didn't bilk

15   Errol when she saw him cutting a fine
Figure on the studio courts, instead
Dispatching a sweet little valentine
In calling a sexy hello which led
To an invite Errol couldn't decline:
Drinks back at Lili's place—which in turn sped
Them straight to bed and under the covers
Where we will now leave our red-hot lovers . . .

16   That's no short version[35] —it *happened* that fast
(God bless a woman who's willing to take
The lead and Byron's fateful die to cast!)
She just the item for our handsome rake
Since by this stage Lili had amassed
A wealth of erotic technique to slake
Flynn's every desire—although he was fussy
About licking her . . . well, that shameless hussy![36]

17   But this was their sole discord—in the sack.
Though 'tween the sheets the two made a great pair,
Lili excelling while flat on her back
(Errol judging her as beyond compare,
Her own brand of French aphrodisiac)
Outside of sex they had little to share,
For it regretfully has to be said
That Lili Damita was a total airhead.

18   As we know, Errol had an active brain,
One that required constant stimulation,
But after the sex-play and the champagne,
With him indulging in speculation
On some abstract theme that didn't pertain
Directly to *Lili* then the conversation
Would screech to a halt, her face going blank,
For which it'd the void behind it to thank.

19   (Oh yes, there was one occasion she did
Display a "flicker of interest"—when Flynn
Spoke of the ancient Egyptians and bid
Her glimpse a photo, a rare specimen
Of time-honored beauty, to wit: the splendid
Great Royal Wife Nefertiti, she in
Regal pharaonic headdress, whereat
Lil vowed that she'd have a hat made like that!)

20   And when Lili's eyes weren't glazing over,
They flashed out with anger and jealousy,
A state to which Errol probably drove her
Through his *roving* eye. But all the same she
By nature was a possessive lover
Who liked throwing vases and crockery,
And choosing an apt image: though petite,
Lil was a tigress defending her meat.

ERROL FLYNN

21 From the South Sea girls all this a far cry—
  But because Errol was schooled in New Guinea,
  In fact our tigress was meat for a guy
  Groomed in a world where a man's destiny
  Was guided by how well he could apply
  The law of the jungle, he using any
  Ruses that he might have at his disposal,
  Which in this case meant a marriage proposal.

22 Flynn had no liking for the wedded state—
  Not then, not ever: much too confining.
  But if a marriage can help to create
  Opportunity by intertwining
  Career and love-life to facilitate
  Your own ascent to Hollywood's shining
  Galaxy of stars then you might abstain
  From seeing the wife as a ball and chain.

23 Errol claimed Lili threatened suicide
  Would he not make theirs a conjugal bed
  And that this notion first came from the side
  Of crony Bud Ernst, the real spearhead
  Behind the marriage, who offered to ride
  Them in his plane out to Yuma to wed—
  Which tale leaves me with a certain disquiet
  Since, to be honest, I don't quite buy it.

24 Perhaps it did happen exactly that way—
  I'd never wish to outright dismiss it;
  Nevertheless, be all that as it may,
  I'd wager Flynn was far more complicit
  In getting hitched than he cares to portray,
  This story in *Wicked* just to elicit
  Our pity for something that he now laments,
  But which at the time made good career sense.[37]

25   Flynn couldn't have been sure of his talent
     At this early stage; but if his acting
     Was still inexpert, our self-aware gallant
     Knew that he was a pro at attracting
     The ladies—and the film capital lent
     Itself to just such marriage-contracting
     Because the whole town was fueled by raw fear,
     Its sole aspect which was *truly* sincere.

26   Damita's own star was now on the wane.
     She still looked dazzling and had enough fight
     (As Flynn could attest!) in her to sustain
     A career of a kind, but now the twilight
     Years were upon her, that infamous bane
     Of sex goddesses who still crave the spotlight
     Even if creeping up on middle age,
     But Lili seemed ready to turn the page.

27   Now over thirty years old,[38] Dynamite
     Damita was finding it hard to explode
     The myth that a woman of her age might
     Not in fact still play those film roles which owed
     Their lure to men's sexual appetite;
     The future would be a prolonged threnode
     To Lili's career, what of it remained,
     So to hang on there seemed scant to be gained.

28   Then along swaggers this Australian lad,
     More thrilling and handsome than any leading
     Man she'd yet starred with (and Coop not half bad)[39]
     Who all the same might yet still be needing
     Some help in the biz, a small launching pad,
     Which she could furnish—and his succeeding,
     In turn, would help to secure her own life
     Were they to become lawful man and wife.

29   But not to be *overly* cynical:
    It does seem that Lili really did love Flynn,
    Hers not merely some coldly clinical
    Project to keep her own little hand in
    The Hollywood game, her star-pinnacle
    Already attained—no!—it'd be a sin
    Not to mention her heart and how Flynn awoke it,
    Which he must have done, since later he broke it.

30   And did Flynn love *her*? Well, he certainly
    Loved what she stood for: sophistication,
    Glamour and fame. And on her womanly
    Charms Errol placed a high valuation,
    As noted, her body uncommonly
    Alive to sexual stimulation . . .
    Was it her body, though, or her *connections*
    That most excited our hero's erections?

31   Connections she had—and chief among these
    Was head honcho Jack Warner's fiancée,
    With whom Lil was close, so with the big cheese
    She'd a mouthpiece and could also make hay
    Of her contact to Michael Curtiz,
    Gifted director and Warners mainstay,
    Helming a new film, now stuck in the mud,
    A swashbuckler bearing the name *Captain Blood*.[40]

32   The film was bogged down since its chosen star
    Had pulled out over a contract dispute;[41]
    So Lili got busy doing PR,
    Curtiz gave Flynn a screen-test that bore fruit,
    And then Warner Brothers' studio czar,
    Jack Warner, who had sunk plenty of loot
    Into this movie, thought he'd take a chance
    On Flynn who was "vivid" (if lacking nuance).[42]

33 Chances were something that Jack liked to take.
    His was the first studio, after all,
    To commit fully to sound and to make
    Partners of "audio" and "visual"
    With *The Jazz Singer*,[43] and first man to stake
    His reputation as well as no small
    Amount of money on that great annuller
    Of black and white film—two-strip Technicolor.[44]

34 "Looney Tunes" and "Merrie Melodies" he
    Also brought into the fold and later
    Promoted 3-D to combat TV[45]
    (Which he soon entered) this innovator
    Whose pictures weren't some writer's fantasy
    But ripped from the news headlines, this trader
    In risk, this gambler just spoiling for a fight,
    Like Errol a buccaneer in his own right—

35 Though quite a cost-conscious one at that!
    But Jack Warner's parsimonious ways,
    His stringent economizing, begat
    Those movies which made "fast-paced" a catchphrase—
    With Raft, Cagney, Bogart and each a gat
    To speed things along and set screens ablaze
    With sizzling tempos that owed to tight-scripted
    Plots the result of Jack being tight-fisted.

36 The shooting schedules were tight so as to keep
    To the tight budgets. But though Jack was rough
    On stars, directors and crews with his cheap
    Approach, the *writers* liked him well enough:
    While other studios caused them to weep,
    At Warners far more original stuff
    Of theirs made the screen—delight of delights—
    Since tightwad Jack wouldn't pay for rewrites.[46]

ERROL FLYNN

37   Gangsters, lean budgets, the Great Depression
All came together back then to create
A no-nonsense style and all of it meshin'
To make Warners the unadulterate
Macho studio, virile aggression
Its sine qua non, no actors castrate
Here nor among the *actress* personnel—
Spunky broads like Davis, Stanwyck and Blondell.

38   The lineup of Warners directors socks
You right in the eye with all its hell-men—
These running the gamut from Howard Hawks
To ex-fighter pilot "Wild Bill" Wellman
To ex-pug John Huston, the school of hard knocks
Likewise producing Raoul Walsh (pray tell, man,
Who else sports a black eyepatch?) but my hunch
Is Michael Curtiz was the toughest of the bunch.

39   Curtiz was a native Hungarian
Who'd fought in the Great War and since its end
Had acquired his filmcraft in Europe where he an
Expert director became, an odd blend
Of sadistic authoritarian
And tasteful artiste whose work can contend
With all those *auteurs* whose lingua franca
Is high art, his masterpiece *Casablanca*.[47]

40   (His grammar was film—not that of English,
His grasp of the latter precarious,
Like that one time when he made a clownish
Remark the film crew found hilarious,
Leading him to spout yet more gibberish,
Reviling their language nefarious:
"You think that I know fuck nothing," screamed the tall
Ramrod martinet, "but I know FUCK ALL!")

41   Lili Damita, Mike Curtiz and Jack
Warner were the three main ingredients
In getting our Aussie on the fast track
To stardom[48]—and Errol's obedience
Expected as their well-deserved payback.
But Flynn wasn't one for subservience
Or for that matter humble gratitude,
His revolt increasing in magnitude

42   The more this troika tried to dominate
Him in the private (Lili), artistic
(Curtiz) and career (Warner) spheres. Some great
Films though emerged from these antagonistic
Relations, this clash of four heavyweight
Egomaniacs, a synergistic
Mix that aroused what made Flynn *magnifique*
Up there on the screen—his defiant streak.

43   And dauntless defiance was the keynote
Of Errol Flynn's first major starring role:
Dr. Peter Blood, no Monmouth turncoat,[49]
Condemned still for treason to spend his whole
Life at slave labor out in the remote
West Indies where he then seizes control
Of a ship and begins a pirate career—
There's more to the tale, but that's enough here.

44   Important to know, however, is that
In this here film it was not just the case
Of a classic Flynn *role*—an aristocrat,
At least in spirit, attempting to efface
Injustice through guile and stirring combat—
But classic Flynn *elements* were in place,
Starting with Curtiz, that jodhpurred despot,
Whose gusto could quicken the limpest plot;

45   And then Olivia de Havilland,
Errol Flynn's radiant love interest,
And not merely in film-fantasyland
But real life too, this fact manifest
In all their pictures, their fondness first-hand,
A mutual affection that caressed
Their mutual scenes like a delicate breeze,
Offsetting the swagger of Flynn and Curtiz;[50]

46   And then so in order to underscore
And heighten the romance and heroics,
Allowing emotion to nobly soar,
Even that of inflexible stoics,
You needed Flynn-elements 3 and 4,
Those fellows who were the studio ex-
Perts for music in major and minor:
Erich Wolfgang Korngold and Max Steiner.

47   Between the two of them, these artists scored
A full twenty-two of Flynn's films, Korngold
Earning his second Academy Award
For *The Adventures of Robin Hood*—old
School romanticism of one accord
With Errol Flynn's dash and serving to enfold
The tale in rich lyric tones and transport
Us back to Sherwood and Prince John's court.

48   With Korngold and Steiner you had a pair
Of Viennese *Künstler* who had inhaled
Their Richards Wagner and Strauss like the air
They breathed and whose film scores duly entailed
Leitmotifs and unceasing melody, their
Orchestrations lush, and best of these hailed
Today as symphonic tone-poems since springing
From an impulse to write operas sans singing.[51]

49   There would be other directors (Keighley,
Goulding, Walsh, Sherman) as well as leading
Ladies (Davis, Garson and the highly
Under-esteemed Alexis Smith)—ceding
Also the evident fact, though shyly,
That *Gentleman Jim* is wholly unheeding
Of Flynn-elements[52] —but Curtiz et al.
Comprised the matrix for Flynn's immortal

50   Movie portrayals of those early years.
And we should note that in Errol's first role,
Captain Peter Blood, this matrix appears
To've been the crucial if not quite the sole
Thing helping Flynn, so wet behind the ears,
Give a performance that critics extol;
At risk though of sounding irascible,
Much of it I find merely passable.

51   Flynn overplays it in more than one scene,
Which one is able to forgive in view
Of the fact that he's not only so green
But that a theatrical residue
Still clings to this effort for the big screen—
One can forgive such, but just *entre nous*,
It's verging on camp, a bit of a hoot,
When done in a plumed hat and pirate suit.

52   It could have been worse: Warner had Curtiz
Return to the set and made him reshoot
Flynn's earlier scenes—and not because these
Were so horrendous (though it does impute
They simply weren't good, at least when one sees
What *did* make the cut) but was a tribute
To Flynn who improved as the filming progressed,
The first scenes now needing to jibe with the rest.

53   It was December 1935
When *Captain Blood* had its lustrous premiere,
And notwithstanding the charges that I've
Leveled at Errol's performance, through sheer
Personal charisma it comes alive,
Exuding a romantic atmosphere,
Ample Flynn magic bestowed to the part
For us to overlook his lack of art.

54   The night of the movie's premiere they threw
A lavish party, and one of the first
Guests to arrive was a screenwriter who
Poor Lili received, very unrehearsed,
In a tearful state and begged him not to
Tell Flynn "how wonderful he was" and burst
Into more sobs, going on to expand,
Wailing: "Tonight I have lost my husband!"[53]

55   Just like Byron, Flynn awoke the next day
To ascertain he was famous,[54] and he
Meant to enjoy the rich banquet that lay
Before him and sample each delicacy
With supreme relish, brooking no delay,
For who knew how long this fine feast would be
Granted to him? And as Flynn drank and fed,
The wine of success went straight to his head.

56   By God he'd done it! Risen to the top
Of the Hollywood world—a star!—and to think
A mere year ago he had made the hop
Across the Atlantic and just tickled pink
To've gotten a chance, if only to flop,
In the film capital. Now in a wink
He'd outdone Dad whose fame was a scholar's
And meant very little in terms of *dollars*.

57   After *Captain Blood* had proved a success,
Errol Flynn's earnings would take a sharp jump
To 800 dollars a week and progress
To 5000 bucks before long, he no chump
Prepared to obligingly acquiesce
To Jack Warner's will but garnering plump
Pay hikes till by 1941 he
Was earning all the aforesaid money.

58   Of all the big studios, Warners paid
The lowest salaries. Errol had to fight
Each step of the way to get a fair trade
On the increasing joy and delight
The planet was taking in this gay blade—
A favored ploy to give Warners a fright,
Being to skipper away on his yacht
And holding up filming as likely as not.

59   Flynn always played for extremely high stakes,
Of course, but added to this was the fact
That he had gotten so many good breaks
En route to the top that he sorely lacked
An appreciation for the *work* it takes
To make the Big Time with a hefty contract,
His career lacking a single pitfall,
And so he less fearful of losing it all.

60   But in contract talks the real decider
For Errol (his own sub-rosa loophole)
Was he perceived himself as a *writer*.
By no means would Flynn just laughingly stroll
Away from fame now that he was bestride her,
But Errol in his pay disputes could enroll
This self-view to shed his acting fetters
And think: "Blast Warners!—I'm a man of letters!"

ERROL FLYNN

61 In point of fact he'd been doing far more
Writing than acting in the year gone by—
Witness "The White Rajah" script which sold for
A cool thirteen grand; and that tale of high
Adventure at sea—as well as ashore—
About a quartet of young fellows who try
To sail a small yacht, in their naiveté,
Out to New Guinea, braving come what may.

62 The *Sirocco* trip! That youthful joyride!
And what the devil had ever become
Of that crew with whom he had risked his hide—
Charlie, Trelawny and Rex, the big bum?
Flynn now felt a belated surge of pride
And urge to artistically profit from
This odyssey with his trio of friends
By writing the novel entitled *Beam Ends.*

63 That first year in Hollywood, Errol began
Thinking back to the South Seas and New Guinea.
He liked California, being a man
Who loved the outdoors and the ocean and he
Prizing the seemingly endless caravan
Of women both starstruck and amatory—
But although L.A. was damn near ideal,
The whole thing struck Flynn as slightly irreal.

64 This is how all of it struck Errol Flynn
Since it had been not all too very long
Before that our big movie star had been
A drifter camped out by a billabong
And living by his wits and by the skin
Of his teeth in New Guinea, far from the throng,
Poor and obscure in a Stone Age land,
And now with the world eating out of his hand.

65   By day he filmed *Charge of the Light Brigade*,
      Which happened to be, by Flynn's own account,
      The toughest movie that he ever made,
      All the time trying to keep a fine mount
      While pushing his steed through the stunts that they'd
      Concocted for him, and the body-count
      In terms of horses, at least, rather high,
      A process that Errol would later decry.[55]

66   But evenings he would doff his riding boots,
      Take up his pen and leave the Crimea,
      Setting sail with his *Sirocco* recruits
      To primordial New Guinea via
      Australia's Great Barrier Reef, in cahoots,
      This gumptious quartet, against the idea
      That prudence, not nerve, should dictate our lives,
      That principal rule of the world's nine-to-fives.

67   As it would for the rest of his career,
      Flynn's displaced mind was now occupying
      Two opposing worlds at once—that one near
      To hand, which Errol felt unsatisfying,
      The Hollywood world of style and veneer;
      And then the world which was underlying
      His primary self—that island nation
      Light years from Western civilization.

68   Errol Flynn's bifurcated consciousness,
      His detached and oft-haunted quality
      Is what caused people to frequently stress,
      In accounts of him, his complexity,
      Saying how hard to make any ingress
      Into his tangled personality:
      That there was a certain something about
      Flynn they weren't able to quite figure out.

69   And that certain something, naturally,
Was the adventuresome youth Errol spent
In the uncharted wilds of New Guinea,
A secret but tangible side that lent
A semblance of danger and mystery,
A man with a past and not just a present . . .
We've touched upon this already, of course,
So there's little reason to beat a dead horse.

70   Dead horses, oh yes—after *Charge* Flynn was kept
Busy making films into the next year,
Becoming more confident and adept,
The next one *Green Light*, our erstwhile cavalier
Playing a surgeon whose life is upswept
In tragic events; and jerk one more tear
For Flynn in the picture *Another Dawn*
(If only because it's one long talkathon);

71   Cheer for him in *The Prince and the Pauper*,
Laugh at him in *The Perfect Specimen*,
This latter light fare that Errol felt proper
To his chief gift of a deft comedian,
Albeit he'd hardly come a cropper
In previous roles—both his masculine
And female public able to enjoy
Him in all parts, just mad about the boy.

72   And here I'll extend an apology
For the apparently unseemly haste
With which I've sped through my chronology
Of movies—though *not* having *Wicked*'s outpaced,[56]
Flynn's bio mirroring his psychology
Back in those early days when he was raced
From one Warner Brothers picture to the next,
His nerves overtaxed and his spirit vexed.

73   Moreover, Errol was feeling entrapped
By marriage to the possessive Lili,
Leaving him psychologically sapped,
Ceaselessly fighting with this French filly.
It seemed like most every day the two scrapped
And one brawl that year was a real dilly,
She using a bottle of Veuve Clicquot
To brain him and issuing in his KO—

74   But not before Errol uncorked *his* best shot,
Knocking out Lili as well as her tooth,
Both of them flattened and later distraught,
Errol for having been very uncouth
In smacking a girl, and Lili for not
Just taking a bat to him like Babe Ruth
And rendering Errol a bit less agile
While saving her natural movie-star smile.[57]

75   Last but not least, Errol's very first book
Beam Ends had been published and gotten some
Quite decent reviews, so Flynn undertook
To get out from under Jack Warner's thumb
And stow the acting and no longer brook
All of that Hollywood madness—in sum:
Fleeing errant bottles of French champagne
For the safe haven of war-ravaged Spain.

76   Flynn wished to renew his old notion of
Himself as a worldly and intrepid
Adventurer with a genuine love
Of real-life risk and not just some tepid
Hollywood celluloid version thereof—
Leaving behind this morally decrepit
Realm where *Action!* meant just another take,
At worst hearing *Cut!* if you made a mistake.

77 Errol had a longing to fortify
 His own self-conception of a writer,
 A full-fledged member of the literati,
 Not just some dilettante fly-by-nighter
 But a man willing to both do and die,
 Riding to the guns, as in *Charge*, if brighter
 His honor in this certain instance—all hail
 The hero who *survives* to tell the tale![58]

78 Errol would travel to Spain's civil war
 In the veritable role of journalist.
 In the past year he'd penned articles for
 A couple trade papers (and their basic gist—
 Surprise!—his life as a Hollywood actor)
 And *Beam Ends* afforded a kindly assist
 By way of its prior serialization
 In *Cosmopolitan* (mass circulation).[59]

79 So, taken together with his *Sydney
 Bulletin* pieces of some years back, yes,
 Errol had enough published stuff to be
 Credentialed as part of the global press.
 And his photographer was someone that we
 Have already met—but just take a guess—
 And I'll be so good as to give you a hint:
 He rivaled Jack Warner as a skinflint . . .

80 In Spain our Quixote's Sancho Panza
 Was Hermann F. Erben, late of Flynn's trip
 Through Asia, that raucous extravaganza
 When they had forged an enduring friendship;
 But maybe I should redo this stanza,
 Perhaps I'm guilty of a careless slip—
 Let's keep with Byron and stay Hispanic
 By speaking of Don Juan and *his* man (sic!).

81   But who in fact was Don Juan's manservant?
In Byron's version I don't recall he'd
Given him one, and I've been observant
In all my readings . . . Ha!—there was indeed
A manner of squire, a scholar fervent
Of languages, but just as in *Candide*,
He meets the same fate as a gluteal cheek,
Namely he's eaten. (I just took a peek.)

82   Thus let the Sancho-Panza stanza stand—
Errol's Spain adventure was *quixotic*
From the beginning since it had been fanned
By his fanciful and periodic
Urge to be a reporter in the grand
Tradition of scribes who craved war's narcotic—
Crane, London, Hemingway, Richard Harding Davis
(Now we've got clowns like Geraldo—God save us).[60]

83   But Erben—he'd tracked down Errol, a few
Months prior, to Hollywood where the two had
A heartfelt joyous reunion; though you
Couldn't say Lili Damita was glad
To see this fellow, for it seems they knew
Each other from his having once done a tad
Of work as a medic on some Viennese
Movie sets where he'd met Michael Curtiz.[61]

84   Lili wasn't fond of Errol Flynn's friend
—In fact she called the good doctor "that pig!"—
And consequently unable to pretend
That she found anything sound in this big
Junket to Spain, let alone to commend,
Instead being ready to flip her wig,
Going on a rampage like Medea,
Since the whole thing had been *Erben's* idea.

ERROL FLYNN

85   Say what you like about Lili but she
Was "a little ball of intuition,"
As Flynn himself put it so cogently;
And it wasn't just her disposition
In wanting Errol in proximity,
But she'd a powerful premonition
That Hermann Erben was up to no good
(Her instinct for such honed in sweet Hollywood).

86   She followed the two of them all the way
To New York then London and on to Paris,
La Tour Eiffel and the Champs-Élysée,
A town where the cheapest little affair is
Set all ashimmer just like a Monet;
And in my view, if a city there is
Where estranged lovers can mend a deep rift
It's Paris (who chose Aphrodite's gift).

87   At Lili and Errol's initial contact
They quarreled (what else) and violently so,
She reading her husband the riot act
For blithely abandoning her to go
Off with this Erben; apart from the fact
That Lili herself might end up a widow—
How thoughtless, how base, how cruel, how obscene
To do such a thing . . . are you listening Fleen?!

88   But then they made up—not to say that he
Would alter his plans but at least Flynn could leave
On good terms with Lili, this something to be
Celebrated with Paris granting reprieve
To their doomed romance. So now let us see
If the two might yet their old love retrieve,
Lili proposing that they hit a local
Club with the quaint name of "Le Monocle."

89   Lili swore it was *le dernier cri*
Where it concerned Paris night life—but
On entering it Errol couldn't quite see,
The *boîte* faintly lit and along with what
Seemed to be alcoves with long and roomy
Benches and discreet nearby doors that shut
Fast as they opened, these doors issuing
On chambers not designed for public viewing.

90   And in the weak light, Flynn's eyes adjusting,
He sees that everyone wears a tuxedo.
My God it's all men, he thinks, *how disgusting!*
And just like Lili to foil my libido,
Hauling me out to a club where the lusting
Is male on male, her unfailing credo
To keep my attention riveted on her—
This judgment emerging as premature.

91   For Errol soon notes that the clientele
Is on the short side, as Frenchmen can be,
But each of these patrons . . . a mademoiselle!
All of their tuxes with very starchy
Shirts to encumber the natural swell
Of their chests and their hair styled mannishly—
In fact these ladies aren't at all ladylike,
Most bringing to mind the expression "bulldyke."

92   One of them seems to be queen of the place—
Or king—no matter: Her name is Frankie,
With schoolboy haircut and finely drawn face,
Flowing bowtie and breast-pocket hanky
Cascading forth, and she moves with a grace
Imparted to her by a pair of swanky
Suede dancing shoes and undulating hips
That set tongues to running along wanton lips.

93   But that which really attracts your attention
    Is her stance, her pose, since she has a way
    (Which in fact might be a very French one)
    Of radiating a kind of blasé
    Arrogance and lofty condescension,
    One hand in tux pocket and, as they say,
    Looking "down her nose," which you must agree
    Is a good trick when you're just five-foot-three.

94   Errol at first is intrigued by all this,
    Even enchanted, for what real man
    Finds *any* fondness for women amiss?—
    Unless a particular one began
    To make a play for your own comely miss,
    She then responding according to plan,
    With you yourself feeling as useless now
    As the perennial balls on a cow.

95   Frankie and Lili take to the dancefloor,
    Gliding along to the snaky music,
    Between them a silent rhythmic rapport,
    Everything seeming to perfectly click,
    Unlike Flynn's marriage, that grim tug-of-war,
    Even pertaining to whether he should lick . . .
    It dawning on Errol now whence might be traced
    Lil's acquisition of *this* certain taste.[62]

96   As the two dance, Errol Flynn can discern,
    At other tables, beneath the dim lights,
    Young ladies necking with grand unconcern
    For the onlookers and trading love bites
    And soft caresses and kisses that burn
    With carnal hunger for taboo delights,
    Some leaving in pairs by those secret doors
    So they can partake of the evening's main course.

97   Flynn sits there feeling an "illicit wonder"
At the proceedings while at the same time
Sensing the error it had been to blunder
Into this sweltering Sapphoist clime.
And as for Lili, he could have gunned her
Down on the spot with her partner in crime,
So riled is he at this usurpation
Of his rightful role—this tacit castration!

98   But what can he do? Flynn orders champagne—
When in doubt drink, that is Errol's motto;
Should things continue along in this vein,
He'll have no recourse but to get blotto,
Dulling the humiliation and pain;
But in a show of gallant bravado,
In a display of gentlemanly class,
He offers each girl at his table a glass.

99   They accept—impressed by his self-possession.
And before long, Lili comes back with Frankie
Who wears a very placid expression,
Which just makes Errol all that more cranky,
Ready to perpetrate some indiscretion,
So as a dumb adolescent prank he
Says he'll find out what's beneath Frankie's shirt,
And reaching out pinches a breast soft but pert.

100   As soon as he does, Errol's arm goes numb,
One of the dykes having given his wrist
A shattering blow—though Lili's new chum
Is wholly unfazed by our crude chauvinist,
The tranquil set of Frankie's face now become
Yet even moreso, as if she'd been kissed
And not merely groped, she spurning self-pity,
Since Captain Blood had just squeezed her titty!

ERROL FLYNN

101   Moreover, she's now the bone of contention
Between two glamorous Hollywood stars,
The object of their delicious dissension,
Assuming the nature of a chic farce,
While taking on the added dimension
Of a *scandale* in those cafés and bars
Where Paris gossip has its propagation,
Thus doing wonders for her reputation!

102   Flynn rubs his wrist and just for a fleeting
Moment he contemplates counter-violence;
But then he ends up merely retreating
Into a sullen simmering silence,
Frankie and Lili forthwith repeating
Their previous tête-à-tête in defiance
Of pouty Flynn with their strictly two-way
Chat while the dykes put the bubbly away.

103   At length comes the bill—but rather than six
Glasses it is for six bottles! Flynn is
Incensed and tells them that they're lunatics
If they think he's paying—it takes no wiz
To see that their Gallic arithmetic's
Ever so slightly awry and that his
Princely champagne offer didn't include
An invitation to be royally screwed.

104   The dykes surround Flynn while suggesting that
It would be better for him to just pay.
But Errol's not one to avoid a spat,
So he suggests they get out of his way,
Since if they don't then he'll knock 'em all flat!
But in the midst of this grandstand play,
Before he's able to mount an attack,
Flynn finds *himself* lying flat on his back.

105   He gets up swinging and fur starts to fly,
The nightclub erupting in screeches and shouts,
Tuxedoed lesbians going banzai,
Errol enraged now and scoring knockouts,
Striking at any and all those nearby,
This one of his more spectacular bouts—
But then things coming to one of those stops
Often occurring at the entrance of cops.

106   These are protectors of the *maison*,
Who promptly toss Errol into the clink,
A grimy old cell, not quite the place on
Which he'd depended to finally sink
Down in a silk-sheeted bed and gaze on
The city of Paris by night with a drink
In hand and Damita right by his side,
Her sex-charms deployed and the two pacified.

107   Errol Flynn's overnight plans are waylaid
(Or any plans as a matter of fact)
And even though he may have left unpaid
The bill with which he'd been rudely bushwhacked,
He's surely paying for his *escapade*,
Not just his pockets now being ransacked
But the police having filched his shoelaces,
Which Errol finds just a tad bit predaceous.

108   Placing his shoes outside of his cell,
As one might do when staying at the Ritz,
Errol commences to raise holy hell,
Banging around and protesting that it's
Time someone cleaned his *chausseures*—fine hotel
This rotten joint is!—an outburst that sits
Not well with the prison caretakers, whose
Job's not to polish a detainee's shoes.

ERROL FLYNN

109   They take Errol out and slap him around
Then throw him back in (*chausseures* still unclean)
And now he discerns the familiar sound
Of Lil's dainty voice—ah!—pleading for Fleen
To be set free and she paying a mound
Of cash for the bail and also quite keen
To settle the bill for all that champagne—
How politic of her, how sober, how sane . . .

110   "Throw that bitch out!" yells Errol. "If you take
Her money you're bums, French bums, you hear me!"
But this would seem to have been a mistake,
A gaffe, a faux pas, Errol Flynn's repartee
Being cut short with a cruel whack to make
Him feel they'd broken the fingers that he
Had gripped the bars with, and so our hard case
Proceeds now to spit in a French bum's face.

111   This is met strangely with the same ill will
As his shoeshine plea, three beefy gendarmes
Invading his cell and with consummate skill
Jerking his coat o'er his head with Flynn's arms
Pinioned inside while two hold him until
The third cop has fully exhausted the charms
Of pounding a star, whom they say can go
Since the bail's paid and you tired, Monsieur, no?

112   Hell no, Flynn's not tired, he'll outlast 'em all!
Still really heated and still breathing fire,
Invoking his rights and threatening to haul
Each of them 'fore the World Court and entire
League of damn Nations and put in a call
To Pope Pius himself! And yet Errol's ire
Doesn't subside when they bring back his things,
Also including the pilfered shoestrings,

113   For he demands that those who removed them
Put them back in. This the sergeant ignores.
Then Errol, looking for some other item
To fuel his anger, now quickly explores
His cigarette case, detecting a problem:
"Who stole my cigarettes? You're thieves!" he roars.
"I refuse to go until they're returned."
They aren't—so Errol is once more interned.

114   It was 5 a.m. before he got out
On the streets again, but not going straight
To the hotel, Flynn just roaming about
In the grey dawn as if bearing a weight,
His shoulders drooping, his footstep without
The usual spring, it being his fate
To've wed a woman who presently filled
Him with crazed thoughts—like kill or be killed.

115   He couldn't endure it, all the insults
And injuries followed by desperate lovemaking—
Only to start up again and convulse
Their marriage and this all the more heartbreaking
Since there'd been intervals where the impulse
Between them hadn't been of their taking
Cruel vicious swipes at each other but true
Fondness and authentic happiness too.

116   Like those first days in the "Garden of Allah,"
Quite suitably named, this cottage complex
On Sunset Strip, like the Muslim Valhalla
Where fallen warriors are given blank checks
To pursue pleasure and each day a gala
Affair with fine wines and limitless sex—
A heaven whose whole conceptual basis
Is of a sense-gratifying oasis.[63]

117   Lili had lodgings at this earthly version
    Of Saracen heaven, where Errol joined her
    To spend their nights in erotic diversion,
    The Hollywood air's ambrosial *douceur*
    Embathing their bodies just like immersion
    In a pool heated the same temperature
    As your warm blood, theirs racing with the thrill—
    Though not too long before that blood would spill.

118   Battle lines were firmly drawn when they left
    Garden of Allah for Appian Way[64]
    (This latter place-name itself not bereft
    Of symbolism, if I might portray
    Their spousal journey and deepening cleft
    As one long hard stony road, let us say)
    On Lookout Mountain, right off Laurel Canyon,
    Lil hoping to make her lover a companion.

119   Cohabitation, though, harrowed the nerves—
    And as they always represent warfare:
    Stretches of tedium with abrupt swerves
    Into sheer terror when tempers would flare.
    And although Lil had the sweetest of curves,
    All her thrown objects were fastballs—howe'er,
    Not being pitched over plates but instead
    That's what she *hurled*, the strike-zone Flynn's head.

120   So Errol moved out—to North Linden Drive,
    Beverly Hills, with chum David Niven,[65]
    Flynn doing his level best to revive
    His bachelor life, he and Lili now riven;
    And unfettered David, still yet to wive,
    Was himself no less sexually driven,
    A worthy sidekick, on the uptake not slow,
    And taking up Flynn's female overflow.

121   From time to time Flynn and Lili would make
A cautious attempt at conciliation,
Practicing the fine art of give-and-take,
Oft taking the form of fornication,
Giving them both a temporary break
From squabbling or a long separation—
But even if good, the sex never spawned
Lasting concord since it was their sole bond.

122   Apart from the incompatibilities
In their own natures, the built-in dynamic
'Tween Flynn and Lili was one of the keys
(Although not during their idyll Islamic)
Why all their meetings required referees:
While Errol was getting a panoramic
View of the world, his star fast ascending,
With opportunities sheer unending,

123   Fading star Lili Damita was trying
To keep Errol on a very short line,
An arduous thing these days with him flying
Higher than a kite—but now this feline
Stunt she'd just pulled, there was no denying,
Had brought him down low; though not one to whine,
Indulging in feelings verging on sappy,
Flynn was admittedly deeply unhappy.

124   What the hell was all the fortune and fame
Worth if you're utterly miserable?
What good success and what use acclaim
If finally subject to considerable
Abuse at the hands of some nutty dame?
In short, Errol felt death preferable
To living with all of this psychic pain,
All of his efforts to allay it in vain.

ERROL FLYNN

125   Errol left Paris that day—though not 'fore
A final climactic scene with Lili
Who threatened to leap from the upper floor
Of their hotel room; Errol fit to kill, he
Yelling up, "Do it! What are you waiting for!"
So she came down from the window sill, he
Still flinging taunts, then she took his suitcase
And promptly flung *it* downward in her place.

126   Flynn took a while to collect all the stuff
—The luggage had spewed out onto the street—
The whole time thinking that he'd called her bluff,
But she'd still captured a win from defeat,
Which she was good at. Well, he'd had enough,
This time the whole thing was set in concrete:
They two were done—finito!—as am I,
Since Flynn needs to be off for Spain by and by.

127   In '37, the spring of that year,
The Spanish Civil War was nine months old,
Kindled when Franco refused to adhere
To fair elections, these finally controlled
By the Left; that is, he a mutineer
And suitably welcomed into the fold
By Mussolini as well as the Führer,
So for fascist friends he was none the poorer.

128   They sent the Condor Legion and the Black
Shirts to do battle on the Franco side.
And there was hardly what you'd call a lack
Of support for the "Loyalists," they fortified
By Soviet Russia and an eager pack
Of volunteers lending commie-implied
Service to the Republic, which for Flynn
Was the wronged party and he hoped would win.

129   That was the side for which Errol struck out
       (Though he'd have gladly joined up with their foes
       Just to flee Madame Damita, no doubt)
       Flynn entering Barcelona at the close
       Of March, he and Erben hardly without
       Concerns as to their reception—but those
       Worries dispelled when our Hollywood star
       Was met by two men and a government car.

130   They spent some days in this graceful town and
       Got heroes' welcomes wherever they went—
       Perhaps due to Flynn's now taking a stand
       As well as his being the first prominent
       Actor to witness the fighting firsthand?
       Because indeed that was Errol's intent,
       Taking the car to embattled Madrid,
       His mood at this time best described as *morbid*.

131   He still felt strongly that he'd come to die
       And that the bottom wouldn't suddenly drop
       Out of folks' lives if he did—and so why
       Not pack it all in when you're still on top?
       They'll say: *He was always a noble guy,*
       That Flynn, not your standard Hollywood fop.
       And matter of fact, it would sure be funny
       To die on Warner—who'd grieve his lost money.

132   They passed through Valencia and then motored
       Through Albacete where the Brigada
       Internacional was now headquartered,
       Errol once again *persona grata*,
       Posing for photographs with the assorted
       Troops of this multinational squad, a
       Group there consisting of men from Germany—
       The Republic's ostensible enemy.

133   And they continued to receive the royal
Treatment in Madrid, Doc Erben and Flynn
Meeting with all kinds of top brass loyal
To the Republic—but making a din
Were Franco's soldiers, fomenting turmoil
By shelling a building right near Errol's inn,
Shells whistling by with a loud blast of air, a
First acid taste for our boy of *la guerra*!

134   Flynn spent that day exploring the city,
He taking notes while Doc Erben took photos
Of him taking notes—the pictures aren't pretty:
Flynn with a grim look, in hunched-over pose,
The landscape ruined and bleak and gritty.
And yet for all of the setting's pathos,
Flynn's still a sight for some passing sigñora,
In his trenchcoat and rakish fedora.[66]

135   Making good use of his safe-conduct pass,
Reserved exclusively for VIPs,
Flynn roamed about in his prime function as
War correspondent to gain expertise
On the situation and to amass
Inside dope appertaining to the squeeze
Madrid found itself in now and the brunt
Borne by the troops—which led him to the front.

136   The Guadalajara Front was where he
Arrived when both sides had been through the mincer—
Yet a great Loyalist victory,
Stopping their foe from closing the pincer
Movement that would have effectively
Surrounded the government's capital since her
Supply lines would've been cut front to back,
She helpless against any further attack.

137   A moral triumph and morale was high
Among the Republican forces when
Errol arrived and they not camera-shy,
Doc Erben snapping away at these men,
All of them happy and thrilled to comply,
The Hollywood hero at hand!—Flynn again
Receiving a welcome he didn't expect,
Since *they'd* done the fighting while he rubbernecked.

138   But back in Madrid was where Errol got
Involved in the war in a real way.
Both he and Erben evidently thought,
Having seen the shelling only by day,
That it'd be fun to observe the onslaught
With sundown affording a fireworks display,
Producing the splendidly menacing sight
Of deathly hellfire profiled against the night.

139   With Madrid blacked out, the guns' stabbing flashes
Lay fulgent and brilliant against the sky,
Like strokes of luminous paint, bright lashes
Of orange on a velvet backdrop, the reply
From across the valley lending more splashes
Of hue to the scene—then a boom and a sigh
Of the shell as it hurtles straight into town,
Far overhead, still you keep your head down,

140   Which Errol Flynn did, and yet all the same,
When a shell burst less than fifty yards off
It jarred loose plaster from off of the frame
Of a house so shot up you just had to cough
To shake it, ensuring that something then came
Plummeting down at you from up above,
The plaster colliding with Flynn's famous head
And news going out that he'd been struck dead.

141   He wasn't, of course, but just knocked out cold,
      Staying so for quite a while—a lifeless
      Cadaver were somebody Flynn to behold,
      Far beyond succor, no more storm and stress,
      And maybe already starting to mold;
      You might surmise such in passing *unless*
      You're a physician who should know better—
      But Doc Erben was the tale's begetter.

142   Why the deliberate fabrication?
      I've no real inkling.[67] But still there can be
      Small doubt as to Erben's motivation
      In spreading a second fictitious story,
      This one involving some imagination:
      That Errol had brought the Loyalists money
      In the amount of one million smackers
      Collected from other Hollywood backers.

143   Neither did Errol have any such sum
      Nor would it seem that he was aware
      (Since Erben the whole time was keeping mum)
      Of strictly why it was that everywhere
      They traveled in Spain they would get a welcome
      Befitting indeed a star millionaire,
      Erben having wished to travel in style
      And Flynn just the man our Spaniards to beguile.

144   This reprobate also wanted to gain
      Access to people and places and things
      That even *with* Flynn would not, in the main,
      Have been feasible without pulling some strings;
      An access enhanced, in civil-war Spain,
      Through Doc Erben's skill in applying dressings
      And placing disabled Loyalists in traction,
      All serving as a blind for covert action.[68]

CANTO IV

145   Not all the photographs that Erben took
During the progress of his Spanish stay
Were destined to end in his private scrapbook,
Many of them later making their way
To Berlin where the Nazis gathered a look
At which of their countrymen had gone astray
In opting to join the Republican side—
Their families accordingly crucified.[69]

146   So Lili was right—Doc Erben was a swine,
Using Errol Flynn as star-camouflage,
As glamorous cover for his malign
Deeds of betrayal and espionage
For that dictatorship transalpine,
Inflicting not only untold damage
On innocents but he not giving a hoot
If bringing his friend into disrepute.

147   There are certain questions at issue here,
The first of them being—for God's sake WHY?
Why did the Jew, Erben, seek to endear
Himself to the Nazis? Just why be their spy
As an American? It's far from clear,
And Erben's Spain-journal doesn't supply
Us clues—in fact there aren't any entries
For the last month, which can't just be caprice.

148   Doc Erben's motives are hardly transparent,
So they are really anybody's guess—
One thing about him, though, is apparent:
The guy always looked for ways to pay *less*,
And to such persons there's often inherent
Another impulse to try and finesse
The system in whatever cagey way,
This hopefully coupled with a big payday.

ERROL FLYNN

149   And the next question is: Did Errol know
About Hermann Erben's debased subterfuge?
Flynn knew he wasn't pure as driven snow
And found out later he'd been Erben's stooge
In the whole million-dollar hoax—but no,
In Flynn's Spain-journal,[70] his doubt-filled refuge,
He frets as to what he merely *suspects*
Are goings-on that could have ill effects.

150   Thus meaning that Errol was in the dark
As to the spying; and Doc Erben made,
Some time later, the uncaring remark
That Errol could be quite easily played
For a fool—so let there be no black mark
Next to Errol's name, he never betrayed
Republican Spain nor the U.S., and I
Am sick of hearing he was some Nazi spy.[71]

151   And now Errol Flynn, after having got
A quickening dose of reality
In this historical trouble spot,
Is once more ripe for the Dream Factory—
Having borne witness to a war which wrought
Division that cut across virtually
All social lines but then finally a war
Which might be described as between rich and poor;

152   Having entered a vicious combat zone
Where a duly authorized government
Was in danger of being overthrown
By outlaw rebels; after having spent
Time with a Loyalist faction that'd shown
The meaning of bravery and commitment
To a cause greater than oneself in face
Of fast mounting odds; after taking his place

153   Alongside people who seemed to *cherish*
Their burdensome lives and were not, like Flynn,
Hoping to catch a bullet and perish,
A people with scant time to wallow in
Morbidity since they had a nightmarish
War to wage trying to save their own skin;
After having learned the obtuse folly
Of cultivating one's melancholy,

154   And having finally shaken the feeling
Of our life's ultimate futility,
Thus undergoing a kind of healing
Process where a dose of humility
Came to replace it and thereby *steeling*,
As often happens (paradoxically),
His penchant for JOY—Errol Flynn was rife
To play the great movie role of his life.

CANTO V

Apotheosis

(1937-1942)

. . . He learn'd the arts of riding, fencing, gunnery,
And how to scale a fortress—or a nunnery.

Don Juan, canto I, stanza 38

With director Michael Curtiz (left) on the set of
The Adventures of Robin Hood, 1937

1   Abe Lincoln had his *Gettysburg Address*,
      Martin Luther had his 95 Theses,
      The Gershwins and Heyward had *Porgy and Bess*,
      Charles Darwin had his *Origin of Species*;
      Bobby Fisher had his great game of chess,
      Bill Gates and Microsoft have their PCs,
      Horatio Nelson had his Trafalgar,
      Rags-to-riches tales their Horatio Alger.

2   Lindbergh had the first transatlantic flight,
      Bannister had the first four-minute mile,
      Billy Conn had the first Joe Louis fight
      (Till round 13 but going out in style);
      Francis Scott Key had the dawn's early light,
      Clarence Darrow had the Scopes Monkey Trial,
      Immanuel Kant had *Critique of Pure Reason*,
      And Neville Chamberlain was tops at appeasin'.

3   Rodgers and Hammerstein had *Oklahoma!*,
      Scott Joplin had his *Maple Leaf Rag*,
      Brave New World figures all have their soma,
      Pasteur that process of which he could brag;
      Chanel No. 5 maintains its aroma,
      The Italian soldier waves his white flag,
      Somerset Maugham had his faultless short stories,
      All Blacks their "Haka" kiped from the Maoris.

4   Carmichael had his immortal *Stardust*
      And petrol-rich sultans have their Brunei,
      Jayne Mansfield had her va-va-voom bust
      And rum-based tiki drinks have the Mai Tai;
      North by Northwest had its Cary crop-dust,
      Sammy Davis Jr. had his glass eye,
      Peggy Lee had *Fever*, that deathless scorcher,
      The Spanish Inquisition its "Judas Cradle" torture.

ERROL FLYNN

5   Louis Armstrong had his *West End Blues*
And Jesus of Nazareth had his cross,
The Grand Canyon has its breathtaking views
And bayou cypresses have Spanish moss;
Tennis star McEnroe had his short fuse,
Bonanza had Pa, Little Joe and Hoss,
Chopin had all those études and nocturnes
And Hagler his KO of "Hit Man" Hearns.

6   Vladimir Nabokov had *Lolita*,
Alexander Pushkin *Eugene Onegin*,
40s sex goddesses have their Rita,
Fictional pickpockets have their Fagin;
White suburban hellholes have Reseda[72]
Kern and Hammerstein (yes, Oscar again)
Had *Showboat*, and the man to deliver
Its showstopper, Robeson, had *Old Man River* . . .

7   Enough Cole-Porter whimsicality!
The point is that Flynn found his incarnation
In that quintessence of rascality:
Robin Hood—an artistic summation
Of his own rousing personality,
Errol emerging with a creation
To take pride of place with the aforesaid—
Though dumb luck is what him to glory sped.

8   The role at the outset had been slated
For Jimmy Cagney who'd walked off the lot
In a contract spat, so they activated
Errol for the role (also how he got
Picked for *Captain Blood*—this facilitated
By the departure of Robert Donat)
Flynn coming in from the wings to snatch the prize
And thus lending wings to the whole enterprise.

9   You know the movie, I assume, otherwise
It's not likely you'd be reading this now;
But on the off chance that you've not laid eyes
On this masterpiece, I can't express how
I envy you the delightful surprise
You're in for when you see Errol endow
The role with such color and vibrancy,
It's like taking a trip on LSD.

10   Never did one see a myth come alive
The way it does in Flynn's capable hands,
His personality able to thrive
In the role, as written, since it demands
That combination of masculine drive
And dapper cool which serenely withstands
All hostile threats to its perfect aplomb,
As if endorsed by the twenty-third Psalm.

11   The man and the part were an ideal blend
Owing to the film's source-material,
Permitting it thus to skillfully wend
Its way 'tween a staid, nay funereal,
Portentous approach[73] and one that would tend
To render the myth too ethereal,
Making it into a cute fairytale,
The Merry Men romping over hill and dale.

12   Flynn's Robin Hood is a canny composite
Of bandit and gallant from Scott's *Ivanhoe*,
Reviving the legend and which did cause it
Sixty years on to be given a go
By Howard Pyle who narrates *and* draws it,
Pictures and prose that strike another blow
For a blithe Robin, a version that bids
Fair to remain the great classic for kids.[74]

13   Never does Robin Hood act ignobly,
Never behaving in a gratuitous
Fashion in love or in warfare, and he
Having a wondrously fortuitous
Alloy of courage, wit, zest and mercy,
His ways neither false nor circuitous
But straight and true as the arrows he shot—
This is the figure that Howard Pyle wrought.

14   And imparting that added lyrical
Note to this mix were Reggie De Koven
And Harry B. Smith, whose own musical
Treatment was not like weighty Beethoven
But lightsome, this hardly illogical,
Much of the play's schema being woven
From Pyle's plot strands, now before the footlights,
And Warners just happened to own the rights.[75]

15   And finally the movie's heart was infused
With the great spirit of the senior Fairbanks
Whose own *Robin Hood* did not leave unused
The daredevil grace of its star (and thanks
To which you can still be more than amused
By this extravaganza since it ranks
Among the great tour-de-force spectacles,
Doug Sr. performing his stunt-miracles)[76] —

16   So Errol was stepping directly into
The swashbuckling shoes of the fellow whose
Mantle he'd donned and whose sword he first drew
As bold Captain Blood—those very same shoes
Of the man whom Flynn would in fact outdo
In most every way except the raw juice
Doug brought to the role . . . . So precisely what,
You ask, did Flynn have that Fairbanks did not?

17   When folks think of Flynn they will call to mind
Both his Greek-god form and his sculpted face
To which costume drama was never unkind;
Or they might dwell on his natural grace,
His patrician bearing and manners refined;
While some would certainly make a strong case
For Errol's high spirits and impudent dash,
Nicely set off by that rakish mustache.

18   Then there was the irresistible grin,
Quite different from Fairbanks', which was hammy
If still endearing, expressing joy in
Sheer bodily verve, whereas flimflammy
Flynn's smile was that of a brash larrikin,
Both boyish and sly—a double whammy
Fatal to hearts who were caught in its beam,
Above that cleft chin and those white teeth agleam.

19   And then you had the eternal twinkle
Dancing about in Flynn's hazel eyes,
And which he needn't so much as crinkle
To make them laugh or take on a guise
Less friendly, this owing to a fair sprinkle
Of tiny gold flecks that could vitalize
Any emotion—glowing hot when riled,
Radiating warmth each time that he smiled.[77]

20   Added to all this, the son of a bitch
(I doubt that Errol would differ with us *there*)
Was the possessor of ever so rich
And wavy and lustrous golden brown hair
That matched perfectly to a skin tone which
Was burnished by years in the tropic air,
With flawless hairline not too high or low,
For cueballs like me just the crowning blow.

ERROL FLYNN

21   And let's not neglect the man's name: Errol Flynn.
No reason to modify *that*—no clinker
Like Ira Grossel, or try to cash in
On Spangler Brugh or that other stinker
Archibald Leach[78]—better Rumpelstiltskin!
But with "Errol Flynn" you didn't dare tinker,
Straight out of Sir Walter Scott or Malory
And thus playing well to the Anglo gallery.

22   Here was a highborn and handsome name—
Do it up in scrollwork! Edge it in gilt!
And alongside its proud and noble claim,
It was imbued with a fine Gaelic lilt,
Suggesting a fellow you'd best not defame,
Who could resent any slight to the hilt,
Dispatching his foes with a hearty laugh,
And be it with sword, arrow, lance or staff.

23   Most bankable asset for Errol, though,
Integral to his ineffable charm,
Was a lambent voice, quickened by brio,
Utterly winning but no hint of smarm;
Its lightly mellifluous ebb and flow
Could well the bitterest cynic disarm,
Conveying an unfeigned sincerity
That defied any mocking parody.

24   His voice at the same time was hardly weak,
Quite manly, in fact, betraying toughness—
Understatedly, in manner oblique,
Never displaying unwonted gruffness,
Owing to a cultivated technique
Smoothing out any Down-Under roughness
While still preserving that rogue Aussie tone—
A voice no one since has been able to clone.

25   Of course Doug Sr. hadn't much of a chance
To speak in his films nor have benefit
Of Technicolor's pomp and circumstance,[79]
Both of these helping Errol to acquit
Himself in a style which milked the *romance*
From Robin Hood and make plain he had "It"—
A term invented by Elinor Glyn
To designate people like Errol Flynn.

26   Miss Glyn's eponymous story defined
"It" as a sexual magnetism
Appealing to males as well as womankind—
No preening type of eroticism
But rather one where its owner combined
A rare and compelling vitalism,
Indifferent to the impact he or she
Was having, in other words *star quality*.

27   In contrast, however, to Clara Bow,
To whom the mystical "It" was ascribed,[80]
Flynn brought a bit of enchanting moonglow
Coupled with what is perhaps best described
As consummate *style* to the vulgar show
That was Hollywood; and ever inscribed
In memory is Flynn's poise and bearing,
His presence vivid—yet never glaring.

28   In Hollywood, Errol reprised the roles he'd
Assumed in his freebooting South Sea days,
Roles which had been, as it were, pedigreed
Through dress rehearsal in a testing showplace,
And consequently not your common breed
Of young actor whose main asset's a face
That photographs well (though God knows Flynn's did)
But whose life-experience is that of a kid.

ERROL FLYNN

29   Long before Flynn the actor there was Flynn
The man. I doubt if guys like Russell Crowe,
Tom Hanks, George Clooney, Brad Pitt or Sean Penn
And myriad other fine actors know
At their *present* age, to say it again,
The brand of adventure that Flynn had in tow
When he hit Hollywood age twenty-five,
Emerging the dashingest actor alive.

30   You can use the "method" all that you like,
Doing all manner of research into
Your role and all kind of cool poses strike
With Strasberg technique, attempting to woo
Impulses from sundry sources and psych
Yourself to a point, coached by your guru,
Where your own person you then reinvent
(In the trade called "stretching your instrument");

31   You can work like a man possessed to capture
A character and inhabit a role,
However the sad fact remains that your
Professional thespian rigmarole
Can't vie with the talented amateur
Who embodies a certain figure's *soul*—
Or do you see any earthly excuse
For Stauffenberg to be played by Tom Cruise?

32   One loves the natural, not the workhorse,
Talent far more than industriousness,
Which garners respect—the use of main force,
Exerting one's will to score a success—
But this not a style I tend to endorse
For acting because we *want* to acquiesce
In the charade, it always a relief
When not *compelled* to suspend disbelief.

33   Errol's compeers also saw it that way,
Putting his face on the cover of *Life*
Magazine on the 23rd of May,
1938; and so as to drive
Home the point of his mega-stardom they
Then placed it in a time-capsule archive
So people in five thousand years could see
Life's face in the twentieth century.[81]

34   Will Flynn be around in five-thousand years
Or movies by then be wholly unknown,
Technical strides having pushed the frontiers
Of entertainment, people having outgrown
The whole medium and shedding no tears
At its death, unmarked by a single gravestone,
Its fortune to briefly flourish and die as
Forgotten as Shelly's Ozymandias?

35   Although not a king, still Errol could state,
"My prestige was high in the land at that hour"—
Or as David Niven, good friend and housemate,
Would later put it, Errol's star power
Made him feel absolute king of his *fate*:
"Legs apart, arms folded defiantly," our
Boy "crowing lustily" over his steep
Rise to the top of the "Hollywood dung heap."[82]

36   And so, having scaled that Great Manure Pile,
Errol desired to construct an abode
Upon it so he could triumphantly smile
Down on his minions—a home that bestrode
The crestline of hills that loomed half a mile
Above the city and reached by a road
Called Mulholland Drive, a name with some charm,
So Flynn dubbed his new address "Mulholland Farm."[83]

37   The place was far more than a house, you see,
       Eleven acres of extended grounds
       And home to a good-sized menagerie
       Of geese, hens, cats, peacocks, horses, swans, hounds
       And cows and some pheasants and a wallaby
       Pair ferried in from Australia, the sounds
       Of ducks and a chattering monkey, too,
       Could be heard at what was less farm than zoo.[84]

38   Oh yes, he also had cocks for fighting,
       Which was in contravention of the law,
       But which made things all that more exciting
       For Flynn Sunday nights when he oversaw
       Bouts in his barn, he always inviting
       Gamblers and cowboy-stuntmen to the straw-
       Strewn venue to come and lay down their bets,
       The air peppered with salty epithets.

39   He also constructed a riding ring,
       With jumps, so that he could mount his swart steed,
       Onyx by name, a beloved plaything,
       And owing to this appellation we'd
       Be gravely remiss in not mentioning
       His flashy saddle that didn't concede
       A thing to notions of renunciation,
       So larded it was with ornamentation.

40   And the man whom Big Bill Tilden once said
       Possessed all the skills of a top-ranked player,
       Didn't neglect to equip his homestead
       With a tennis court, having his surveyor
       Level a section of hillside and spread
       A concrete surface while growing a layer
       Of ivy all up and down the high fence
       To ward off the odd prying camera lens.[85]

41 And what is the home of a big movie star
    Without the compulsory swimming pool?
    Like no champagne with your caviar!
    And Errol no exception to the rule,
    His basin an outstanding exemplar,
    And hardly what you would call minuscule,
    Of the Hollywood natatorium,
    This proud centerpiece of Flynn's imperium.

42 The long white frame-house is laced with windows,
    To let in the California sunshine,
    The bright light driving out shadows morose,
    The walls and the ceilings of pickled pine,
    A forest fragrance to tickle the nose
    Albeit no carpet of needles to line
    The floor but instead one of the wall-to-wall
    Variety, no quick snap to install,

43 Since though the rooms can be counted on two hands,
    Most of them are exceedingly spacious
    (The house, by the way, built to Errol's own plans)
    Which they must be—that is, capacious—
    Seeing as how they're replete with the man's
    Fine art, his books and all kinds of gracious
    Antiques and keepsakes from near and afar,
    And there must of course be some space for his bar.

44 The walls of the house are hung with great art,
    Including Monet, Van Gogh and Gauguin,
    This latter's work transporting Errol's heart
    And thus allowing him to go again
    To that place where he had gotten his start—
    The balmy South Seas—and to know again
    That sense of Nature which had taken seed in
    Him as a youth in this tropical Eden.

ERROL FLYNN

45   But if instead Errol wishes to feel a
Life and death thrill, the Mexican bullfight
Painting behind the bar, with his tequila
In hand, can provide it; and here's the sight
Of a Flynn who seems he might want to kill ya—
An unsettling portrait which is hung right
Over the livingroom's brick fireplace,
An unlovely aspect marring its face.

46   For an abode so enlivened and bright,
The portrait was strikingly saturnine,
As if the thing had been painted at night,
So sunless it was, with a black-outline
Technique to delineate and to highlight
Errol Flynn's features, effecting a malign
And decadent likeness that largely smacked
Of the picture of Dorian Gray in fact.

47   Of course I'm aware that we discussed this
In a prior canto but nonetheless bears
Perhaps just a bit more analysis,
Though it won't emendate but only squares
With former remarks: While Dorian put his
Grim portrait safely out of sight upstairs,
Flynn's wasn't where people wouldn't enter
But in his livingroom—front and center.

48   No hypocrite Flynn—he lived his *life* front
And center. What's more, there is little doubt
He liked the painting, it not just some stunt
To shock and appall but verily flout
His fabled good looks and insofar shunt
Aside his beautiful cardboard-cutout
Image (and oh what tripe he did find it!)[86]
To show his star-face had something behind it.

49   Mr. John Decker was the portrait's artist,
Quite popular with the Hollywood crowd,
A painter who was very frequently pissed,
In the British sense, who was an avowed
Drunkard, blasphemer and cheerful nihilist,
A gifted wastrel whom Errol was proud
To call a good friend[87] —though what friend would make
You appear so *villainous* for goodness sake?

50   Where was I? Oh yes—the things in Flynn's home.
We've done his art so why not now his books?
There's so very many, but let's take that tome
In the bay window, the volume that looks
Like it'd break your wrist—Ed Gibbon on Rome;
And in another of Flynn's reading nooks
Is P. G. Wodehouse; and stacked over here
Are Joyce, Walt Whitman, James Cain and *King Lear*.

51   What about Errol's record collection?
Though it may come as a small surprise, he
Inclines toward musical introspection,
Loving the classical repertory
And with a very strong predilection
For Russians like Borodin and Tchaikovsky
As well as a sizable dollop of
A neighbor named Sergei Rachmaninoff.[88]

52   And as for the home's prevailing decor,
There aren't any feminine fripperies,
Zebra and bear skins bedecking the floor;
And serving as male conversation piece
Are flintlocks and other engines of war;
With random exotica like a Chinese
Chest and while others may style Persian rugs,
Errol has lamps made from Persian milk jugs.

53   The home's only actual formal space
Is the large dining room with its accent
On refined elegance and cultured grace:
Bedraped French windows with their complement
In the mirrored walls so as to showcase
The moonlight while munching your aliment
And seated in chairs very *ancien régime*;
And still in keeping with the Gallic theme,

54   Just round the corner from the dining room,
Lies the vast kitchen where ruling the roost
Is Marie the cook, Frenchwoman to whom
Flynn owes those rich banquets right out of Proust,
She shooing us out so she can resume
Her culinary chores;[89] now to an underused
Part of the house where cobwebs are forming
And where I trust we'll not catch Flynn "performing" . . .

55   Though the bedroom may have been Sigmund Freud's
Specific area of expertise,
For our erotic athlete on steroids
The bedroom's just somewhere to hang his shirt, he's
A man who instead intently avoids
This space, in his *den* taking inert ease—
Active ease, too, albeit horizontal
(Or top or bottom, or rear or frontal).

56   Errol Flynn's second wife, Nora, later wrote
That his master bedroom, all done up in blue,
Seemed to be almost unlived in—I quote:
"Like a museum" where you're "allowed to
Look but not enter," a chamber remote,
So it's no wonder that Errol withdrew
To his cherished den, which we'll do as well,
But let's here for one final moment dwell.

57   Near the door is a model of a ship,
Its glass case embellished by a brass plaque
Engraved with some wisdom for life's one-way trip,
A snippet of verse it seems didn't lack
Meaning for Errol who strove to outstrip
The winds of Fate by assuming a tack
That'd speed him past all the menacing rocks—
And now I cite Ella Wheeler Wilcox:

One ship drives east and another drives west
With the selfsame winds that blow.
'Tis the set of the sails,
And not the gales,
That tells us the way to go.

58   So let us herewith proceed to the den,
The nautical theme being on full bore,
In praise of wooden ships and iron men,
With a barometer, ship's clock and more,
The focal point being a Spanish galleon
Gracing the mantle—and were it not for
The pine of the ceiling and walls, Errol may
Have painted the whole room battleship gray.

59   And it's a pity that the waterbed
Still as of yet hasn't been invented,
With bare-breasted mermaid as figurehead,
Lack of such must be sorely lamented;
A pull-out couch, though, stands Flynn in good stead,
Quite ample for two and so he's contented
Putting the bedsprings into fast motion,
Thus replicating a wave-tossed ocean.

60   In fact that's a term that does very well
       To peg Errol's house as a whole: shipshape.
       Not fussy, not cluttered, nothing pell-mell,
       As if we're all set to round the fierce Cape,
       Low-beamed ceilings and below-decks wood smell,
       A place of peace and quiet and escape—
       The purpose yachts serve—yet rugged and hearty,
       Like rich dark rum (not that paint-thinner Bacardi).

61   But hardly content with just a land-yacht,
       Errol the sailor had purchased the real
       Thing—and because he still had a soft spot
       For the *Sirocco*, he decided to steal
       It's name for his vessel, which you ought *not*
       To do, says maritime lore, but Flynn's zeal
       Both for the name and its associations
       Trumped any thought of later complications.

62   While shooting at Warners it was Flynn's habit
       To stay ensconced in his mountain retreat—
       With filming done, though, off like a rabbit
       For the *Sirocco* to inhale the sweet
       Sea air and make an eager and rapid
       Departure by setting his ketch's mainsheet
       To sail for Mexico or Catalina,
       Albeit skirting this latter's marina.

63   He liked to anchor in secluded bays
       Where he might then go dynamite fishing,
       Just as he had in his New Guinea days;
       Or as alternative, he perhaps wishing
       To hunt wild boar, undertaking forays
       Onto the isle, from dynamite switching
       To bow and arrow (having learned this skill
       From *Robin Hood* archery coach Howard Hill);[90]

CANTO V

64   Or go skin-diving to hunt with a spear,
Flynn having scant time for reel and rod,
Needing fast action, his great single fear
That of stark dullness; he liked to maraud
And *attack* so as to evade the drear
Pastime of sitting around all slack-jawed,
Waiting and hoping that something might happen—
Like fickle fish at your hook to start snappin'.

65   As concerns women there is the adage
Of fish in the sea, and on land or skipping
His boat Errol was secure in the knowledge
They'd come to *him* and some even stripping
And swimming out nude to his craft, no shortage
Of these brash ladies, their crotches dripping
And nipples erect now aboard with our yachter,
Their aroused state not due just to chill water.[91]

66   So back to the den—I still had something
To say on this room, a Flynn favorite,
And like the Gauguin it tugged at his heartstring,
Causing that string to blissfully quaver, it
Being the place where he did his writing,
In solitude (and how he did savor it!),
Seated at a handsome leather-topped desk,
His fancy indulging in flights picturesque.

67   Weekends alone in his den, the doors barred,
A log in the fireplace behind the brass
Horse-head andirons, our scribbler tries hard
To put down words that will not merely pass
Muster but vibrate with life while not marred
By vulgarity or a lack of class,
So many factors . . . causing Errol to rise
And pace through the room while rubbing his eyes.

68   Those weary eyes of his fasten onto
The words he has posted right near his chair:
"The only worthwhile people are those who
Are always beginning again." To repair
The problem in a piece of writing, you
First had to know unmistakably where
To *find* the problem so as to unmask it—
And failing that: your best friend the wastebasket.

69   No, that was dumb, a dramatization
You saw in bad Hollywood films—the man
Alone at his desk in contemplation,
The score resounding with tragic Chopin
To highlight the anguished act of creation,
Wadded-up sheets spilling from the trashcan . . .
Errol knew that since the writer sweats blood,
He throws out little—unless total crud.

70   At the last count Flynn had written eighteen
Articles since he'd arrived in L.A.,
In the first one Errol venting his spleen
About all the hardships of his workaday
World as fostered by the stringent routine
On *Charge of the Light Brigade*: "I'd Rather Play
Tennis"—and most recently, in typeset:
"The 10 Most Sensational Women I've Met."

71   Most of these pieces—published as they were
In film magazines—thematized Hollywood
And therefore were of a frothier nature,
Flaunting the Beautiful (not the True and Good);
But Flynn now felt himself far more mature
As author and sensed that he understood
The town to the point that in his den-hovel
He was now penning his Hollywood novel.

72   The odd thing about Errol's novel, though,
Is that it would seem to have first started
Out with the main figure ready to go
Out to Hollywood, but this then discarded
For a very different scenario
Where the main figure *never* departed
New Guinea, the hero's home base, Flynn he
Instead bringing Hollywood out to *New Guinea*.[92]

73   The book's title would metamorphosize
As well, starting life as *Charlie Bow-tie
Goes to Hollywood*; and Flynn would revise
It several times more (*The Show-Off*; *The Eye
On the Stump*; *Be Good, Sweet Maid*) but the prize
Going to a title that would imply
A Western—and therefore hardly terrific
Since the book's set in the South Pacific.

74   *Showdown* might not have been so very bad
As the book's title had Flynn's storyline
Served as mere *basis*, it playing nomad
And vagabonding to Hollywood and Vine,
Flynn's central figure an actor now clad
As one of those "boys" who's good at bovine
Herding and roping and not prone to shun
Deadly shootouts with his holstered six-gun . . .

75   Or something like that. But we never get
Out of New Guinea because of the plain
And simple truth that Flynn still was beset
By thoughts of it and had to glean his brain
Before adopting an altered mind-set
And bidding the South Seas *auf Wiedersehen*—
In short, such musings, no use to resist 'em
If you've not gotten them out of your system.

ERROL FLYNN

76   Flynn was reliving those New Guinea years
When life was young and the world brand new,
Before the stardom and deafening cheers
And big bucks and starlets and the whole slew
Of hangers-on with their smiling veneers,
Before all that Hollywood hullaballoo—
And mythic New Guinea preoccupied
Flynn's consciousness till the day he died.

77   Part of Flynn's effort those years to recapture
Was to restore his former habitation
By the Laloki, that joyful rapture
Of managing his tobacco plantation,
Where all unpleasantries he could abjure,
With enough time for his avocation
Of writer, his mainspring identity,
To be plied in all peace and serenity.[93]

78   Errol was re-inhabiting his past—
Or, if you like, bringing it up to date,
The hints everywhere, you just had to cast
An eye about his extensive estate,
For instance the bougainvillea that massed
Beneath his home's eaves, serving to punctuate
Its white wood-frame's colonial optics,
This clambering plant native to the tropics.

79   And in returning to the pool you'll see
Something that might seem like an erratum—
Though hardly occurring mistakenly
But due to a certain desideratum
Of our homeowner whose rich fantasy
Decreed that the pool should have a black bottom
For taking a swim of an afternoon
In water resembling a depthless lagoon.

80   And standing in for the native lasses
Were those amenable Hollywood gals,
With figures resembling sleek hourglasses,
Whether coy cuties or hot femme fatales,
All of them primed to plunge their bare asses
Into Flynn's pool for depraved bacchanals—
His only frustration that when submerged you
Could do lots of things but not actually screw.[94]

81   Please be so kind to consider as well
His household staff, Flynn with a "manservant,"
As he calls his butler; then the bombshell
"Secretary," she her master to serve; and
The man Flynn relies on, his *maître d'hotel*,
As it were, a guy both sharp and observant,
And I'd not be shocked if Flynn did employ,
In speaking to him, the byname "Boss Boy". . .

82   But last we left Flynn he was pacing his den,
Warm on this cold night in January,
Casting his mind backward to the time when
He was a drifter—a plain ordinary
Guy on his uppers—and back to those men
Whose fine example had taught him to carry
Himself like a man, somewhat rare this type
In Hollywood where the "he-men" were all hype.

83   Where was Jack Ryan? Whatever became
Of Dusty Miller and old Basil Hoare?
Ryan was doubtless still working some claim
And likely, as ever, just as dirt poor.
And had they got wind of Flynn's movie fame?
News of it *had* reached the New Guinea shore,
Because our star had received legal threats
From fellows down there to make good on his debts.

ERROL FLYNN

84 And what of Erben? Flynn's intervention
  On his behalf had been to no avail,
  Doc Erben finally denied retention
  Of his passport—he then hitting the trail
  To Mexico so as to dodge detention
  And wartime internment—and then setting sail
  Across the Pacific where that dang guy
  Was now up to something covert in Shanghai.[95]

85 That was the last time that Flynn had seen him
  And likely as not for some time to come,
  What with the world being torn limb from limb,
  Marching to the beat of Hitler's war drum.
  So much had changed in the short interim
  'Tween Errol Flynn's having been on the bum
  And his present lofty situation,
  His soul undergoing a transmigration

86 Of sorts by moving from its prior form
  To that one gracing the cinema screen
  In this or that swaggering uniform,
  Then reproduced in some film magazine,
  All instigating a passionate storm
  Of fan mail each week, the women all keen
  On meeting this star in the flesh—which was swell,
  But Flynn would've liked to have met him as well.

87 So in a way a kind of *dis*embodied
  Presence was this new or parallel or
  Proxy version of precisely what he'd
  Become: not some face up on Mount Rushmore
  Or what Michelangelo Buonarroti'd
  Chisel from a white marble block but more
  Or less one of moviedom's flat inventions
  And thus comprising just *two* dimensions.

88   And so not only was Errol Flynn's soul
Suffering serious psychic jet lag
By his arriving so fast at his goal
But it lacked even the merest fleabag
Hotel where it might be able to hole
Up for a while and obtain a ragtag
Semblance of self in a Hollywood where
(To adapt Gertrude Stein) there was no there there.

89   A good metaphor? Yes, 'tis a bit strained—
But all I'm really attempting to convey
Is that though outwardly he had attained
His dream house and own bachelor hideaway,
Homeless his *internal* self yet remained,
Still not quite knowing just where to find CHEZ
FLYNN to whom all that fan-mail was addressed
And just how its resident might be accessed.

90   So was *that* metaphor any improvement?
I'm dropping them, anyhow, for all the rest
Of this section so as to hasten its movement—
Not that I'm feeling in any way pressed,
I could long dwell in what you've likely meant
Is an uneventful canto at best;
But like with diaries, entries slow their pace
When nothing much bad in your life takes place.

91   Life for Flynn now was a bed of roses,
So his motto was (it stands to reason,
Since it of course for all lotharios is):
"Gather ye blossoms while they're still in season!"
A mindset which, as everyone knows, is
Carpe diem, be the moment seizin'
So you won't later be seized by regret,
Playing life safe is like Russian roulette.[96]

ERROL FLYNN

92   It was a good time and place to be Flynn:
Southern California—that hedonist's delight.
For starters you had the loveliest women
Flocking to Hollywood, our sybarite
Not exactly going on a slimmin'
Diet in handling their sex appetite
Since his *own* simply grew with the eating,
Flynn not one to be the same dish repeating.

93   And what greater treat for a sailor than
To have the Pacific in his own backyard!
With Anacapa, Santa Cruz and San
Miguel and such islands to interlard
Your ocean trips and impart to them an
Air of adventure, no picture-postcard
Resorts these isles, no tourist destinations,
And hence suitable for rugged explorations.

94   Then south of the border lay Mexico,
Just like New Guinea with its brown-skinned maids,
Whom Errol found *muy simpatico*,
With its cantinas and brothels in spades
To blow off steam and get a bit loco,
A hot-blooded land where your escapades
Weren't to be read next morning in the paper
After your having pulled some drunken caper.

95   California was a consummate fit
For Flynn's multiform personality;
That is, being Flynn was more than a bit
Like *life* in the Golden State already,
With myriad facets whereby you could flit
From one to the next, a rich potpourri,
So when you put our Aussie gadabout
In California . . . well, brother, watch out!

96   Not to forget the stuff which enabled
This lavish lifestyle—his movies of course.
Fact of the matter is that his fabled
Existence was most often spent, perforce,
Not on his yacht or in his white gabled
Home but in being a real workhorse
Six days a week and within the confines
Of a Warners soundstage reciting his lines.

97   From 1938 to 1942
Flynn made a total of thirteen movies,
Three of them classics[97] and most of which you
Can still view today without saying "Puh-leeez!"
Pretty good record for somebody who
(Exempting a handful of devotees)
People will contend couldn't really act—
So here's a rundown in hopes they'll retract:

98   Errol's next picture after *Robin Hood*
Was fast-moving farce, the film *Four's a Crowd*,
In which our man is amazingly good,
Playing a light role and being allowed
To show comic chops—and how on earth could
He *not* have dazzled, as he was endowed
With a co-star named Rosalind Russell,
No slouch at flexing her own comedic muscle.[98]

99   At the time Flynn felt the role which he played
In *Four's a Crowd* was closest to his own
Personality—but the next film he made,
The Sisters, in fact is the picture I'm prone
To regard as what would later, I'm afraid,
Emerge as a kind of filmic touchstone
For his true character, very in sync,
Playing a charmer with a weakness for drink,

ERROL FLYNN

100   Who also harbors the burning ambition
To be a writer; but when this fond hope
Finally fails to come to fruition,
He finds that he is unable to cope
And goes to sea in an act of contrition,
Spiritually at the end of his rope
And searching for something that he can't find—
Not a fresh haven but just peace of mind.

101   In playing a less than reputable
Film character for the very first time,
Errol is perfectly creditable
And *had* to be in the challenging clime
Generated by the formidable
Miss Bette Davis in her acting prime,
Garnering her second Oscar that year[99]
And playing Flynn's consort in her role here.

102   In just four years Flynn had come a long way—
From a mere unknown on the English stage
To starring with *the* actress of his day;
However if you want to truly gauge
His skill at this time then watch him portray
A pilot in World War I and him wage
Both war in the sky and in his own soul,
Sending men to their deaths in *The Dawn Patrol.*

103   This was the absolute best pure acting
That Errol had done in a film hitherto,
Displaying great range, and only extracting
A single scene there's that one in which you
Have David Niven charged with an exacting
Mission next day, likely his waterloo,
Flynn as Commander Courtney then bedding
Him down and systematically getting

CANTO V

104   Him drunk so that he'll miss his assignment
        Next morning, and so as to lull him to sleep
        He soothes him with sweet talk of home, his intent
        To fly Niven's mission instead and keep
        His own, as we'll later see, appointment
        With gallant death, Errol showing here deep
        Tenderness, wistfulness, nobility—
        That is, showing consummate *acting* ability.

105   'Tis said, "Greater love hath no man than this,
        That a man lay down his life for his friends."
        And in this film with no women to kiss,
        None at least for which Flynn's heart contends,
        One might argue that David Niven is
        Object of an unselfish love which sends
        Flynn to his death in the skies above France,
        This being *Dawn Patrol*'s central romance.

106   Errol and Niven, in any event,
        Had a close friendship and this comes across
        Onscreen; moreover, Flynn's in his element
        With all the hijinks and wartime pathos
        Of male comradeship—and his evident
        Ease in this setting, I would propose,
        Was he could love a man but not a woman.
        A statement which he himself saw fit to summon.[100]

107   Let me dispel any rumors right now
        That Errol came from, as the Germans say,
        The "opposite bank"; nor can I allow
        The notion that if he weren't outright gay,
        There were occasions when his vessel's prow,
        While piloting life's twisty waterway,
        May briefly have touched that counterposed bank,
        Errol then strolling across the gangplank.

108   Let me state clearly: Errol Flynn was *straight*.
       And it's not as though I'd have any trouble
       Conceding that he liked to fornicate
       With men, his sexuality double,
       That it would somehow his stature deflate,
       Leaving my view of him in a rubble,
       Since my man *Byron* indulged in such joys
       As to be relished with comely young boys.[101]

109   I've not a thing against man-on-man sex,
       Which would come under my motto *Don't knock*
       What you've never tried. And with Errol's reflex
       To glean new sensations it would be no shock
       If search for them in erotic respects
       Led him to man-love—but it's poppycock
       To *claim* this happened since there's not a shred
       Of proof to suggest that he shared a man's bed.

110   Certain heterosexual males tend
       To do this, trying in their own way to smear
       This man with it all—a breathtaking blend
       Of looks, charm, brains, talent and big-time career,
       Too very POTENT, so they will contend:
       Sure, but the guy was a big fucking queer,
       While gay guys will do it because it's a plus
       If they can point out: *You see—one of us!*

111   The Western *Dodge City* was next film on tap,
       And though Errol made half a dozen of these,
       For me there's a credibility gap
       'Tween the suave Flynn and the roughhewn types he's
       Always thrown in with—but I'll shut my trap
       Since the fact is that he doesn't displease
       As a tough sheriff who's able to dislodge
       The bad guys and get them all out of Dodge.[102]

CANTO V

112   The next film of Flynn's was *The Private Lives*
of Elizabeth and Essex, Errol starring
With Davis again. He more than survives
This second skirmish (that is, debarring
Film's end, when he dies); in fact he contrives
To *best* Davis in their on-screen sparring—
She twitching, nervous and almost affected,
Errol unforced and supremely collected.

113   It also tests viewers' credulity
That the devastatingly handsome Flynn
Should be in love with Bette's old biddy
Of a queen—shaved brows, bald pate, pasty skin—
And *not* de Havilland's more than pretty
Lady-in-waiting; though our paladin
(If any still dare at his acting scoff)
Does the impossible and pulls it off.[103]

114   Following *Essex* came *Virginia City*,
Errol playing opposite Randolph Scott,
Great Western film star; and it's a pity
The script wasn't better (a decent plot
But flat dialogue) because in it he
Holds his own quite well, which is a whole lot
More than I can say for Humphrey Bogart,
Made to look bad by the kid from Hobart.[104]

115   Then came *The Sea Hawk*, in all likelihood
Flynn's most enduring motion-picture role
—If of course leaving aside Robin Hood—
Similar though in that Geoffrey Thorpe stole
From his sovereign's foes for the greater good
Of England, and by the time that credits roll
His sword duel's won and he's captured the girl
And is dubbed a knight, as was Robin an earl.[105]

ERROL FLYNN

116   My dad experienced old Hollywood,
That of the 30s and 40s, those years
Encompassing his Angeleno boyhood,
And so his *imaginative* frontiers
Were boundless, in his direct neighborhood
Diverse "film palaces," those storied spheres
Where dream and fantasy came to engender
A sumptuous aura of cinema splendor.

117   The Pantages with its coffered barrel-vault
Ceiling rising from the top of ornate
Columns graced with golden statues that exalt
Airmen and moviemen and decorate
Two stately stairways, this optic assault
Cresting in three chandeliers to create
An opulent air while not being snobby—
And that's not the theater but just the *lobby*.

118   Nor did the Hollywood "Warner" forego
A lavishness verging on the febrile,
What you might call Renaissance-Rococo;
And the Wilshire "Warner" with its green-tile
Facade and golden cove ceiling was no
Less grandiose for its Art Deco style;[106]
Then Grauman's "Chinese" and Grauman's "Egyptian,"
Their names all you need by way of description.

119   My dad was a real Hollywood kid,
Spending countless hours of his youth inside
These shimmering film palaces amid
Tapestries, murals and friezes and wide
Marble staircases; chandeliers that outdid
Versailles in their pomp; arched entries that vied
With the Alhambra; and then those brocaded
Curtains over which rajahs would've salivated.

CANTO V

120   These movie palaces helped to transport
        You to a rare time and place by leaving
        Behind the prosaic world to consort
        With beauty and romance and thus achieving
        A synthesis with the more glamorous sort
        Of picture—a seamless interweaving
        Of this enchanting, spellbinding setting
        With the film-magic that viewers were getting.

121   All that as preface to a stray remark
        That my dad tossed off while chewing the fat
        One day about all the old stars like Clark
        Gable and Tracey and Muni, our chat
        Diverting this Hollywood patriarch
        Into some fond reminiscing on that
        Picture-show venue which now, alas, is
        All but extinguished—the film palaces.

122   Grauman's Chinese was just round the corner,
        But where my father would normally go
        Was to his cherished Hollywood Warner,
        Down on Cahuenga, with its long ago
        Renaissance-Rococo to adorn her,
        Where of necessity they'd always show
        Those action-packed Warner Brothers films that a boy
        Of his (or any?) time could best enjoy.

123   And though I can't firmly attest that he
        Had 1940's *The Sea Hawk* in mind,
        With its great sweep and its proud majesty,
        It might as *well* have been when Dad opined,
        In our exchange, that in all honesty,
        It was the coming of Flynn and his kind
        Of flick with its noble sword-fighting gents,
        That those film palaces "really made sense."[107]

ERROL FLYNN

124   *Santa Fe Trail* and *Footsteps in the Dark*
And *Dive Bomber* were Errol's next three efforts—
None of them being decreed a landmark
Of movie history by the experts,
But Flynn as always imparting his spark
To the proceedings, even if he skirts
The edges of pure balderdash in *Footsteps*—
No fast-paced farce but just one that schleps.

125   After *Dive Bomber* with Michael Curtiz—
His intemperate tongue ever tyrannizing
The cast and crew as had Simon Legree's
Lash his poor slaves, forever chastising,
Treating them all just like trained chimpanzees,
If even *that* well, and victimizing
Above all Errol—our boy decided
That he was tired of being derided.

126   Errol Flynn's leverage now let him dictate
Who was to be his director, a new
Seven-year contract secured as of late,
With cast and script approval and a slew
Of other clauses so as to placate
His sense of entitlement—quite a coup—
And in this spirit of clearing the decks
Lili Damita had become Flynn's ex.[108]

127   Ah, darling Lili! When we saw her last,
Some five years ago, with Flynn off to Spain,
He walking the streets of Paris downcast,
Having concluded that he'd go insane
If Lili were not consigned to his past,
Life with her simply too much of a drain
On his affective and other resources—
Sole antidote for which a divorce is.

128   However, the two somehow reconciled
When Errol returned from his Spanish jaunt,
Petition for divorce never being filed,
They arriving at a kind of détente,
With Errol continuing to run wild
But doing his best not to rashly flaunt
All his amours—or at least it would seem—a
Bit hard to figure out the precise schema.[109]

129   But then this glamour pair's situation
Clarified in quite an unforeseen way
When Lili Damita missed her menstruation
In the Fall of '40—and late that next May,
Following eight months of further gestation,
She bore a son; though far and away
From being abject, Flynn plainly was not
Thrilled by what Lili said he had begot.

130   Flynn didn't question the paternity,
Perhaps well knowing that Lili'd been true
(As concerned *men*) and Sean grew up to be
So very "Errol" that it's déjà vu
(Though this is something that I'm afraid we
Haven't time really to delve into)
And few kids have so resembled their sires—
At least that's the thesis of Jeffrey Meyers.

131   Meyers' book's name is *Inherited Risk*,
A title that pretty much tells the story,
Sean making his span thrillseekingly brisk,
Conscious of life being transitory,
*Sub*consciously hoping that death might whisk
Him off, he daring its dark territory
One time too frequently as a hardcore
Photo-journalist in the Vietnam War.[110]

ERROL FLYNN

132   Sean's birth was under an ominous star
Since it was kind of an act of revenge
On Tiger Lil's part, she hoping to jar
Errol by throwing a large monkey wrench
Into his bachelor life (Errol's memoir
At least makes this claim)[111] and as all those French
Well know with their Laclos and their Dumas:
"La vengeance est un plat qui se mange froid."[112]

133   So with their alliance now closing out,
Lili Damita had no intention
Of doing a quiet and docile fadeout,
Grabbing instead her husband's attention
One final time, like a punch in the snout,
Hatching a future bone of contention,
Knowing that she, no matter how reviled,
Would stay in Flynn's life as mother of his child.

134   And Lili would exact her pound of flesh
In her vindictive divorce settlement,
Not leaving Flynn poor as Bangladesh,
But more or less taking fifty percent
Of all his assets; and she would enmesh
Her life in his to a further extent,
Even without any matrimony,
Through regular payments of alimony.

135   Her lawyer had given Errol a choice
Of alimony or pay a lump sum,
He choosing the former because our playboy's
Mulholland Farm had presently become
One big whopping bill, a massive invoice—
And what did she think, that Errol was *dumb*?
She'd wed again, that's for sure, this honey,
At which point he could stop shelling out money.

136   Ah, but Lili, that bloodthirsty tiger,
    Would she remarry? Or would she persist
    A single mother, just she and the tyke, her
    Alimony payments frequently missed,
    Flynn made to look like a first-rate piker,
    Lil then proceeding of course to enlist
    Her lawyers again to squeeze Errol dry,
    Her claims exceeding the old boy's supply?. . .

137   Could be, let's see—but one thing was certain:
    This deranged union had witnessed its end,
    No hope of repair, no Taylor and Burton,
    No chance that they would their differences mend—
    This was the finish, the final curtain,
    Like in *Captain Blood*: "And that, my friend,"
    Says Errol to conclude the duel he's just won:
    "Ends a partnership that should never have begun."

138   The line's a good one, and very apt too,
    Since it was Lili who'd chiefly wangled
    The choice Captain Blood role for Errol who
    Snapped up the stardom for which he'd angled
    In wedding Lili—and if *Errol* slew
    The partner with whom he'd become entangled
    In the film, the old adage can't be ignored
    That if living by it you'll die by the sword.

139   Main thing for now, though, Errol was free,
    Lili with no more *emotional* claims,
    Flynn also gaining his prized liberty,
    As mentioned, from Michael Curtiz, his fame's
    Other enabler—and for his next three
    Films he would team with one of the big names
    From the silent days, under whose direction
    Doug Sr. had worked (again that connection).[113]

ERROL FLYNN

140   Raoul Walsh and Flynn were a splendid pairing—
       Both of them red-blooded buccaneer types,
       Both with a love of adventure and sharing
       A taste for liquor and winning their stripes
       With the ladies as well; and actors faring
       Much better with Walsh, who didn't take swipes
       At them like Curtiz, that vicious warmonger,
       Walsh having been an actor when younger.[114]

141   Perhaps a film by Raoul Walsh didn't plumb
       Great psychic depths and all that kind of stuff;
       And on occasion maybe he'd succumb
       To fear that there wasn't action enough;
       But a Walsh movie was *tight as a drum*,
       Bereft of the smallest semblance of fluff,
       So it's of some note that Walsh was quite keen
       To make clear his films were about the "love scene."

142   Proof enough for me of this quotation
       (Which on the surface of things would appear
       A mere apocryphal declaration)
       Is Flynn having played his two most sincere
       And poignant love scenes, in my estimation,
       Under the direction of Walsh—for sheer
       Unalloyed feeling few others come close,
       Just *thinking* of them makes me lachrymose.

143   The first of these scenes occurred in the first
       Picture that they made together, it called
       They Died with Their Boots On, where we're immersed
       In George Armstrong Custer's world, he enthralled
       By pursuit of glory, this chase interspersed
       By scenes with de Havilland who is installed
       As his wife Libby, the last time that she
       Would play the sweet girl upon Errol's knee.

144   She'd grown sick of it, Olivia had,
      Being typecast as the cute ingénue,
      Leaving her thwarted and so very mad
      That she would bring suit, with her legal crew,
      To break what was seen as an ironclad
      Contract with Warners—a case she'd win, too,
      This break effecting a first little crack
      In the contract system (while sticking it to Jack).

145   So, de Havilland, that iron maiden,
      Who'd played Melanie in *Gone with the Wind*
      (Later gaining acting's top accolade in
      To Each His Own and *The Heiress*) felt sinned
      Against by Warners and not afraid in
      Expressing her view that she had now grinned
      And borne long enough second billing to Errol,
      Ever consigned to the his-lady-fair role.[115]

146   There had in fact been a falling out between
      The two of these stars—somewhat hard to say
      How much was due to the internecine
      Warfare of those in the same métier
      (She'd accused Errol of certain onscreen
      Misdoings)[116] or if the feelings in play
      Were of a far more "personal nature"—
      To use that discreetly vague nomenclature.

147   Their relationship had never been clear,
      At least from an outsider's point of view,
      Since there were times when from her you would hear
      That there'd been nothing between both the two,
      Except screen kisses, in the carnal sphere;
      While other times she might drop a coy clue
      That yes, as a matter of fact, she had
      Done stuff you'd expect with this winning cad.[117]

148   Errol, for his part, in *Wicked* confessed
      That he'd been in love with de Havilland
      From the beginning, but that he had messed
      Things up through his failure to understand
      Just how to woo her, he making a pest
      Of himself through his impetuous brand
      Of fun—not presents of flowers and candies
      But one time placing a snake in her panties.[118]

149   And yet no matter the nature of their
      Relationship, by the start of production
      On the Custer picture the crass underwear
      Prank was long past and posed no obstruction
      To warm shared feelings, both of them aware
      That even barring some sudden ruction,
      This story of General Hell-for-Leather
      Might be their very last film together.

150   And this is one of the movie's virtues:
      The contrast between the flashy Custer
      And a tender love that wholly eschews
      Any bravado, bombast or bluster,
      Errol here learning just *how* a man woos
      One like Olivia—please don't disgust her
      With snakes in her drawers or a similar jest
      That will run counter to your ardent quest.

151   For instance right at the start of our tale,
      Custer is pulling guard duty when strolls
      Up Libby, a hitherto unknown female,
      And they march back and forth till his patrol's
      Finally completed; and he doesn't fail
      To walk her home where a date he cajoles
      For a promenade, saying he can't construe
      Much finer "than walking through life with you."

152   Errol as Custer is perfectly cast—
        Meaning he's suitably *terrifying*,
        Charging straight into the massed cannons' blast,
        Always and everywhere gratifying
        A valorous urge that remains unsurpassed,
        And Custer himself ultimately dying
        In manner to which his whole life had been sworn,
        At that bloodbath called the Little Big Horn.

153   This battle looming, George still at the fort,
        There is this one scene in which he provokes
        A drinking match where he goes snort for snort
        With his foe, the beverage not just rum & cokes
        But glasses of whiskey, near on a quart
        In just five minutes, too much for most folks,
        Vastly too much for our plastered victim
        Who passes out—Flynn having done licked him.

154   It's during this scene, while tossing 'em back,
        That Custer/Flynn vaunts the merits of glory,
        A thirst for which he himself has no lack,
        His own taste for drink rather desultory
        Compared with his parching desire to rack
        Up countless honors in the great gory
        Business of warfare—and his last battle
        Proving that this isn't just empty prattle.

155   Fine thing about glory, Custer opines,
        Compared to money, which his rival lauds,
        Is not only that the martial type shines
        All that much greater the greater the odds
        But that a man's dying on the frontlines
        In a pitched battle finds favor with the gods
        Who in their bounty have arranged it so
        Glory goes with you when it's your time to go.

156 And Flynn as Custer expresses these thoughts
With an intensity that is scary,
Not lessened any by the monstrous shots
Of hooch, to be sure; and military
Zeal for duty and a proud patriot's
Love of country are not the primary
Concern, but judging from his wild gaze he
Is a bit touched if not outright *crazy*.

157 This scene has a certain centrality
In showing the feral barbaric side
Of Errol's complex personality,
Here now both focused and purified,
A man who possessed the ability
To venture mass carnage and suicide,
Just bent on *destruction* and no matter
If it be the former or the latter.

158 Next morning after the night in the bar
There is that scene which I wished to adduce
As among the most affecting by far
That Flynn ever played, George knowing his goose
Is pretty well cooked, seeing as how there are
"Quite a lot of Sioux" with no taste for truce
Lying in wait for him in the Black Hills—
No wonder he'd gotten stewed to the gills.

159 It's in such knowledge that they say goodbye,
Custer and Libby, this devoted pair,
And if you are in the mood for a cry,
Here is your chance as they banish despair,
Or try to, endeavoring to dignify
This leave-taking with a touchingly rare
Display of tenderness under pressure,
Leaving filmgoers with a lasting treasure.

160   Of course your emotion is helped right along
           If you're aware that this love scene is not
           Only the farewell between George Armstrong
           And his beloved wife Libby but what
           Will also be Errol and Livy's swansong
           In terms of movies—this private subplot
           Fueling it all, helping them to emote,
           While putting a sizeable lump in your throat.

161   And magnifying one's appreciation
           Of this scene might also be knowledge that
           Four decades on, at a celebration
           Of Livy's pictures our heroine sat
           Watching the film and before culmination
           Of this tableau she wept tears and went scat
           Out the door, Olivia not up to bearing
           This last movie moment the two were sharing.

162   As well she might have—since the tear looks real
           Which runs down her cheek in the scene, her chin
           Trembling convincingly just before she'll
           Be given a fervid smacker by Flynn,
           After conveying to his beau ideal
           That he would do it all over again,
           "Walking through life" with her wearing his ring,
           Their stroll having proven "a very gracious thing."

163   The next Walsh-Flynn film was *Desperate Journey*,
           Wartime adventure again the main theme,
           Flynn so heroic (at every turn he
           Pulling off yet one more fantastic scheme)
           That it is verging on the Jules-Verney,
           Like science fiction and thus quite a scream—
           But of note here: Errol plays an alien
           Not from deep space, but himself, an Australian.[119]

164   Third of the Flynn-Walsh collaborations
Was *Gentleman Jim*, that neglected gem,
Jewel in the crown of Errol's creations
(And pearl in Alexis Smith's diadem)
Which under Raoul Walsh's ministrations
Emerges as a kind of film-requiem
To the Gay Nineties, when Walsh was a lad,
A requiem therefore that's anything but sad.[120]

165   *Gentleman Jim* is an absolute must,
The one film of Errol's not to be missed
If you want some notion of the robust
Nerve, cunning, smarts, cockiness and the list
Goes on of attributes that helped to thrust
Flynn to the top like the opportunist
He plays, Jim Corbett, a man who likewise
Set his sights on it—then took the big prize.

166   Errol was very at home with boxing
And Gentleman Jim's take on the "sweet science,"
Flynn using Corbett's style of *outfoxing*
Rivals instead of straight brute defiance,
Uttermost hand-speed to make punches zing
Into their target along with reliance
On rapid footwork to get out of range
And avoid a slogging inside exchange.

167   However the scene I wish to depict
Was not in the ring but just right before
James Corbett enters it for a conflict
With tough Joe Choynski that bodes to be war,
And no small number who're willing to predict
That he'll use Corbett to mop up the floor,
Nobody giving too much of a chance
To Gentleman Jim, that fistic fancy-pants.[121]

168   So just as Corbett is leaving his home
       For the bout, both he and his retinue
       Going out the door, our fighting coxcomb
       Spies his grieved mother who's all in a stew,
       An Irish one at that—and this a syndrome
       That might be ascribed to the movie if you
       Aren't feeling terribly charitable,
       Namely "Hollywood Paddy," a veritable

169   Wealth of clichés being bandied about
       As to the Irish—their penchant for booze,
       And all liquored up or sober to clout
       Each other like mad, but still they all ooze
       Ebullient charm (even that churlish lout
       John L. Sullivan) and finally whose
       Mothers are sacred, which is underscored
       Here in this scene where Jim sees his adored

170   Matriarch weepy and whom he embraces
       In filial hug and tells not to fret,
       He won't be injured; then Corbett chases
       The tears from her eyes by saying she'll get
       A fur coat with all his prize money, then places
       His hand 'neath her chin, maternal upset
       Fleeing her features as Corbett beguiles
       Her with his blarney till finally she smiles.

171   It don't sound like much, begorrah, I know,
       Lasting no longer than half a minute,
       But somehow Errol is able to show
       More love and tender emotions in it
       Than all those scenes where he played the Romeo—
       And in the especial instance of Flynn it
       Was displaced yearning, one can't help but add,
       For the caring mother that he never had.

CANTO VI

Errol's War

(1942-1945)

. . . We left him in the focus of such Glory
As may be won by favour of the Moon
Or ladies' fancies—rather transitory
Perhaps; but who would scorn the month of June,
Because December, with his breath so hoary,
Must come? Much rather should he court the ray,
To hoard up warmth against a wintry day.

Don Juan, canto X, stanza 9

Flynn with legal team Jerry Giesler (left) and Robert Ford (right)
and behind them Peggy Satterlee, 1942

CANTO VI

1   Sometimes I ask myself if maybe I
When young wasn't far too fastidious
Where it concerned girls, too squeamish and shy,
Which in the end had the perfidious
Effect of preventing me from getting my
"Fair share," a thought which is insidious
Because you may then repent at your ease
A long list of missed opportunities.

2   But even if this is somewhat galling,
Because I live in the German *Hauptstadt*
—Which let me tell you is fairly crawling
With single women who are hot to trot,
Making it effortless to go trawling
For pickups in this Teutonic fleshpot—
I can assure you, dear reader, that I'm
Doing my best to make up for lost time.

3   All of this easy availability
Of women who are pliant but who vary
Markedly in their desirability
(Some luscious, some lovely, some quite scary)
Has made me ponder my inability,
When young, to do what was necessary
In landing those girls—I can't disclose all—
Who placed themselves freely at my disposal.

4   I was hard to please, a fact which reduced
The already very limited pool
Of sex candidates for whom I enthused,
My having attended an all-boys high school;
Then Catholic college, the girls there not used
To sharing their charms as a general rule;
Then graduate school where hyper-intellectual
Women don't spawn thoughts running to the sexual.

ERROL FLYNN

5   In other words I was a diffident
And fault-finding youth who wasn't willing
To do the little required to cement
The deal with girls who were neither filling
Me with a feeling described as "ardent"
Nor who promised to be all that thrilling
In satisfying my finicky lust,
And therefore things tended not to combust.

6   But over time I have learned to relax
My own youthful standards a bit, and now here
In Berlin where no aphrodisiacs
Are needed (if you don't count German beer)
To spur sundry female sensuous acts,
It's clear you can sate any day of the year
An appetite carnal or otherwise
If willing to settle for burgers and fries.

7   Errol was both a gourmand and gourmet,
His palate refined but with appetite
Amply robust so that he wouldn't say
No to a burger and fries and just might
Now and again go out of his way
To hit on a girl who if not outright
Ugly would often enough be that strain
Of female wont to be labeled as "plain."

8   The sexual *charge* was of primary
Importance to Flynn. And if great beauties
Happen to make up your customary
Fare then it might occasionally please
You to eat something quite ordinary—
Slumming, as it were, so as to appease
Your taste for cuisine both cheap and exotic,
Which in Flynn's case made the *common* erotic.

9   Miss Betty Hansen was just such a girl,
Mousy midwesterner who was mundane
As they come and thus for Flynn a rare pearl!
And in late '42 she would maintain
That Errol indeed had given her a whirl,
And even if he didn't actually chain
Her to the bed or throw her in a cage,
It seems Betty Hansen was slightly underage.

10   In California a "minor" will mean
A boy or a girl who has yet to attain
The minimum legal age of eighteen;
And if it's the case that you entertain
Relations with someone who's just seventeen,
Like Hansen, and even if she'd been fain,
You can wind up in a big legal scrape,
Such being classified "statutory rape."

11   Events now unfolded in a hurry.
After the complaint, next morning the case
Was brought before an L.A. grand jury—
Which nixed an indictment. But did that then place
Errol Flynn out of harm's way? No sirree!
For almost before Flynn and friends could raise
Glasses of champagne in sweet victory,
The DA brought in Peggy Satterlee.

12   Quite unlike Hansen was Peggy LaRue
Satterlee and more like what you'd expect
Errol to take a real hankering to:
A gorgeous showgirl with proud and erect
Carriage, dark hair, clear green eyes and lulu
Of a figure—a babe with scarce a defect—
And everything would have been just peachy keen
If not for the fact she was only sixteen,

13 And *fifteen* at time of her little run-in
 With Errol one year before on his boat,
 Sirocco, which he'd taken out for a spin
 To Catalina so he might devote
 Himself to a small bit of fun; hence Flynn
 Accused now of having sown one wild oat
 Too many in defiling shapely Peggy—
 Not only busty but long and leggy.

14 With Peggy on board, the city's DA,
 "Honest John" Dockweiler, quashed the judgment
 Of the grand jury and went straightaway
 To a full hearing to once more present
 His action and this time a judge to weigh
 Its merits—and to Errol's bedevilment
 The judge ruled for trial, he having sustained
 The state's arguments, so Flynn was arraigned.

15 The charge was three counts of statutory
 Rape (Satterlee saying Errol had twice
 Violated her, plus Hansen's story)
 And fifty years was the maximum price
 To pay for each count (though likely just four), he
 Now pleading innocent, and the judge nice
 In setting the bail at what seems a very
 Low thousand bucks and the trial for January.

16 Hearing, indictment and arraignment took place
 In autumn when *Gentleman Jim* was released.
 For Warner Brothers it had been a race
 With time to get it out before Flynn ceased
 To be a draw if it turned out the case
 Against him proved true and Warners got fleeced
 At the box-office (but too late to trim
 The title and change it to just plain *Jim*).

17   Flynn was the scapegoat—or rather: fall guy
In an elaborate scheme on the part
Of the DA's office to crucify
Him not in fact by besmirching his art
But his peccadilloes and morals, thereby
Striking at Warners' penurious heart,
The studio having declined to bankroll a
Spiteful DA through sufficient payola.

18   According to this certain version as told
By Flynn in *Wicked*, the gentleman who
Resented Warners for not having doled
Out enough money in fact was the new
DA Dockweiler who'd broken the hold
That ex-DA Fitts had had not just for two
But three straight terms in the post for a grand
Total of twelve years with him in command.

19   Till 1940, for those dozen years,
When any big star got in a tough fix,
Mr. Burton Fitts would assuage the fears
Of studio heads through slick legal tricks,
Saving both stars and their precious careers,
Able at drop of a hat to deep-six
The charges and warding off all kinds of flak—
Although at the price of a juicy kickback.

20   When DA Fitts came up for reelection
In 1940 in his camp were all
The film studios by dint of protection
He'd given them against any hardball
The law might have played with their collection
Of bright shining stars when one took a fall,
They freely giving now to his campaign
To foil "Honest John," who'd be a damn pain.

21   And so when Dockweiler won a landslide
      Victory—all of this still Flynn's version—
      He was in no mood to just let things ride
      But sought to make very clear his aversion
      To any and all acts not sanctified
      By law (not least to any *perversion*)
      And the first Hollywood guy out of line
      Going down hard as a stiff warning sign.

22   Flynn was convinced that his case, externally,
      Was Hollywood morals (or lack thereof)
      On trial whereas the case internally
      Was the unsavory push, pull and shove
      Of town politics, at its kernel he
      Himself and the vagaries of his own love
      Life—which if a broad generalization
      Is, I believe, a fair evaluation.

23   What other reading of the case is there
      When DA Dockweiler doesn't abide
      By a grand-jury decision (quite rare)
      And digs up a case the cops shunted aside
      A full year prior if *not* to ensnare
      One of the dozen or so bona fide
      Worldwide stars of which Hollywood could boast—
      This debauched "swordsman" who'd earned a riposte.

24   Not that John Dockweiler had a weak case
      With Betty Hansen or Peg Satterlee.
      For one, this latter showed more than a trace
      Of vaginal bruises and rips directly
      After arriving back from the two days
      At sea with Errol when she weepingly
      Told her mother how Flynn may have knocked her
      Up—all this confirmed by a cop-doctor.

25   Satterlee's mom wanted charges to be pressed—
      She then dissuaded though by the police
      Who said her daughter'd be put to the test
      By the judicial authorities,
      Posing sharp questions as if to suggest
      She were the felon; and so the Satterlees
      Decided that if the prospects were thus,
      Maybe they wouldn't kick up such a fuss.[122]

26   (All of which makes someone wonder, of course,
      Why "Honest John" didn't *then* seize his chance
      To show Hollywood it'd bet the wrong horse,
      Catching our mega-star Flynn with his pants
      Down and engaged in taboo intercourse?
      Seen from this angle it doesn't advance
      Flynn's theory—or maybe it simply imputes
      That cops and DA weren't yet in close cahoots.)[123]

27   The DA's office also placed a large hope
      In the Hansen case with its share of slings
      And arrows with which Errol had to cope,
      A girl *hearing* both of them on the bedsprings
      (Mainly Betty Hansen giggling like a dope)
      And later another one of the things
      Not aiding in Errol's peaceful slumber
      Was Hansen possessing his telephone number.[124]

28   The point here's that Flynn was in very deep shit
      And badly in need of a lawyer who would
      Restore his good name and duly acquit
      Him of profaning pristine maidenhood;
      Not someone who had to bristle with wit,
      Just someone who knew how these Hollywood
      Cases were handled—a fellow named Jerry
      Giesler, Flynn praying he'd be his good fairy.[125]

29   Giesler had first made his name in defending
      Theater potentate Alexander
      Pantages against a rape charge, upending
      The guilty verdict since able to brand her,
      The female plaintiff, a fake; contending
      That Eunice Pringle was, in all candor,
      A bimbo; and strongly hinting that she
      Was pawn in a vicious conspiracy.[126]

30   This was exactly the three-pronged attack
      Which Giesler took up in Errol's defense—
      That the girls' stories had adequate lack
      Of inner cohesion to make real sense,
      Their sexual compasses way out of whack,
      The whole thing a fix; accusing them, hence,
      Of being that which all the world deplores:
      A couple unprincipled lying whores.

31   The girls were good, though, up there on the stand,
      Their tales forthright with plenty of telling
      Detail to make things sound very first-hand,
      Hardly as if the two might be dwelling
      In the far reaches of cloud-cuckoo land,
      Both of their stories pretty much jelling
      With the known facts of each of their cases,
      As Jerry Giesler put them through their paces.

32   Peg Satterlee was the best of the two,
      Poised and well-spoken for someone so young,
      Handling most everything that Giesler threw
      Her way with nary a slip of the tongue,
      All of her tale ringing perfectly true
      Except when she spoke of a moon that hung
      In the evening sky, Flynn able to cajole
      Her below-decks to view it "through a porthole."[127]

33   In Errol's stateroom she'd mounted his bed,
      Peering through the porthole to glimpse the moon,
      At which point then it was full steam ahead,
      Errol Flynn mounting this sweet macaroon,
      She though resisting his effort to wed
      Their intimate zones—yet the big baboon
      Eventually able to overpower
      Her and a second time pluck her flower.[128]

34   This here was serious testimony:
      Not just a case of statutory rape,
      For Flynn had come on like a cyclone, he
      Now assuming a nefarious shape—
      This meeting of our dramatis personae,
      Afloat on that lovely moonlit seascape,
      Not smacking of misplaced sexual zest
      So much as diabolical male conquest.

35   Errol felt there was tacit agreement
      Between the jury and himself that if
      Giesler could demonstrate there'd been consent
      On part of the one or the other plaintiff
      And that Flynn hadn't been rough or indecent—
      They'd let him off; but let there be a whiff
      Of force or depravity on Errol Flynn's
      Part then they'd make him pay dear for his sins.

36   Here the idea was that your average
      Person might see fifty years as too hard
      A sentence for what in everyday usage
      Wasn't quite "rape" by a lowdown blackguard
      But sleeping with girls just a bit underage;
      And also a factor in this regard
      Is that the two *looked* older than their years,
      Both of them long beyond training brassieres.[129]

37   And if moreover you managed to show
That they had hardly been young innocents
Barely aware of their own libido,
That the whole thing was a phony pretense;
And if withal you were able to sow
Reasonable doubts (for those on the fence)
As to their *motives* in testifying,
Jurors might feel one or both were lying.

38   Again, all this was the same strategy
Giesler had used in the Pantages case,
His research finding that Peg Satterlee
Had an abortion, while Hansen's disgrace
Was that she'd gladdened a man orally,
Felonious acts in that time and place;
So Giesler implied they'd agreed to squeal
On Flynn if the DA cut them a deal.

39   Unprincipled whores—but lying ones too?
This was de facto where the whole case hinged,
Since if the jury believed it was true
That Errol Flynn had ungallantly impinged
On Peggy's honor then he was all through;
But if her story could somehow be tinged
With the odor of willful fabrication,
Said tacit accord would be Flynn's salvation.

40   To read Jerry Giesler's cross-examination
Of the girls is to have leap out at you
All the extremely detailed information
He sought to extract, he taking them through
The three alleged acts of fornication
Step by step, unhurriedly, so as to
Show up their stories' inconsistencies
Or virtual impossibilities.

41   This latter he did with a masterstroke,
     Having a federal meteorologist
     Testify that though Peg Satterlee spoke
     Of a starboard moon at her second tryst
     In Errol's cabin, she might like to revoke
     Her story since it would be hard to twist
     The fact that the moon this night wasn't spied
     From starboard but rather from the *port* side.

42   But still there was Flynn yet to testify.
     Throughout the trial, now in its fourth week,
     Folks crowded the courtroom to see him try
     And beat the rape charge, this *opera comique,*
     Just what it'd become, able to gratify
     Their yen for farce, as opposed to the bleak
     Reports from a war which Flynn did upstage
     By moving it off the newspaper's front page.

43   With an enormously large area
     Of the earth's surface still in Axis hands,
     Errol Flynn's trial was diversionary, a
     Respite from battles in faraway lands,
     The public now roused to mild hysteria
     As Errol's case met their clamant demands
     For all manner of salacious detail
     About this sex-fiend and his San Quentin quail.[130]

44   Throughout the trial, as I was saying,
     Flynn kept his cool, remaining composed
     Despite the tremendous pressure weighing;
     And if at some juncture he diagnosed
     A guilty verdict, a plane for conveying
     Him to Mexico (as later disclosed
     In *Wicked*) awaited him out at Burbank
     Airport—his future beyond that a blank.

ERROL FLYNN

45   Errol was damned if he'd serve prison time—
The whole trial process was bad enough;
Although the public saw a man with sublime
Sang froid it was all more or less a brave bluff:
At Mulholland Farm reigned another clime,
Flynn dropping all that jaunty "old sport" stuff,
And in a desperate attempt to throttle
His desperation he reached for the bottle.

46   Long weeks of the trial did take their toll—
Flynn pale, losing weight, his nerves badly frayed.
Waves of excitement, though, started to roll
Through the courtroom when Jerry Giesler played
His ultimate card, his ace in the hole,
And one might have blown a fanfaronade
When Giesler stood up from his seat and in
A soft voice stated, "I will now call Mr. Flynn."

47   Day in and day out the people had stood
In line to obtain a privileged seat
For high drama auguring to be as good
As any film where they'd seen Flynn defeat
The bad guys—but now the question was would
He as defendant be able to beat
Off the indictments of a pair of teenage
Girls, this not merely some Warners soundstage.

48   As Errol arose and approached the stand
A sigh made the rounds all through the courtroom,
It chock-full of women, you understand,
And the air fragrant with scent of perfume,
Some of it wafted by a jury here "manned"
Mostly by ladies—though one might assume
That none let slip any deep yearning sighs,
And certainly none from the three juror guys.

49   That was another Jerry Giesler coup—
      Obtaining a jury three-quarters female:
      What woman could resist Flynn? Nor undue
      Concern for the girls would likely assail
      Ladies who might also hold to the view
      That any femme must be nuts to bewail
      Being taken by Flynn, which in their own dreams
      He'd done to *them*—and to ravishing extremes.

50   Today there was no debonair cravat
      Adorning his throat but just a gray tie
      (Though speckled with orange); and rather than that
      Colorful swatch of silk catching the eye
      And flowing from Errol's breastpocket there sat
      A crisp white hanky; and that old standby,
      A plain dark suit, all capped the impression
      Of someone beyond all rash indiscretion.

51   And whether premeditated or not,
      There also was the notable absence
      Of something that looked stylish in a mugshot
      But not opportune in Errol's defense,
      Something that might be termed Errol's "mascot,"
      Back then worn by a fair number of gents,
      Lending Flynn, though, a bit too much panache
      Since somewhat rakish—his pencil moustache.

52   Flynn enters the box, he seeming at ease,
      Externally calm, hands folded in lap,
      Giesler commencing with: "State your name, please,"
      And it is all they can do not to clap
      When comes the reply: "Errol Flynn"—and these
      Two simple words starting a renewed flap;
      'Fore the whole courtroom, though, can unravel
      The uproar is silenced by the judge's gavel.

53   Giesler's next bidding is: "State your birthplace."
And when Flynn says: "Hobart, Tasmania,"
A ripple of low moans through the court race
—Which, to be honest, Scranton Pennsylvania
Would have excited if *that'd* been the case—
But all these ladies' avid Flynn-mania
Is only compounded by a place-name
That's so exotic and, like Flynn, *untame*.

54   After some more basic information,
Giesler starts into the case. It is clear
That Flynn's tactic is the affirmation
Of all those things falling within the sphere
Of "proven facts" and the *refutation*
Of everything that should fail to adhere
To law or the rules of befitting conduct,
His word against Peggy's and Betty's they'd fucked.

55   All Giesler's questions are easy to field,
And Errol's true test arrives the next day
When the state-prosecution comes to wield
Its secret weapon, a young lawyer they
Have hired to smash Errol's defensive shield
By grilling him ruthlessly, this man's forté,
He hoping to show that Errol's depiction
Of events is riddled with contradiction.

56   This Giesler had done, or had tried to do,
With the girls—but John Hopkins, the state's hotshot,
Was solely focused on Flynn and now drew
On copious notes he'd managed to jot
Down at the Giesler-Flynn court interview;
Flynn had been readied, though, for the onslaught
By Giesler who warned that the prosecution
Might make this last-minute substitution.

57   As Hopkins, a big brawny guy, arose
Approaching the box, Errol folded his arms
Across his ribcage and got a hardnose
Look on his face, knowing he was in harm's
Way and that all his wisecracks and bon mots
Would be here wasted as too all his charms,
Hopkins now trying to make his reputation
With his first movie-star incarceration.

58   Hopkins began to review in detail
The *Sirocco* trip, he probing the subject
From every angle, trying to derail
Errol on whatever point; but Flynn wrecked
His scheme, never straying from his portrayal,
And leveling Hopkins with a direct
Gaze, his voice calm, jawbone set, eyes alert,
Errol's execution no less than expert.

59   Cross-examination continued through
The morning session and then extending
Into that same afternoon with the two
Of them tooth and nail, Hopkins unbending
In his attempt to put Errol askew,
Ever setting traps, but Flynn defending
Himself in great style, no question refusing,
So his Fifth Amendment rights not abusing.

60   All of this was yet another facet
Of our defendant Errol Flynn's contract
With jury members, yet one more tacit
Agreement: that they'd get to see him *act,*
To not let them down, that he should acquit
Himself with aplomb on the stand—the pact
Duly fulfilled, Flynn well in conformance
Through his unerring command performance.

61   And though it may sound as if I nitpick,
The sole problem here was that perhaps he
Was a bit too good, too practiced and slick—
In short: just a little too *actorly*,
Not missing a beat or a single trick;
So two days later when the sworn jury
Retired so as to obtain a verdict,
It was no cinch that they wouldn't convict.

62   As Flynn sweated out the jury's decision,
He swigged black coffee and played solitaire,
Smoked cigarettes and fought back the vision
Of soon being led away in a pair
Of handcuffs and the naked derision
To be heaped on him and of course no prayer
Of ever restarting his movie career:
Errol fought back his overwhelming fear.

63   The fact was his odds of exoneration
Diminished with every minute that passed,
The notion here being that vindication
Would come about quickly, while much less fast
Would be a (reluctant) condemnation.
So as the minutes crawled by and amassed
Into long hours leading to the next day,
Flynn's fate—if not black—looked decidedly gray.

64   And then that morning, after twelve or thirteen
Hours of the jury's deliberation
—And for Errol countless jolts of caffeine,
Just helping to fuel his agitation—
The court was permitted to reconvene,
The jury returning and the whole nation
Waiting to hear what would be Errol's lot.
(And here one wonders what *Tiger Lil* thought.)

65   Under the table Giesler grips Errol's thigh
As foreman Ruby Ann Anderson
Reads out the verdict, the *vox populi*
Now concentrated in this single person,
Moment of truth and reality nigh,
Moment for which there can be no rehearsin',
Flynn sitting frozen with hands in his lap,
Staring down the muzzle of a three-count rape rap . . .

66   "Not guilty!" says Anderson to the first count,
Giesler's grip on Errol's leg growing tighter,
This a good start but will hardly amount
To all that much if his sanction's no lighter
Than fifty years for each charge, tantamount
To a life sentence—a real nail-biter,
And Flynn himself one, so perhaps more wise
To batten his hands and not one of his thighs . . .

67   "Not guilty!" she declares for the second time,
Giesler's grip tightening down like a vise,
Almost complete now the long upward climb,
Those magic words having been uttered twice,
And who the hell cares about my next rhyme,
Let us just see if she'll utter them thrice,
Attesting that Errol is not a pervert,
And since his leg's really starting to hurt . . .

68   "Not guilty!" she says for the third time running[131]
And our defendant leaps up from his chair
While cheering breaks out, this verdict stunning,
The man the DA had tried to ensnare,
That man for whom the state had been gunning,
Found wholly innocent in this affair . . .
However the question that we can't escape
Is whether in *fact* Flynn was guilty of rape.

69   Let's put it this way—if we're to define
"Rape" in the very broad statutory
Meaning of the term and do not confine
Ourselves to the time-honored category
Of *forcing* yourself upon a fräulein,
Of stalking and pouncing your female quarry
And thereby profaning an innocent lass,
Then Errol indeed was a snake in the grass.

70   Just how exactly can I be so sure?
There is first the fact that Flynn *liked* them young
(The death knell to him liking them "mature,"
In my estimate, would seem to have rung,
At latest with Lili Damita's departure);[132]
Secondly, that Errol loosened his tongue
In *Wicked* by ultimately rejecting
Notions of underage "rape," one detecting

71   An undertone of: *So what if I did?*
Both of them women in all but their age,
Neither of whom one might label a kid;
An undertone of: *How is someone to gauge*
If a girl's "legal" or not if not bid
Her show proof of birth and your doubts assuage;
An undertone of: *How to curb your penis*
When the girl in question is built like Venus?

72   This last line referred to Peg Satterlee.[133]
In fact it was almost as if Errol's stance
In *Wicked* were: *Just between you and me,*
I will confess I got in Peggy's pants,
That gorgeous creature; however, I'll be
Damned if admitting to any romance
With Betty Hansen—whom Errol termed "gruesome"
(If only *after* enjoying their twosome).

73   But all in all, justice may have been served.
The right-minded jury had closed its eyes
To the key "statutory" clause and observed
Native common sense, which oftentimes flies
In the face of punishment that is reserved
By law for the man whose action defies
All of the abstract legal definitions,
Jurors harking to life—not its theoreticians.

74   Maybe the verdict was indicative
Of a shift in U.S. morality,
Its citizens now willing to forgive
A bit of sexual rascality
(Even if somewhat manipulative)
Provided there'd been no brutality,
For brutal enough was the war being fought:
So what if Flynn strayed—least no one was shot.[134]

75   Errol became more popular than ever,
In fact, as a consequence of the trial,
Not serving to come between or sever
Him from his public but serving to *beguile*
Them if it were some kind of clever
Publicity stunt to keep the turnstile
Clicking and the box-office cashing in—
Ergo the still current phrase "in like Flynn."

76   I guess there are plenty of ways of using
This phrase but mostly when you've got a lock
On a girl or a job and you're just cruising
To victory, nothing able to block
Your final triumph, not a chance of losing,
A question of time, just you and the clock,
Even if at some point your progress slows,
Still fated to come up smelling like a rose.

77   Flynn's name had entered the language and he
    Himself was now a folk hero—but though
    His career wasn't hurt, he was still badly
    Wounded by this unforeseeable blow:
    The fact that in the public mind he'd be
    Long linked to the sordid rape charge and no
    Matter if he had been finally cleared,
    His name a catchphrase but also besmeared.

78   The public henceforth saw only the rake,
    Errol Flynn's name now equated with sex,
    A "male Mae West"—as Errol would make
    The point—thus pairing this highly complex
    Man with a trite image he couldn't shake
    The rest of his life, like some evil hex,
    Nor after his death (one reason I hit
    On Byron's *Don Juan* stanza, I will admit).

79   And adding to Errol's unhappiness
    Was that he'd no active role in the war,
    Our cinema warrior denied access
    To all the guts and concomitant gore
    Of that big world-historical mess,
    Greatest conflict going straight back to yore—
    The Nips in Rabaul, the Krauts in Kiev,
    And Errol at Warners since he was 4-F.

80   One year prior, back in February
    Of '42, Flynn had tried to enlist
    In the American military
    But his petition for service dismissed
    As the result of a pulmonary
    Condition, namely there seemed to exist
    A spot on his lung and the diagnosis
    Being that Flynn had tuberculosis.

81   This was no "doctored" deferment but fact.
       Flynn knew he had a heart murmur as well
       As malaria and often been wracked
       By long coughing fits which *he* thought befell
       Him from his smokes—but our Greek god contract
       Galloping consumption? That was just swell,
       Flynn the great robust masculine ideal
       Was ailing, anemic—a male Camille!

82   Errol and Warners kept his rejection
       A secret—which did nothing to allay
       Thoughts that he had a nice line of protection
       With powers-that-be and that the fault lay
       Not in some physical imperfection
       (*How could it—just* **look** *at the guy*, they'd say.)
       But one of character: that this Flynn fellow
       Was a malingerer—or simply yellow.[135]

83   This preyed on Errol—he wanted to show
       That he could make a true contribution
       To the war effort; and he wasn't slow
       In his attempt to find a solution,
       Refusing to take as his answer no,
       Showing great energy in prosecution
       Of his agenda and writing the chief
       Of the OSS to share his belief

84   That as a famous Hollywood actor
       He could perform service for the U.S.
       In Ireland where he might be a factor
       In helping America gain access
       To naval bases and make an impact—or
       At very least not retard the progress—
       Of mutual U.S.-Irish defense
       While providing some useful intelligence.[136]

85 There failed to come a positive reply;
   But Flynn had a better idea—he'd
   Achieve the front lines and see action by
   Being a war correspondent, that breed
   Of wordsmith for whom Flynn's esteem was high,
   A breed to which he belonged, pedigreed
   Through his reporting in civil-war Spain,
   But now in a place where he knew the terrain.

86 It took some time but finally in the Fall
   Of '42 he received assignment
   To report on the global free-for-all
   With Hearst, thus ending his stateside confinement,
   The talk being that his new boss would install
   Him in Australia where his byline meant
   Quite a lot to Flynn, now entering the fray
   Where his own prose had first seen light of day.

87 For Errol it'd be a triumphant return, he
   Just then starring in a movie that wraps
   Up with the final line (*Desperate Journey*):
   "Now for Australia and a crack at those Japs."[137]
   But just days later the District Attorney
   Torpedoed these plans, which had to collapse
   In face of the rape charges, Randolph Hearst
   Placing his syndicate's good repute first.[138]

88 Junked was Flynn's plan for combining his two
   Deeply felt passions, adventure and writing,
   While living up to the popular view
   (This certain view of course coinciding
   With his *self*-image) of a fellow who
   Wanted to get up close to the fighting
   And slim the gap and perchance bridge the span
   Between his screen roles and Errol the man.

89   So Errol would remain a denizen
Of film fantasy, his wish coming to naught;
And playing a Norwegian partisan
In *Edge of Darkness,* a role where he fought
Alongside the "Oomph Girl," Anne Sheridan,
Would be the closest that Errol Flynn got
To any combat that year—but no joke
His work on the film when the rape case broke.

90   Errol's performance in *Edge of Darkness*
Is skilled largely due to its restrained mood.
And I suppose that it's anyone's guess
As to just whether this might be construed
As in spite of or the *fruit* of duress
That Flynn was under—whether raw fortitude
Held him in good stead or rather did our
Actor's upset make him suitably dour?

91   But there's small question that genuine pluck
Was called for in Flynn's ensuing onscreen
Presence in a film aimed at the starstruck—
A fundraiser for the Hollywood Canteen,[139]
A musical spree with stars run amok,
Errol performing a little routine
In one of East London's working-class bars,
A movie entitled: *Thank Your Lucky Stars.*

92   Errol Flynn's number was comic satire
On his heroic screen image while not
Himself ever having come under fire—
A Cockney drunkard who talks tommyrot
About his brave wartime feats, the entire
Time hoping to cadge, this engaging sot,
But yet another half-pint mug of ale
In swap for his grandly ludicrous tale.

ERROL FLYNN

93   Errol's at his jaunty and sprightly best,
Very light on his feet as he imparts
Great waggish zest to the role as expressed
In the bright ditty by Loesser and Schwartz;
And though he's spoofing his own manifest
Lack of any role in the war, this part's
One of the more temerarious things
Flynn ever did since he *dances and sings.*

94   Not only did Errol both sing and dance
For the first time, which exampled some grit,
But there was also the tough circumstance
Of strictly *when* that Canteen-benefit
Was produced, with Errol breaking a lance
For the troops—that is, filming of this one bit
Where Flynn does his comic turn in high style,
Took place just four days before his rape trial.[140]

95   "Thank your lucky stars"—that's what *soldiers* thought
Should be Flynn's motto: He'd gotten the shaft
With trumped-up rape charges, but still he had not
Been sent up, and he had beaten the draft
And now was right back to sailing his yacht,
Festooned with beautiful girls fore and aft,
Choice pieces of ass for Errol's caprices
While GIs got *their* asses shot to pieces.

96   Errol might have cracked: "In like Flynn *my* ass."
He didn't feel lucky, not in the least,
Because things have come to a pretty pass
And qualify as exceedingly triste
If seeing no way out of your morass
And feeling it better to be deceased—
Our big life-affirming matinee idol
Possessed now by thoughts that were suicidal.

97   But wait a minute—was it really so bad?
From traumatized Flynn's point of view indeed.
And if it's the case that you've never had
A long drawn-out court battle intercede
In your life, I can only say just be glad
And let me perhaps bring you up to speed:
The stress on defendants can be so high,
They don't *have* to kill themselves—they just die.

98   The strain is huge when so much is at stake,
A physical and emotional test,
But not a mere question of make or break,
For after *acquittal*, studies suggest,
Defendants will oftentimes fail to shake
Off the effects of the trial, hard-pressed
To restore their health and to cauterize
Their wounds, all leading to an early demise.

99   Not only did Errol Flynn's reputation
Never recover from the rape trial,
Even after his complete vindication,
But Errol himself (who made no denial)
Suffered profound psychic devastation,
Now branded a borderline pedophile,[141]
His mental distress not some fleeting state
But throughout his life an eternal weight.

100   Of course this alone might not have sufficed
In nurturing Flynn's suicidal thoughts,
But now that his 4-F status had iced
His *film*-hero status (just fighting ersatz
Wars on the screen) and having sacrificed
Much to a fame that had his life in knots,
Getting him in this rape mess from the start—
All this could well make a person lose heart.

ERROL FLYNN

101   But just *what* had Flynn sacrificed to be
        A star—for which half of our great nation
        Would give their firstborn if it served as passkey
        (Others perhaps with *slight* hesitation)—
        To answer: Soon after the trial, he
        Had his dad forward the accumulation
        Of letters that Errol had penned when he'd been
        Out in New Guinea, mere lad among men.

102   The letters were simply so as to compare
        The fellow back then with what he'd become—
        To see how his Hollywood self might fare
        In stopping to calmly regard it from
        The standpoint of ten elapsed years (a bare
        Decade but one in which Flynn, on the bum
        At its beginning, had soon made his mark)
        The contrast now boding to be rather stark.

103   It was—Flynn liked the younger man better:
        That guy who still had a whole host of dreams,
        These perhaps vague but Flynn a go-getter
        Once he had fastened on one of his schemes
        For striking it rich, and one certain letter
        Voicing frustration at what Errol deems
        An onerous fact—enough to shed tears—
        That he'd be dead in some two hundred years.[142]

104   The youthful Errol had been intensely
        Interested and engaged in the act
        Of living, he ever seeking to densely
        Pack life with incident and to extract
        Its pap, a task which he was immensely
        Suited for due to the manifest fact
        (In his spirit, I think, it's evincible)
        That he *embodied* the life-principle.

105   But if suicidal then obviously
       Much of Flynn's great will to live was now gone;
       Though he had everything, ostensibly,
       He'd lost the one thing he'd craved early on:
       To somehow be taken *seriously*,
       Impressing his father, that great paragon
       Of dignity and enshrined in *Who's Who*,
       His son just a Hollywood-actor yahoo.[143]

106   Not only his person but Errol felt
       That his *film* roles had been relegated
       To objects of sneering—a red garter belt
       In one hand and sword in the other—he hated
       The boiler-plate parts he was being dealt
       By Warners. He thought that his talent rated
       More complex stuff and that this paucity
       Of roles had made him a mediocrity.

107   For Errol this was "the cardinal sin,
       To be middling was to be nothing" (he
       Once wrote in a piece)[144] —his rule *play to win,*
       With which we Americans would agree,
       A mindset perhaps best summarized in
       Those words of the football coach at Navy,
       Who said that a tie—here now citing Mr.
       Ed Erdelatz—"is like kissing your sister."[145]

108   Or in Flynn's case it is not the word "tie"
       That would apply but instead "stalemate"—
       A vicious circle, this endless supply
       Of so-so roles doing little to sate
       His creative lust and the main reason why
       His acting was judged to be less than great
       And he to be just a good-looking hunk—
       This in turn leading to more roles that stunk.

ERROL FLYNN

109   Let us be clear—this was Flynn's view, not mine.
Sure, he'd appeared in a couple of duds,
As Warners was predisposed to confine
Him to adventure fare since *Captain Blood*'s
Resounding success—but the bottom line
Was how many other Hollywood studs
Could ride, wield swords, kiss hands like our hero?
And you guessed the answer if you said zero.

110   Of course one can see Errol's point, and I
Don't think, among actors, that he's alone
In *not* hungering to transmogrify
Into a self-parody like Stallone,
That clever fellow (hence his nickname "Sly")
Whose fame has been based on testosterone,
His public now coming so to expect it
That in old age he's started to inject it.

111   To his roles Errol brought a style and grace
Of which Sylvester can only but dream
(I'm just saying that as a turn-of-phrase—
His reveries are surely per the theme
Of pecs and lats and how best to showcase
Them in his latest *succès d'estime*),
Though he might *learn*—and here's hoping he can—
That full-body workouts don't make a full man.

112   Of course this is something that has been lost—
The full-man view—so perhaps I should cut
Sylvester some slack; this ideal's been tossed
Boorishly aside in favor of what
Is termed the "specialist," a word that's embossed
With rare qualities; but due to the glut
Of so-called specialists, I can't concede
Much rareness or specialness in this new breed.

113   Neither did Flynn realize quite how good
He was in the swashbuckling roles nor just how
Perfectly suited parts like Robin Hood
Were for his talents—which we can see now
Clearly with one of the top Hollywood
Stars, Russell Crowe, having tried to endow
This dashing free-spirit with rude gravity
That divests him of all verve and suavity.

114   I'm sure Crowe would say that he didn't want
To play Robin Hood in the Errol style—
That it'd be phony to make war a jaunt
And not to mention a blatant denial
Of its rare horror to be nonchalant,
Playing the role with that big roguish smile,
And who gives a toss if folks like it Flynn's way,
I simply refuse to flog that cliché!

115   Crowe was right in not striving to repeat
Flynn's take on Robin because otherwise
Why do it at all?—though quite a conceit
On his part to even *try* to reprise
The role after Flynn and thereby compete
With him while attempting to exorcize
Flynn's specter, perversely, by ensuring
His star-turn lacked all that made Flynn's so enduring.

116   No esprit, no pizzazz, no light-hearted joy
Are ever permitted to interfere;
No lusty laughter from Crowe to destroy
The downright funereal atmosphere;
No bracing razor-tongued wit to alloy
Our thickset lummox who's there to strike fear
Into the hearts of his various foes.
(And struck fear in *me* he'd style Lincoln green hose.)

ERROL FLYNN

117   If Russell Crowe is the Robin Hood you
Should fancy then by all means be my guest;
His version, however, is less a breakthrough
Interpretation than a manifest
Bid by our ACTOR to make a virtue
Of his shortcomings since he's neither blessed
With the face nor form nor *je ne sais quoi*
Of Flynn—thus showing up Crowe's major flaw:

118   The man has no charm. Now this word is thrown
Around quite a bit, but I'm indicating
A certain something like Dom Pérignon,
That prestige champagne for celebrating
Special occasions, a sine qua non,
With its superbly intoxicating
Effect, so easy to quaff that it throws ya
All the while swearing you're drinking ambrosia.

119   Flynn brought this champagne magic to bear
In his early roles, a fact of which he
May not at all have been fully aware
Nor of their very real difficulty,
Since he in playing them had such a flair,
They coming to him far too easily,
So Flynn may have underestimated
Their worth, leaving him unjustly frustrated.

120   Although a Freudian psychoanalyst
Might trace Flynn's decline to whatever trauma
(Which I dislike since it's so fatalist—
For instance his relationship with his mama)
Without any doubt the main catalyst
In adult years was the rape-case drama,
Killing himself not by pulling a trigger
But in slower fashion, jigger by jigger.

121   He now the butt of jokes for his amorous
      Exploits as well as for winning the war,[146]
      All the while safely ensconced in glamorous
      Hollywood, Errol began to abhor
      Not just the whole movie biz and clamorous
      Public but deplored the loss, furthermore,
      Of the sole thing which a man can't expect
      To lose and love life—namely self-respect.

122   But as an antidote to suicide,
      And perhaps yet still to even regain
      A sense of self-worth and restore his pride,
      Flynn plunged into prose, diverting his brain
      With *Showdown*, his novel, he tucked inside
      His Mulholland study and giving free rein
      To his own writerly imagination
      While stemming his gloom through mounting pagination.

123   Errol invested himself in the book
      To thwart what he called an increasing "sense
      Of futility," scribbling in his nook,
      Line upon line, amassing evidence
      That he was not just some profligate schnook
      Given to anything but abstinence—
      A playboy, boozer and general dissolute
      Whose sole creed was pleasure and its pursuit.

124   What does a man do to impart meaning
      To his existence when he comes to view
      Life as a hollow pursuit and gleaning
      No purpose in it, youth's fresh morning dew
      Burnt off by adulthood's sun, intervening
      To show things in clear light of day, the blue
      Firmament above revealing no sign
      Of angels or heaven, let alone the divine.

125   Having no faith in a being called "God"
    Nor in some kind of celestial plan,
    What does one do to make sense of this odd
    World that we live in—how fill our brief span?
    Some race after thrills, others work and plod
    (Camus styled Sisyphus "a happy man");
    Some will raise families, others breed dogs,
    One fellow gardens, another guy blogs;

126   Some try inventing a better mousetrap,
    Others are bent on saving the whales;
    Some try to lower their golf handicap,
    Others love shopping at Bloomingdale's;
    Certain individuals like to wrap
    Up public monuments in giant veils;
    Some get their jollies by joining with cults,
    Others through acts with consenting adults.

127   In short, whatever gets you through the night.
    And now in Errol's dark night of the soul
    He once more started in earnest to write,
    Hoping to crawl from this bitter black hole
    And bring a semblance of sweetness and light
    To a life spiraling out of control,
    Thereby employing artistic creation
    To lull his feeling of earthly damnation.

128   The writing, though, was not just an attempt
    To prove that he was a man of substance
    But was expression of Errol's *contempt,*
    An ostentatious act of defiance,
    For even though he'd been rendered exempt
    From wartime service, he still would enhance
    His reputation for being no stranger
    To high adventure and mortal danger.

129   *Showdown*'s main figure is positively
       Errol himself, the captain of a ship
       Plying the dread waters of New Guinea,
       Facing down tempests with stiff upper lip,
       Taking on cannibals and the odd sea
       Creature and always with very firm grip
       On tiller and nerves—and though the plot creaks,
       You feel the author knows whereof he speaks.

130   The main figure is undoubtedly Flynn,
       Which he would like to have readers believe,
       Resemblance between them more than just skin
       Deep since their psychologies interweave
       And any differences are paper-thin,
       Flynn with his heart on this character's sleeve,
       A likeness that's drawn with great delicacy,[147]
       Except that his figure vows *celibacy*.

131   In my humble view the book's a protest
       Against the post-trial image Flynn had
       Of someone obsessed with female conquest,
       A sex psychopath, not the true Galahad
       Of his films, that walking and talking *beau geste*,
       Which by itself wouldn't have been so bad,
       But Errol the warrior, which he also played,
       Was missing the war—was the fellow *afraid*?

132   So it was in this besieged state of mind
       That Errol attended a party thrown
       By David O. Selznick (the fellow behind
       Gone with the Wind, one of Hollywood's own),
       Toward end of the war, Flynn there to unwind,
       A glass in his hand and standing alone
       In O. Selznick's hall and just sort of roostin'
       When along ambled director John Huston.

133   Huston at this point had already made
The Maltese Falcon, his directing debut,
Humphrey Bogart as gumshoe Sam Spade;
Aside from that, though, he'd only done two
More movies—or maybe we can downgrade
That to *almost* two, this last not quite through
When Huston was drafted by the Signal Corps
To film documentaries of the war.[148]

134   Huston had been in the thick of action,
Exposing himself to enemy fire,
The war for him not some mere abstraction,
He wading through all its blood, muck and mire,
Film heroes holding but small attraction
For him, he not finding much to admire,
Especially when alleged hero's the sort
Who wears silk cravats and calls you "old sport."

135   Major John Huston and Flynn had a nodding
Acquaintance, the former also employed
By Warner Brothers and both of them trodding
The same movie turf and having enjoyed
(Huston similarly a marauding
Male who women didn't seek to avoid)
The company of the same ladies and
One of these being Miss de Havilland.

136   Flynn of course harbored a great affection
For Livy, but it continues unclear
If there'd been sexual intersection
Between the two stars, while it *does* appear
That with John Huston she'd had a connection
Predicated equally on sincere
Feelings and serious fornication,
Which was (or had been) Flynn's own aspiration.

137   And lastly John Huston was also known
       For being, like Flynn, handy with his fists,
       He having entered the combat zone
       In this regard, too, for manly-art trysts,
       Exceedingly able to hold his own,
       Since it would seem that this pugilist's
       Semi-pro record was twenty-three wins
       Against two losses, which far outshone Flynn's.[149]

138   And so to quote Huston: "The stage is set,
       Rehearsals are over, the actors are ready,
       The curtain is going up" (all which we get
       In Huston's voiceover to his heady
       Report from the Aleutians,[150] showing the threat
       Posed by Japan, our palms getting sweaty:)
       "But this is not make-believe drama, they
       Will be playing for keeps"—so on with *our* play . . .

139   "Why, hello Huston, what brings you round here?
       Last that I heard you were lending our chaps
       A hand with the war in Adak."—"I fear
       I only shot film and not any Japs,"
       Says Huston, then Flynn with outward good cheer:
       "Sole difference 'tween us is you"—and he slaps
       John's back—"'hind the camera and me out front,
       All those enlisted men bearing the brunt."

140   John cocks an eyebrow: "Say, how did you know
       I was in Adak?"—"Because I was there
       Myself," declares Flynn, "with the USO.
       They said that you chaps had been in their hair
       For quite a while. Well, we gave them a show,
       And boy, that's just what they needed, I swear,
       Their life there is sheerest monotony—
       No landscape, just tundra, not even a tree."

141   "Yeah kid, that's right," says Huston, "not a wide
Spectrum of flora and fauna, but I
Am afraid the Aleutian countryside
Is one thing, the war another—just fly
One of their bombing runs. I took a ride
Or two and can personally testify
That 'monotony' is not a word you
Would use to describe a raid on Attu."[151]

142   "What's more," adds Huston, "if we didn't lose
Our planes to Zeros or artillery flak,
Which happened enough, along with the crews,
The *climate* would then go on the attack,
Like some perfidious Japanese ruse,
We dropping bombs but they getting theirs back
With fogbanks and cyclonic winds that hurled
Our planes from the worst goddamn skies in the world."

143   "I know what you mean," says Flynn, giving John
A look that's more than just a bit wary.
"We also encountered some bad weather on
Our trips to each base—the military
Shipped us like packages, *par avion*,
Thought they'd be writing my obituary
A couple times there, since you will remember
How awful the gales can be in December."

144   Huston says nothing at first, just taking
A swallow of scotch: "Gosh, kid, I had no
Clue to what lengths you had gone to making
A contribution, in striking a blow
For our war effort and not just faking
It up on the screen but effecting to go
Up to Alaska so as to perform
In person for all of our 'chaps' in uniform."

145   Flynn stares at Huston—the implication
Is perfectly clear: that *Errol* is not
In uniform and defending the nation,
Not bearing arms, having never once fought,
Doing mere passable imitation
Of it in movies; a real cheap shot
By Huston, just like a kick to the groin—
But Errol can pay him back in his own coin:

146   "Wasn't that gallant and noble of me?
Like all those figures that I used to play
Opposite Livy—a nice girl, but she
Is nothing like those demure dames she'd portray.
You know her, John, and would have to agree,
That our Olivia's one easy lay!
If fans only knew . . . though I find it funny
That their saintly Melanie fucks like a bunny!"

147   It can perhaps be lent to Flynn's presence
In house of *Gone with the Wind*'s producer
That he'd cite "Melanie" as the quintessence
Of Livy's image versus her looser
Private behavior; but this excrescence
—Flynn's verbal dirt so as to reduce her
To the equivalent of a cheap floozy—
Is to goad Huston, and his goad's a doozy.

148   "That's a lie!" says Huston. "And even if
It weren't then only a son of a bitch
Would repeat it!"[152] And so that their little tiff
Should now attain to the right fever pitch,
Errol suggests they step out for a whiff
Of fresh evening air, a proposal to which
John Huston accedes, both quietly leaving
The party to do some bobbing and weaving.

149   In actuality both of these two
Are orthodox stand-up boxers, Flynn much
In the Corbett mold, attempting to subdue
Foes by employing that sweet-science touch,
Straight jabs and crosses, just what Huston threw,
As tall as Errol and possessor of such
Long apelike arms that he too likes to slide
In far-ranging haymakers from the outside.

150   Similar tactics and both pretty near
In age (with Huston merely being prone
To calling guys "kid" who might be a year
Or two his junior), Flynn with a two-stone
Advantage in weight but Huston with sheer
Weight of prizefighting experience thrown
Into the scales on his own lanky side—
Though Flynn as a scrapper is hardly untried.

151   They quit the party, Flynn leading the way
Down to the bottom of Selznick's garden—
No words exchanged now, what is there to say?
Neither man begging the other's pardon,
Pride not permitting Errol Flynn to betray
His 4-F status and he feeling harden
His heart (and knuckles) as the two proceed
And the fête's music and laughter recede.

152   Finally they reach a secluded place, a
Site where in lightlessness they cannot see
Any vegetation but able to trace a
Sweet scent of jasmine in the air graciously
Mingling with that of sun-drenched acacia
Along with the tang of eucalyptus tree—
Aromas aroused by this soft April night
And making a nice perfumed ring for their fight.

153   They shed their jackets, raise fists and square off,
Feinting and jabbing . . . when suddenly Flynn
Dances in on his toes like Baryshnikov
And shoots a straight right to John Huston's chin,
The punch landing right on the money—BOFF!—
And Huston goes down, his head in a spin,
His body instinctively following suit—
Spinning, that is, presupposing Flynn's boot.

154   But it doesn't come, Flynn now stepping back
And calmly waiting for Huston to rise
Before he once more goes on the attack—
Flynn once more cutting his foe down to size,
John Huston dropped this time with a sharp *thwack*
And busted up nose. (Which had been no prize
To start with because it'd already been bent
As a young boxer—so what's one more dent?)

155   "Huston, you're giving away too much weight,
You don't want to fight," says Flynn with a sneer.
He'd been in a bit of a drunken state
When starting, Huston, his head none too clear,
But having a string of stiff blows detonate
On your face is a great if rather severe
Way to get sober—and though Flynn would scoff, he
Had served up the equal of hot black coffee.

156   John Huston wordlessly climbs to his feet,
Shuffling back in now to prove Errol wrong,
He bloodied and bruised but still far from beat,
Not at all daunted, still feeling quite strong
And (although landing once more on his seat)
His stamina's good, Flynn in for a long
Night of it, come what may, Huston's condition
Tip-top as of taking his army commission.

ERROL FLYNN

157   Flynn cocks his right, Huston able to gauge
      Its advent and slip it, stepping in close
      And digging sharp hooks to Errol's ribcage,
      Hard body-punching, a vigorous dose,
      Flynn clinching while John tries to disengage,
      Both of them trading choice you-so-and-sos,
      Flynn starting it off, now being hurt, he
      A pretty clean fighter but his language quite dirty.

158   So their fistfight commences in earnest,
      Huston clearheaded and starting to score
      On Errol's body, this one of the sternest
      Tests that Flynn's had, Huston not one of your
      Brawling "headhunters"; and though thou may spurnest
      That boxing dictum of kill the body, for
      The head will follow, it's not out of place
      With actors who're vain of protecting their face.

159   The slugfest continues for a good while,
      And though our battlers have plenty of gas,
      Yours truly is almost on empty, so I'll
      Exit the scene with a prudent volte face,
      Leaving the two of them less than docile,
      Going like gangbusters out on the grass,
      Cursing and panting, two jerky silhouettes,
      Grotesque in their throes, like life-size marionettes . . .

BOOK THREE

TRAGIC WAYFARER

CANTO VII

Descent from Olympus

(1945-1950)

"Que sçais-je?" was the motto of Montaigne,
As also of the first Academicians:
That all is dubious which Man may attain,
Was one of their most favourite positions.
There's no such thing as certainty, that's plain
As any of Mortality's Conditions:
So little do we know what we're about in
This world, I doubt if doubt itself be doubting.

Don Juan, canto IX, stanza 17

New York 1948, after a court appearance for kicking
a cop in the shins

CANTO VII

1   The California sun was blazing bright
    Her first time to Mulholland Farm when she saw
    Errol Flynn seated by the pool in white
    Gabardine slacks, his torso in the raw,
    Skin glistening gold, a memorable sight,
    That strong chiseled profile barren of flaw,
    Head as if sculpted, and the sunshine's glare
    Evoking the red and blond tints of his hair.

2   Errol Flynn rises to his moccasinned feet,
    Graceful in movement, just like a big cat,
    A panther who spies something scrumptious to eat,
    This lamb who's strayed into his habitat,
    He drawing near to the succulent meat,
    Tender and juicy, though sleek and not fat,
    Baring his teeth, dazzling white in his tanned
    Face—and bends over and kisses her hand.

3   Nora Eddington was nineteen years old
    When first she set foot in Flynn's domicile,
    And Errol first laid eyes on *her* when he'd strolled
    Past Nora's courthouse cigar counter while
    Heading to that chamber in which untold
    Drama took place at his double-rape trial;
    So Nora was *legal*—as too was her pop,
    So to speak, since he was an L.A. cop.[153]

4   Flynn himself didn't approach her; he had
    His stuntman-crony Buster Wiles go chat
    Her up at her stand, and Errol's comrade
    Did a fine job as the paw of our cat
    In finally getting her up to Flynn's pad,
    Both of them hitting it off just like that—
    Not hitting the *sack*, though, she was a virgin,
    So Dr. Flynn went to work like a surgeon,

ERROL FLYNN

5   Proposing (so as to foster her trust)
That Nora start work as his secretary,
Taking dictation and typing and just
Doing whatever was necessary,
His own girl-friday, she handling the robust
Fan mail and such things epistolary—
Her duties, in short, being none too sparse,
But quite a lot better than selling cigars.

6   This was a smart stratagem on Flynn's part:
While ever maintaining propriety,
It daily exposed her tractable heart
To Errol in all his variety
While laying open her mind to his art,
But *not* that for which he'd gained notoriety,
Her shorthand instead helping Flynn not to slow down
As he dictated his novel *Showdown*.

7   But it was hardly some great admiration
She had for his book let alone fan mail;
He failed to exert a fascination
Which made Nora swoon like your basic female;
He failed to incite that adoration
With which the girls tended Flynn to assail;
Nora fell for him (let her testify)
Since "he was simply a wonderful guy."[154]

8   She fell in love with *him*, not with his fame,
Not with his riches, not with his elite
Hollywood status; it was all the same
To her if he had the whole world at his feet,
This in turn causing Flynn's passion to flame
And his own heart to more ardently beat,
He at last losing his sexual cool:
No surgical kit—he'd use his own *tool*.

9   Though not quite rape, Errol forced the issue,
     Which when you're young and naïve to such things
     (First off just wanting the guy to kiss you,
     Your thoughts then turning to engagement rings
     And then wedding bells and only then *this*) you
     Are likely to feel like one of his flings,
     As if you've been rudely violated—
     This in her memoir is clearly indicated.[155]

10   Errol eventually did marry her
     (Following, though, his stint with Tiger Lil,
     You couldn't find any man warier
     Of the wedded state, that battle uphill)
     With the proviso it'd be temporary, her
     Principal wish to stay married until
     Birth of that child Errol didn't disclaim,
     Thereby bestowing upon it his name.

11   And so Deirdre Flynn the baby was called,
     She born in early 1945;
     Then two years on little Rory installed
     Herself in their home; and the match stayed alive
     Up until 1949 when it stalled
     Once and for all and performed a nosedive,
     Nora having had enough of Flynn's games,
     She leaving him for the singer Dick Haymes.[156]

12   How's that for concision and brevity?
     Though you would not call their marriage long-lived
     (Four years don't rate the expression "longevity")
     We should be happy that it has survived
     This many stanzas since—all levity
     Aside—in *Wicked* you'd scarce know he wived
     A girl named "Nora," whom Flynn tends to gloss
     Over and not due to memory loss.

ERROL FLYNN

13   Shortly before Errol's death he told Nora
That in his memoirs he wouldn't dispense
Particulars of their shared life—and for a
Laudable reason: "the wonderful moments
We had are not for the public to savor"—a
Remark underpinned by fine sentiments,
But Errol had a far better rationale,
One less romantic not to say banal:

14   Those wonderful moments were interspersed
With others less wonderful, in fact horrific,
Their marriage on the whole not blessed but cursed—
And if you'd like me to be specific
How about raising his hand or durst
I say *knee* to her gut, simply a terrific
Clout that decked her; and the five times she tried
To leave him; and two tries at suicide.[157]

15   It must be said, though, that Errol was not
Entirely sane when he'd raise hand or knee
To Nora but had often taken a shot
Or two or three of those drugs to which he
Had grown addicted, even on his yacht,
Conquering even his love of the sea—
Opium, cocaine, morphine, heroin
All vying for the soul of Errol Flynn.

16   But what of Flynn's *heart*? True in things conjugal?
To which I can only say are you kidding!
You can't stuff that genie back in the bottugal!
Flynn of course did his libido's bidding,
The man's womanizing non-stop prodigal,
Shamelessly so, he not even ridding
Mulholland Farm of those telltale traces
That women can leave in the damnedest places,

17   For instance douche bags hanging in the bathroom.
And when wife Nora made bold to complain,
In an even tone, careful not to fume,
Not asking that Errol *wholly* refrain
From other girls but that they not presume
To place their hygienic gadgets in plain
Sight, Flynn quipped, "Now don't let"—not his penis—
"A few old beat-up douche bags come between us."[158]

18   In fairness to Errol it has to be said
That he and Nora weren't living together.
He'd set her up in her private homestead,
Needing his space—that old shibboleth—her
Own heartfelt wish now fulfilled (to be wed)
So she not needing Flynn on a short tether.
(When Rory came, though, they did cohabitate;
Sad case, however, of too little too late.)[159]

19   Thus many "wonderful moments" perhaps,
And with a "wonderful guy"; nonetheless,
Errol Flynn sought to keep much under wraps
—Even in a memoir that flaunts wickedness—
Much where he *wished* that his memory would lapse;
Though his true motive is anyone's guess,
I think he failed to air his more baneful
Conduct because it was simply too painful.

20   He loved her likely as much as he could
Any female, while styling her "a rare
Jewel of innocence," devoid of falsehood,
Which was to just implicitly compare
Her with lesser models of womanhood,
Wenches who'd rendered his life a nightmare:
Marelle and Lili, Peggy and Betty—
All making him want to wield a machete.[160]

21   Just as Damita had signified fame,
       Cop-daughter Nora stood for normality.
       Now that he'd staked his celebrity claim,
       Flynn thought he'd hazard conventionality,
       Which he *achieved* with this Eddington dame,
       Errol rejoicing in nuptiality,
       Leastwise for stretches, until he grew antsy,
       When he would yield to whatever fancy.

22   His pal David Niven, just back from the war
       With a new wife and two children in tow,
       Recounts how Errol would come see the four
       Of them in their closely knit home and bestow
       His help in preparing the dinner or
       Just play with the kids, whom he seemed to adore,
       Saying in a voice with rue underlaid:
       "This is the life, sport, you've really got it made."

23   But Flynn *had* this life (a house and a home,
       A spouse and two kids) so he was just saying
       That he was wishful of that chromosome
       Which would prevent a fellow from straying,
       Stifling that red-blooded penchant to roam,
       Permitting Flynn to *delight* in staying
       True to one woman and make a family
       And not just some Hollywood facsimile.[161]

24   But Errol was doing his level best
       In living a nice settled life in fact,
       Indeed succeeding, and one litmus test
       Being that he had now finally cracked
       His novel *Showdown*, no minor conquest,
       But failing to make any real impact
       On the large public nor on the critics
       When it was published in 1946,

25   A great blow to Errol, who as we've seen
Had lofty literary aspirations—
Though one's not able to expressly glean,
From *Wicked* or elsewhere, his frustrations
With *Showdown*'s reception, which could well mean,
Just like with Nora and their tribulations,
Errol's silence here should likely alert
Us to the fact it concealed profound hurt.[162]

26   Writing *Showdown* had helped Errol deflect
Suicidal thoughts which had arisen
After his trial in ripple effect;
For even though he'd eluded prison,
Yet still held captive was Flynn's self-respect
Because he was still enslaved by showbiz, in
Hollywood of all inelegant places—
That greasy, maudlin, mirage-like oasis.[163]

27   And Flynn himself not only in a cage
But his own "image" incarcerated:
That of the hero who's destined to wage
War on injustice and always fated
To conquer the girl . . . this plight to assuage
Not easy because the image that grated
Owed in large part to the manifest case
That *it* was captive to Flynn's form and face.[164]

28   Rising from his couch, Flynn heads to the bar
And pours more vodka, which he always stocks,
Now viewing John Decker's painting from afar,
There over the hearth, that savory pox
On the famed beauty that's Errol's bête noire,
And an undoubted Pandora's Box
(Outing his demons) then he heads to the den
To sit at his desk and take up his pen.

29   On to the next book! Perchance his life story?
      That would be sure to make an impression,
      All hoping to read of his amatory
      Adventures, that's certain, but this confession
      Not some cheap self-congratulatory
      List of his triumphs, a long succession
      Of victories in the carnal arena,
      From the South Sea girls to Peg of Catalina.

30   No, he would never compose such a book
      (In any event he would need at least two)
      But would instead give the public a look
      Into the *mind* of an actor who knew
      The price of "success"—that it often partook
      Of sacrificing other dreams that you
      Had stored in your heart but then put aside
      To make big bucks and let integrity ride.

31   To do the memoir justice, however,
      He'd have to vacate the Hollywood scene
      Because the kind of sustained endeavor
      That he envisioned would need a serene
      Place where he could effectively sever
      His movietown ties and kick his morphine
      And other vices—and though it would take a
      Miracle of sorts, there was now Jamaica.

32   He had discovered its charms this past year,
      Falling in love with the lush paradise,
      Not just because it recalled to mind dear
      Laloki plantation—come to symbolize
      The natural life in a pure biosphere—
      But he enjoyed getting between the thighs
      Of pulchritudinous Jamaican girls
      (Why there's so many Jamaican Errols).[165]

33   He would buy land and live there, just writing,
As in New Guinea once, putting his cash
Where it was safe and not be providing
For lawyers and agents and courts and a rash
Of others who had a stake in dividing
Whatever it was he had in his stash—
Foremost among them Damita, of course,
Greedy for dough ever since their divorce.

34   Jamaica was where he would make his stand,
Out on the "Errol Flynn Estates"—and if that
Didn't work out (investing in the land)[166]
Then there was always the water: just scat
Onto the *Zaca* and tell the dockhand
To cast off the ropes and in nothing flat
Your cares were cast off and you had surcease,
Which is precisely what *Zaca* meant—"peace."[167]

35   Peace you could find out on the wide ocean
—What Flynn asserted he desperately craved—
Despite now and then a bit of commotion,
Like recently when the *Zaca* crew braved
That West Indies cyclone, a frightful notion,
But all those mountainous waves somehow staved
Off the unrest which made Errol squirm, a
Bane when he dwelled too long on terra firma.

36   He saw the words that were over his desk:
"The only worthwhile people are those who
Are always beginning again"—this grotesque
Hollywood life with its values askew,
The whole damn town just the stuff of burlesque,
Indeed his exit was long overdue,
He had to make tracks, there was little doubt,
And *could* with his Warners contract running out.

37   However, he couldn't just pick up and GO.
Making this move would require preparation,
Not just a matter of presto-chango;
Though he'd a talent for confrontation,
He didn't possess *that* kind of bravado.
Last thing he wanted was more litigation,
Which would result if he ditched his career,
Telling Jack Warner to blow it out his ear.

38   He'd wished to do that for a long time now—
Being an actor was lousy enough
Without playing all those dud roles, endow
Them with what you will, with all your best stuff.
As Corbett or Custer he could take a bow,
But more recent roles hadn't been up to snuff
(Very mildly put)—O, but for one crack
At something like Cyrano de Bergerac![168]

39   The last decent movie that he had made
Was *Objective, Burma!* (a war film) and since
Then five pictures that hadn't made the grade,
In fact they collectively made Errol wince;
In fact to simply call a spade a spade,
His preference would be to nuke all the prints—
Each one a movie designed to entertain
But too often failing in *this* modest vein.

40   In *San Antonio* he'd played a cattle
Baron contending with rustlers—a bad
Notion to start with: Flynn in the saddle
Of an American Western, a tad
Misplaced in such cowboy fiddle-faddle.
(Warners so prizing this stuff that they had
Salvaged Max Steiner's theme from *Dodge City*
Just to save money on a brand new ditty.)[169]

CANTO VII

41   *Never Say Goodbye* was more uninspired
And recycled schlock, the best thing about it
Hollaender's music which gracefully squired
Moviegoers through this comic washout—it
Nonetheless having Errol Flynn (byword
For pluck) to his daughter, who herself would doubt it,
Declare: "You believed in me as Robin Hood,"
And she: "That was just make-believe"—which *is* good.

42   The movie *Cry Wolf* with Barbara Stanwyck
Was a contrived and bewildering mess,
A melodrama where it's laid on thick,
A case where more is definitely *less*.
That apart, however, I mustn't nitpick—
What the film's about is anyone's guess.
(Sure as the grave, though, and that diehard taxman,
You had a fine score by trusty Franz Waxman.)

43   The most to be said for *Escape Me Never*
Is that after just 104
Minutes you may escape *it*. Whoever
Cast Flynn as a musical genius was more
Enemy than friend. (Although quite clever
They were in selecting Korngold for the score,
A musical genius if ever there was,
Upgrading weak films, here just what he does.)

44   Then another oater called *Silver River*
(Steiner on board for the score—no matter
These movies' flaws, music-wise they deliver)
Which started well but became a tatter
When Flynn commenced to punish his liver,
Drinking while filming, and so this latter
Was delayed, thus leading to cost overrun—
And despite no ending, was just declared done.[170]

45   Flynn sips his vodka, leans back in his chair,
The pen he had taken up long put aside.
Co-star Ann Sheridan had made him aware
Of the on-set gains of getting cockeyed
On vodka, one of those liquors so rare
In leaving no trace on your breath, allied
To its water-like hue, and this last shoot-em-up
Like a silver river they'd been lapping it up.

46   This was the nasty circle: Errol drank
As the sole method to get through a role
For which he had his Flynn-image to thank,
Behavior by no means likely to cajole
The brass to forego their "money in the bank"
And cede him a part you *couldn't* pigeonhole—
So Errol Flynn just kept hitting the sauce,
Which kept the brass thinking profit and loss . . .

47   That's where Flynn's own focus was presently—
He had all manner of fiscal obligations,
As never before, and consequently
Had to keep working (with short vacations
Of course between films) just as intently
As ever; and all of the degradations,
Mentally speaking, aren't hard to foretell
In doing filmwork against which you rebel.

48   There was no way out. Could he just retrieve
That former feeling of having some power
Over events in his life or *believe*
He did and not poison the idle hour
With toxic musings that gave no reprieve—
But *life* bid you think them, per Schopenhauer,
Who felt existence a chronic disease
(And *he'd* never worked with Michael Curtiz).

49   Errol leaves the den and ascends the stairs
       To his bedchamber—not to hit the hay,
       He sleeps here rarely, unless of course there's
       Wife Nora around (which she's not today)
       Nor to bang others (she might find stray hairs)—
       En route to his bedroom, along the way,
       At top of the steps his brooding gaze locks
       On the plaque with those words from Ella Wilcox:

       One ship drives east and another drives west
       With the selfsame winds that blow.
       'Tis the set of the sails,
       And not the gales,
       That tells us the way to go.

50   That was the mark of a man: to master
       Lady Luck, albeit not in that one
       Could somehow always forefend disaster,
       For instance death, but the way that you won
       Was if not outlast to've at least *outclassed* her . . .
       Flynn makes his bedroom and then takes a gun
       Out of the dresser and sits on the bed
       And now weighs the merits of ending up dead.

51   That might in fact be the classiest move:
       Offing yourself before doing much more
       To embarrass yourself—if only to prove
       Here was a fellow who did know the score,
       He never *could* act and naught did behoove
       Him as *Flynn* on the cutting-room floor.
       Such would be noble and finally rate
       As you being ultimate master of your fate.

52   You've always admired—haven't you, digger?—
Men who could level with themselves and draw
The hard conclusions. So just take a swig 'er
Two of your vodka to keep your sang froid
And *level* that barrel and *draw* that trigger!
In Westerns fighting for order and law,
You're quick with a gun and the last man standin'—
Or might you care for a stuntman stand-in?

53   No, he should care for a change of costume.
And so in placing the gun to one side,
Rising from the bed and crossing the room,
He opens his closet and reaches inside
And after a bit he comes to exhume
A blue sportscoat that has been modified
To the extent that beneath its breast pocket
Is a question mark—and though you may mock it

54   As a kind of absurd affectation,
For Flynn it isn't at all tongue-in-cheek,
Since he got from it a strange satisfaction
(Like Decker's portrait so baleful and bleak)
As an entirely fitting summation
Of his inner life, allowing a peek
Into a psyche that was obsessed by
The simple but basic question of "Why?"

55   Errol had this question mark on each suit,
Symbolic statement of his confusion,
Which as of late had been rather acute
(Witness his pending self-execution)
But since it's not every day that you shoot
Yourself, it was a foregone conclusion
That Errol should wish to look his very best—
The scarf and gray slacks he wore doing the rest.

56   Perhaps a note saying what they should do
      With his glorious Aussie cadaver?
      No funeral for him, no formal adieu,
      With the adjunct bereavement palaver—
      For all he cared, let him rot *in situ*,
      Just spare him all the concomitant slaver
      And public grief and staged lamentation—
      All that emotional masturbation.[171]

57   But they would not let him rot where he fell,
      They'd want to plant him some place specific
      So they might bid a collective farewell;
      In that case dump him in the Pacific,
      Off of the *Zaca*, he ever to dwell
      Beneath the waves—in fact a terrific
      Idea that was! Just let his corpse be
      Consigned from dear *Zaca* to his cherished sea.

58   They'd want some site, though, to prowl his remains,
      Needing a parcel of sanctified ground
      To "pay their respects," one more of those banes
      Of the departed, some little dirt mound
      Where to lay wreaths till your memory wanes—
      Hence let his bones be Jamaica-bound!
      Buried underneath a native oak tree,
      At least with a *view* down green hills to the sea.

59   Sufficient already was the prime view
      He suffered of Forest Lawn Cemetery.[172]
      Regardless post-mortem what might ensue,
      Under no circumstances should they bury
      Him in that stinking necropolis to
      Half of Tinseltown, his sworn adversary,
      Because he'd long lived on Hollywood's terms
      And be damned if he would feed Hollywood's worms . . .

ERROL FLYNN

60   A knock at the door, very impromptu:
"Yes," answers Errol, as the sound recedes.
"Sir," comes the voice of Flynn's butler, "the new
Studio contract has arrived and needs
Your signature now." For a moment or two
Flynn halts, gulps vodka, and then he proceeds
To place the gun in the drawer with a frown:
"That's fine, Alexander, I'll be right down."[173]

61   The seven-year contract that Errol signed
Was the best to date, they paying a quarter
Million per picture, Flynn no more confined
To being under exclusive order
Of Warners, granting him (were Flynn inclined)
One loan-out each year, be it waving a sword or
Those "serious" parts for which he felt ripe—
Though one more sword-waver now in the pipe.

62   And here's the one we've been waiting for, folks,
Where Byron and Flynn and this poem meet up
In one of Errol's movie masterstrokes,
Here his star-role causing things to heat up
In that film genre of daggers and cloaks
And damsels whose hearts he makes really speed up—
As swashbucklers go, it's not Flynn's swan-song,
But his last great one: *Adventures of Don Juan*.

63   I grant myself use here of the word "great"
Since the film is a triumphant return
To form for Errol Flynn after that spate
Of films he'd seen crash, so just let them burn;
And I'd not weep if a similar fate
—Ending as ashes in some giant urn—
Befell all the movies he made thereafter,
None comic but many still prompting laughter.[174]

64 Though doing a very fine acting job
In some of these films, Flynn never did make
A movie to equal *Don Juan*—not to rob
You of the fun of just seeing him take
The bit in his teeth, and I'm not a snob
Who thinks to proscribe your artistic intake;
Some of these pictures, though, aren't merely bad—
If you're a Flynn fan, they can feel quite sad.

65 Were you to view chronologically
Errol's last films to his death in '59
(A sound approach methodologically,
In any case an approach that was mine)
You can trace—physiologically
Speaking, not actor-wise—Errol's decline,
His looks still that of which mere mortals dream
But no longer kissed by a golden moonbeam.

66 A fellow will age from forty to fifty.
Although his weight's still the same as at twenty,
That weight is starting to markedly shift; he
Is told by friends he's still got looks aplenty,
Mirrors though put him in a mood quite face-lifty;
Far from retirement's *dolce far niente*,
And though regarded as the new forty,
At fifty a guy can still feel less sporty.

67 Errol compounded the aging process
Through drugs but chiefly through excessive drink,
The main brunt borne by his noble proboscis,
Turning it bulbous and a shocking pink,
The liquor also serving to emboss his
Skin with red blotches and make his eyes sink
Into his visage, all puffy and bloated,
The eyes always glassy with Flynn always loaded.

68   It was as if he were punishing the face
Which made his fortune but still had impeded
His own potential to fully embrace
That certain dream gone largely unheeded
Of being able to carve out a place
As a fine writer—although he succeeded
In at least *looking* a bit more like he
Was part of that frowzy fraternity.

69   But in *Don Juan* he is still the Adonis,
And matter of fact the case might be made
That Errol never looked *better*—don't con us,
You say, and I won't, I swear: Flynn betrayed
No tokens of dissipation, that onus
Had not, as of yet, begun to invade
His features and therefore his looks stayed intact—
Plus something that they had earlier lacked:

70   That something was dolor, that something was rue,
Lending to Flynn another dimension
That'd not been present before he'd gone through
His trial, 4-F war, and not to mention
The writing career which hadn't come true;
And there prevailed a delicious tension
Between the outwardly triumphant rake
And his sense that it'd been one big mistake.

71   Errol played a Don Juan heartily sick
Of his well-earned but accursed reputation
As a swordsman whose inimitable prick
(Yes, in that word's twofold implication)
Was feared and yet loved, no effortless trick:
Love counterpoised by a trepidation
Stopping short of *hate*—that casus belli—
And straight from the pages of Machiavelli.[175]

72   Thus was our Hollywood prince the perfect
Actor to handle this prince of a part,
The whole film in fact earmarked a project
For Errol Flynn more or less from the start,
And which took on before long the aspect
Of self-parody, the dialogue smart
As a whip and at Flynn's *image* taking aim
With tart lines that he was pleased to declaim.[176]

73   Who says he had no prime roles or prime scripts?
With Vincent Sherman as the director[177]
And budget to make a guy smack his lips,
Errol then went straight ahead and *wrecked* her—
The filming, that is—through improvised trips,
And boozing sustained by the Russian nectar,[178]
Inciting delays and driving up cost,
Warners each day keeping its fingers crossed

74   That Flynn would show up and then that he would
Be able to *stand* up and utter a line
Or two of dialogue. Here Hollywood
Was at last granting him something quite fine,
After his gripe that the place was no good,
Doing all he could now to undermine
The picture just short of his up and dying—
Which, as we've seen, he might well have been trying.

75   So what exactly was going on here?[179]
The answer's no snap—but the Don Juan role
Itself is a starting point since it's a mirror
Of inner tensions in Errol Flynn's soul:
The movie depicts a Don Juan who's sincere
In the desire to abandon his whole
Life devoted to pursuit of womankind,
So as to pursue higher things of the mind;

76   He wants a scholar's life, but it's beyond
His skill to effect; and at movie's end,
He giving chase to a ravishing blond,
His pal reminds him of his pledge to mend
His ways and not to be overly fond
Of the fairer sex, Juan telling this friend
That there's some Don Juan in each man, you see,
And *since* I'm Don Juan there's more of it in me!

77   Replace "Don Juan" with the name "Errol Flynn"
And we've gotten to the nub of his woe,
For it was our hero's special chagrin
To be well aware of just how shallow
His own life was, lacking self-discipline
To rein in his appetites and to forego
The women and wealth and the adulation
For the quiet joys of a bookish vocation.

78   Every child's character is an alloy
Of mother and father and it here the case
That ever since Flynn had been a small boy
His own sense of self would by turns embrace
One then the other—he able to enjoy
Pleasure and fun in their time and place,
And greatly so, his mother's special gift,
But then just as easily able to shift

79   To a more serious posture of mind—
Of research and study—his father's bequest.
And naturally I don't need to remind
You that Flynn prized his father while *detest*
Is likely the word that better defined
His feelings for mom; the parental contest
For his soul, however, eventually won
By she whom his whole life he'd tried to shun.

80   By the late '40s he'd capitulated
To the glib side of his nature—defeat
Not just because it finally checkmated
His writerly dreams but the rout complete
Since authored by that woman he hated;
Errol though choosing to scourge and maltreat
Himself with the liquor and drugs, which makes
Sense if mom of your own person partakes.[180]

81   Flynn never said this—*I'm* saying it—
He very happy to fasten the blame
On Warners, his "image," his fans, laying it
At the door of whom or whatever came
In for a small share and portraying it
As extrinsic when he should have taken aim
At his own lazy bon-vivant penchant—
But Flynn was rarely if ever this trenchant.[181]

82   The truth is he couldn't afford to be,
For then he would have been rudely confronted
By an unbearable reality:
Rather than swing for the fences he'd *bunted,*
Employing his self-styled tragedy
As alibi onto which he shunted
Personal failings—a handy excuse
As well for his drug and alcohol abuse.

83   It worked out nicely for Errol that way:
By taking refuge in dissipation,
Some might well question but none could gainsay
His own story of frustrated creation
At hands of cruel fate, a dupe of foul play,
For how to disprove his attestation
That he'd been by outer forces bested,
When he's too *drunk* to ever have it tested.[182]

84   This was the self-fulfilling paradox
And wry logic of his predicament—
His anguish and gloom forming major roadblocks
Owing to self-abuse and the extent
That his life, like his vodka, was on the rocks;
And the fact that all those long years misspent
In boozing since forced to play depthless hunks,
Got him roles later as interesting drunks.[183]

85   But in *Adventures of Don Juan* we still
Have the drunk as hunk and fortunately
What a pairing it is, Flynn bringing great skill,
As stated, to this classic role, *malgré lui.*
Yet the film failed to absolutely kill
Them at the box office—and therefore with any
Future Flynn-film Warners saw to begrudge it
Anything like a munificent budget.

86   The booze and delays were simply not worth it.
Don Juan itself got some sterling reviews,
But it'd been just too painful to birth it.
Though no one out there to fill Errol's shoes
(His type of male not swarming the earth) it
Soon would come time to cut this guy loose
Because, since the war, people weren't all that keen
On old-time heroes on that big old-time screen.[184]

87   That is to say, in the *States* they were not—
But *Don Juan* did very well in Europe.
Having turned forty and having just got
Divorced from Nora, Flynn thought to cheer up
By heading out to where he still might be hot,
Also which might move his film career up
A notch in an Old World still to beguile
With old deeds on old screens—so Flynn chose exile.

88   I use "exile" loosely—but Errol did stay
Long enough to pay court to a princess,
He finally making her his fiancée,
Her name Irene Ghika and her noblesse
Obliging Flynn to show her off—so what say
We overtake them in London, the press
There also in droves since it's the premiere
Of *That Forsyte Woman*, for Flynn new frontier.

89   This was the first film that Errol had made
(Per the conditions of his new contract)
Outside of Warners, with MGM, they'd
Tendered a role where at last he could *act,*
And with Greer Garson, this time no clichéd
Hollywood trash but as matter of fact
A character straight out of English Lit.—
Soames Forsyte—that is, artistically legit!

90   And here's where the problem begins: Flynn being
The snob that he was, deep down, was far too
Respectful of the role and thus guaranteeing
Soames Forsyte remains flat and lifeless. (If you
Discount that one scene where Errol is seeing
Red and grabs Garson by her shoulders to
Give her a shake, really blowing his fuse,
And just what the movie in general could use.)

91   The snag is that Errol brings no *Flynn* to bear
—No effervescence, no sparkle, no dash—
And I don't think that I'm being unfair
In stating that the odd lack of panache
Errol displays as the cold millionaire
Could have been *anyone's*: meaning that flash
Of Flynn magic's missing—and now to extend
The magic metaphor, please don't pretend

92 That you'd prefer that the Great Houdini
   Just perform card tricks? Or that you would choose
   To have the maestro Giacomo Puccini
   Whip off a piece for Jew's harp and kazoos?
   You would reduce them to just a teeny
   Weeny of what makes them special and lose
   All that you love, their talent's very soul—
   And hell of it is, Flynn *demanded* the role.[185]

93 Let's shift locales, saying sayonara
   To London and now for southern France heading:
   A nudist colony is where we are, a
   Shy Flynn clothed but his bold princess shedding
   Quite a bit more than just her tiara;[186]
   Her finger soon (let's not be forgetting)
   Well clad, though, in a ring of engagement—
   All prelude to the sting of estrangement.

94 Errol soon broke with her since he'd begun
   To notice that Irene Ghika (or the "Geek"
   As he nicknamed her) did not find her fun
   In brainy converse, while having a streak
   Of anti-intellectualism, for one;
   And for another, she tended to freak
   Out with jealousy (our rake not idle);
   And furthermore she was suicidal—

95 All proof of mental instability,
   Not boosting Errol's hopes for their future,
   But the one thing that then served to *kill* it, he
   Saw she liked spending his cash, this moocher
   From the penurious nobility.
   (And 'fore allowing Flynn even to smooch her,
   He'd been at her financial beck and call, it
   Incumbent on him to make with the wallet!)

96 So let us take one more look at that list:
  Unstable, vapid, jealous, predatory—
  Any pejorative we may have missed?
  Add "small" and "dark" to our inventory—
  These last two not *bad*, but I can't desist
  Because the more anticipatory
  Among my readership already will
  Have grasped that the Geek was just like Tiger Lil.[187]

97 However the all-important factor
  In Errol's resolve to ever disburden
  Himself of Irene—main reason he sacked her,
  Though it may sound just a bit absurd (in
  The telling it seems so)—in point of fact her
  European glamour was conquered in
  That most American of symbols: Irene's
  Blueblood style not so stylish in blue jeans.

98 Flynn had brought Ghika back to the U.S.,
  Outside of Gallup, a location shoot,
  The town's name exceedingly apt since, yes,
  Another horse opera;[188] so maybe Flynn's root
  Concern in Irene's not wearing a dress
  Was the poor contrast it made to his cute
  Yankee co-star who her own blue jeans wore
  As to the manner born: Patrice Wymore.

99 Patrice was the all-American girl—
  And Flynn, like Don Juan, was ever so sick
  Of the whole European social whirl.
  Just as he'd gone from Lil's vampish shtick
  To Nora's wide-eyed innocence, Errol
  Now dropped his Dacian princess right quick,
  Without so much as a backward glance, as
  Soon as he spied this looker from Kansas.

100   In a strange way it made absolute sense:
Flynn with the princess was on the rebound
From Nora, it all an ego-defense,
With the nobility traipsing around
Europe, rebuilding his self-confidence;
And after he had successfully drowned
His sorrows in the Lili-like Geek, it checks
Out he'd fly back to a girl like his ex.

101   On the rebound from the rebound was Flynn.
Apart from the jeans, though, what did he come
To find so pleasing about her? The twin
Of Nora in looks, Pat was warm and wholesome,
Sincere and direct and quite lacking in
Vanity or wiles or tricks and in sum,
To cite Flynn himself, he right on the dot,
Pat "typified everything that I was not,"

102   Furthermore he'd "found something to respect"—
Two telling thoughts in juxtaposition.
And Errol's appeal to *Patrice*? You'd suspect
The usual things but then your suspicion
Would be mistaken since when in effect
He queried what she saw in him (he fishin'
For compliments?) Errol had to make due
With the reply: "I feel sorry for you."

CANTO VIII

Sea Drift

(1950-1956)

Man, being reasonable, must get drunk;
The best of life is but intoxication:
Glory, the grape, love, gold, in these are sunk
The hopes of all men, and of every nation;
Without their sap, how branchless were the trunk
Of life's strange tree, so fruitful on occasion:
But to return,—Get very drunk; and when
You wake with head-ache, you shall see what then.

Don Juan, canto II, stanza 179

London 1952, for the film version of Robert Louis Stevenson's
The Master of Ballantrae

CANTO VIII

1   In 1950 Flynn married Patrice
    —A chapel wedding, she in gown of white,
    The event taking place in modish Nice[189] —
    And it was this year that Flynn came to write
    An article which would be the last piece
    That he'd ever publish in what one might
    Describe as a Hollywood mag, *Screen Guide,*
    Marking as such something of a divide.

2   The piece was entitled "I Do What I Like"[190]
    And in it Errol does inventory
    On past and present and on down the pike,
    Granting it goes with the territory
    To have less peace and solitude alike
    In the star-business—but that its great glory,
    Its saving grace (so he mustn't cavil),
    Is its amalgam of artistry and travel.

3   He also endorses the intrinsic worth
    Of what he labels "sincere, honest work,"
    Prime reason mankind was put on this earth,
    To dig right in, not your labor to shirk,
    This latter Flynn's urge more or less from birth,
    But now the tendency starting to irk,
    He wishing to leave the world a thing outstanding
    To "add to its beauty, knowledge, understanding."

4   "Most of all, however, in the years to come,
    I desire to achieve freedom—to do
    What I like" and not be forced to succumb
    To pretense while also able to eschew
    All that was phony and derived not from
    A place in himself that was valid and true—
    That is: "integrity" as the main factor
    In his life "both as a man and an actor."

ERROL FLYNN

5   This was his credo at just past the age
Of forty—Errol's midlife confession
Of faith—and incumbent on us at this stage
Would be to probe whether his expression
Of basic precepts in fact did presage
The future course of his life and profession.
So let's fast-forward and take a quick look
To see if Errol's resolves indeed took.

6   Let us begin with his quest for "freedom."
In terms of freedom of *movement*, his journeys,
One must concede it'd be tough to beat 'em.
Impelled by his dodging of attorneys,
Taxmen and wives, trying hard to exceed 'em
By showing the lot of them *Zaca*'s stern, he's
Lucky that sailing is still his great passion—
Though fueled by that quart-a-day vodka ration.

7   Free on the outside but inside a slave
To booze, morphine and other addictions.
What about "work," though, did that somehow save
Flynn and resolve his heart's contradictions?
Can it be said that his art at last gave
The world more beauty to soothe its afflictions?
In brief *did* he work and it make him *happy*—
And was that work good, indifferent or crappy?

8   Errol in fact did a sizeable amount
Of movie work in that final decade
Of his shortened life (and that's not to count
All those television guest-shots he made)
But most of it done for his bank account,
His main care being he simply get paid,
So Errol Flynn wasn't likely made glad,
Artistically, by films often plain *bad*.

9   Thus broaching the point of "integrity"—
     Both as a man and an actor. Although
     His pictures weren't good in their totality,
     His acting was mostly that of a pro,
     Errol's *command* having centrality
     In the parts he played, often stealing the show
     (Like in that role where he mesmerizes,
     Playing Mike Campbell in *The Sun Also Rises*).

10   Integrity as an actor?—indeed!—
     But not as a man necessarily.
     Though movie acting might answer a need
     For artful expression, it would verily
     Usurp Flynn the writer and functioned to breed
     Self-estrangement. If you primarily
     See integrity as "the state of being whole,"[191]
     Flynn the man lacked it—he riven in his soul.

11   The paradox is that after Flynn wrote
     "I Do What I Like"—and Errol of course
     More than liked writing—he ceased to devote
     Himself to belles lettres; and one other source
     Of mordancy here is that Flynn makes note
     Of his return from moviemaking chores
     In India, having wished to revisit
     The subcontinent and all its requisite

12   Beauty and strangeness, allure and mystique,
     Spurning the lead in *King Solomon's Mines*
     For a supporting role in *Kim*, a weak
     Movie overall (though Flynn himself shines
     In dashing turban, still raffish and chic)
     Whereas the film that he turned down *defines*
     The white-hunter genre, Africa's danger
     Met in this classic by Stewart Granger.[192]

ERROL FLYNN

13   Although his acting was largely well-meant,
Here his integrity was compromised
By the *choice* of roles, it Errol's intent
To fuse work and travel, as emphasized,
Therefore selecting parts to the extent
That they conform to his own undisguised
Desire to augment his world travelogue—
Better known as the tail wagging the dog.

14   So in an odd way we can truly speak
Of Flynn's integrity, yes, as a man.
If he is going to confront the bleak
Prospect of ditching his own youthful plan
Of writing, his first love,[193] then he would seek
Solace in the prospect that acting can
Sustain his other love (of adventure)
And so we mustn't unduly censure

15   Him for not having quite followed his bliss
With the whole writing scheme, since still intact
Was his precept of not being remiss
In *living*, ensuring that his life be packed
With events, a resolve we discern in his
Youthful New Guinea diary in fact:
"Not to discover when I come to die,
That I have not lived,"[194] which should testify

16   To the case that at a basic level
Errol had stayed and would always stay true
To his inner self, our unbridled devil
Quite principled insofar as all through
His earthly sojourn his rule was to revel
In the act of living—and then if a few
Good films resulted, so much the better;
But life *before* art—life as a jetsetter!

17   In the next decade Errol Flynn would make
Pictures in England, Scotland, Italy, Spain,
France, Cuba, Mexico, and even take
A role in Africa's jungle, his main
Spur no doubt so as to fix his mistake
In nixing *King Solomon's Mines*, this terrain
Completing his six-continent world tour.
(What other intent when the script was so poor?)[195]

18   The reason that Flynn was able to compact
Filmwork and travel so nicely was not
Only the loanout clause in his contract
(MGM, for instance, the outfit that bought
His talents for *Kim*) but later the fact
That both of them, Flynn and Jack Warner, thought
It best to just end the damn thing—this to thank
For Errol no more being stuck in Burbank.[196]

19   For a long time now Errol Flynn's career
Had been slowly slipping, whereas his bad
—For our swashbuckler we'll say *cavalier*—
Behavior gained traction; and then you had
Studios panicked of course by the clear
Threat posed by TV, not some passing fad,
Cutting their payrolls, these Hollywood czars,
By axing some of their priciest stars.

20   De Havilland, Bogart, Davis—all gone
When Errol and Jack Warner finally went
Their own separate ways. Their long liaison
Stretched back eighteen years, Flynn's rise and descent
All under Jack, with a certain élan
Of his own to rival his malcontent,
And why their mutual provocation
Had meantime fostered a shared admiration.

21   Warner had stuck with Flynn long as any
Of the other actors in his old guard.
And though Jack was a noted pinchpenny,
And pinching those pennies extremely hard,
He sent Flynn off in fine style when he
Used frozen funds in Great Britain and starred
Him in a final swashbuckler: *The Master
of Ballantrae* (to the end a typecaster).[197]

22   End of an era but not end of Flynn.
Along with the vodka there was still a lot
Of vinegar in the old boy—but a win
In his column was needed, a serious shot
Over the Hollywood bow announcin'
His super colossal comeback, and not
Just as a star but as a producer
To show *you* Jack Warner a thing or two, sir!

23   Errol would make a film about a guy
Who knew, like Robin Hood, how to propel
A shaft, whose son was the apple of his eye,
Pun intended since he was William Tell;
And Errol not keeping expenses down by
Filming on a soundstage but he would quell
His wanderlust and give things a true feel
By filming in the Alps—mere start of his ordeal.

24   Errol had put up over 400 grand
Of his own money to finance the pic,
Italian investors pledged to command
An equal amount—but they never did kick
In with the loot, not a single cent, and
Weeks into filming it was shut down quick,
The set being stormed, bailiffs running amok
Impounding the cameras as well as film stock.

25   So Flynn wasn't simply out half a mil
       But his prized film would remain incomplete
       (Even to the present day it is still
       In some sealed vault);[198] this agony of defeat
       Not followed by any offsetting thrill
       Of victory but just another downbeat
       Turn of events where Flynn's bad luck waxes:
       $840,000 in back taxes.

26   How could this be? More bad news on the way:
       Errol's financial advisor Al Blum
       Had died and there was the devil to pay,
       Since before Al met his untimely doom
       He'd managed in having a real field day
       With Errol's funds and lowering the boom
       With purchase of homes and a plane and Cadillac,
       Just leaving his client the clothes on his back.

27   Old actor friend Bruce Cabot did the same—
       Leave Errol his clothes—although he did take
       Those of Patrice while also laying claim
       To Errol's two cars, this in Rome, the snake
       Sending along process servers; fair game
       Was Errol because he had failed to make
       Payments to Cabot who'd played Errol's foe
       In accursed *William Tell*—how nicely apropos.

28   And while on the theme of arch-nemeses,
       Pray what would this perfect storm of fell blows
       Be minus Errol Flynn's former main squeeze
       Putting the squeeze on him for all of those
       Past slights and deceits and infidelities
       By making ex-hubby pay through the nose—
       And with Flynn now at the poorhouse door, he
       Recalled the old phrase that hell hath no fury.[199]

ERROL FLYNN

29   After their split in 1942,
      Lili had been after Errol for back
      Alimony which then ultimately grew
      To over a million, and this ransack
      Aided by the Internal Revenue
      Service which required that he also tack
      A tax on the tax on the "tax," a jam
      You'll only get into with Uncle Sam.[200]

30   All of this—Lili, Al Blum, IRS—
      Climaxed in 1955 with the loss
      Of Mulholland Farm to our Gallic tigress,
      She finally able to sink her sharp claws
      Into Flynn's dwelling, and the whole mess
      Having begun when Al Blum scorned the laws
      Pertaining to realty tax (which means
      He'd failed to *pay* it) and so they put liens

31   On Flynn's house and adjoining property,
      Which tallied to some fifty thousand and paid
      Off by Lili when she took "custody"
      Of the estate and who later then made
      A prodigious profit by selling it—she
      Having stalked Flynn all these years and just laid
      Low till the moment was ripe and then *pounced*,
      Her negligent prey effectively trounced.

32   Ah Lili! You did it! Vengeance is yours!
      You took the bastard lock, stock and barrel!
      Though let's have HER speak . . . *Voilà!—this one gores
      Very deep, n'est-ce pas, my beloved Errol,
      Perhaps you now feel a bit of remorse,
      Perhaps you now see that it's at your peril
      That you cross Lili—"Tiger Lil" I'm called
      By you—so don't be so shocked you've been mauled!*

33   *Errol, you **used** me. You know very well*
That I—how they say?—was your meal ticket.
And now that I've made your life a sheer hell,
You surely feel that this is "not cricket,"
Not fair, in fact cheating. But let me tell
You, as they say, that you can just stick it!
All has its price, and sooner or later
That debt's redeemed, you infamous traitor!

34   *I loved you, Fleen, no matter the reason.*
And when a woman loves a man there's no
Winter or summer or fall, no season
But freshly blossoming spring, so to throw
That love away equates to high treason.
And although the price for treason, you know,
Is dying, the guillotine blade—c'est la mort!—
I've spared you because I need money—much more!

35   *And who else but Lili could give you a son?*
*Have either of your two young wives done **that**?*
Only girls, three girls,[201] and no single one
As lovely as Sean, no Hollywood brat
But growing up in the Florida sun,
Far from that imbecile film habitat!
The funny thing, too, my esteemed ex-spouse,
About my now owning your Mulholland house,

36   *Is that my lawyer back then offered you*
The option of paying me out a lump sum.
You needed cash, though, for things still to do
On your dream mansion and thought it'd be dumb
To pay all at once since—merci beaucoup!—
I'd marry of course in the years to come,
At which point you could then finally drop
Alimony payments and it would all stop.

ERROL FLYNN

37 *But it will not stop—and that much I can*
Promise, since so long as you are alive
*I'll **not** re-marry just to spoil your plan!*
You thought the lump settlement would deprive
Your home of funding and be much worse than
Monthly alimony—but seeing that I've
Obtained sole custody, your failure to pay
The lump sum has cost you your house—touché! . . .

38 We'll leave Lili now so that she may crow
Over her victory, though not before
Apprising you that she would indeed go
Unwed till Flynn's death and waiting no more
Than three years to do it and not to some hero
In the Flynn mold but to rather a bore,
I suspect, as it's tough to romanticize
A man who spends life selling Eskimo Pies.[202]

39 Damita was bracing for the long haul
In her running battle with Errol, but he
Himself was bracing for nothing at all:
That fateful year of 1953
He'd gotten a medical wake-up call—
His liver was starting to atrophy,
The doc telling him with no compunction
That it would very soon cease to function.

40 In a strange fashion the bad news would seem
To've given Flynn's sagging spirits a lift,
He getting a surge by swimming upstream
(Countering his inborn penchant to drift)
Imparting a shot to his self-esteem,
This most helpful when the current was swift,
Which it is now, Flynn a bit out of breath
Since he is battling the River of Death.

41   We all swim this river and what does it matter
If with it, against it, or floating along?
I guess most people would fancy the latter,
Going with the flow; others rush headlong
For the climax; and others have at 'er,
Bucking the current while they're feeling strong;
Then there are those who delight in all three,
Depending on the riverbank scenery.

42   Errol was a triple-threat in this way,
Which is why it is not easy to know
Precisely how one ought then to portray
Him from one moment to the next—although
I think it reasonably safe to say
That Errol for the next three years or so
Lived not just a shallow life where he'd keep
On the surface of things but ventured down *deep.*

43   This not merely in a figurative sense,
For in these years Errol Flynn became quite
The scuba diver as a consequence
Of his continuing financial plight,
Attempting to save his dollars and cents
By quitting America and taking flight
For Europe while still remaining afloat
Moneywise by just living on his boat.[203]

44   Most of the time *Zaca* could be found moored
In the posh harbor of Majorca's new
Yacht club—when not in Jamaica or lured
Away to go film in some flashy venue,
Flynn was on *Zaca*, be rest assured,
Not too far distant, leastways, and if you
Would chart that distance (and take a bath) him
You'll find by using the nautical "fathom."

ERROL FLYNN

45   Errol's down there now, in fact, I should think
    Some fifteen fathoms, the shafts of sunlight
    Stabbing and shining down through the green drink,
    Illuminating the fish left and right,
    And Errol hastening down in a wink,
    In hot pursuit of some prey that takes flight
    After he misses it with his spear gun—
    Flynn dogged, though, since it only takes one.

46   The fish weighs about forty pounds, a grouper,
    With thick body and protuberant eyes,
    Flynn well aware that it makes for super
    Eating and constitutes a super-size
    Meal and so he determined to scoop 'er
    Up at any price—although he'd be wise
    To steal a glance at his wrist at this stage
    Since that's where he sports his trusty depth-gauge.

47   As Flynn moves downward in quest of his fish,
    He sees it enter a rock formation,
    But Errol's still bent on his tasty dish
    And follows it in without hesitation,
    Ready to now pull the trigger . . . when *swish*
    Goes its tail and, to Errol's consternation,
    Sand is whipped up from the seafloor, fast work
    That lets the fish scram behind the brown murk.

48   But his dismay is of very short span—
    As the sand settles, Errol Flynn detects
    Stray little bits of what look like more than
    Mere rock or seaweed but what he suspects
    Is some other item; and so our frogman
    Descends to the bottom where he inspects
    The shiny fragments, all covered in paint—
    When without warning he starts to feel faint.

49   He now eyes his depth-gauge—42 meters,
A long way down, precious air getting short—
And pulls the reserve, releasing fresh liters,
Backs out of the cave . . . but then must abort,
Feeling like one of the Lotus Eaters,
A bit high, or drunk, like he's had a snort—
But too deep too fast and the diagnosis
Is axiomatic: nitrogen narcosis.

50   Another label for this condition:
"Rapture of the Deep"—thus hardly unfun—
Main problem being, though, that your cognition
Goes on the blink, you not wholly undone
But on the *threshold* of inanition,
So it's to lesser depths you must needs run
If you'd escape from a watery grave—
But Errol right now is stuck in his cave.

51   Afloat in a world of aquamarine,
Awash in a feeling of cockeyed peace,
He feels no pain but is almost serene,
Like in the arms of his darling Patrice:
So upright, so honest and without a mean
Bone in her, she no creature of caprice
Like me, thinks Errol, not selfish or lazy . . .
And that type of virtue can drive a guy crazy.

52   Try *living* with someone like that—just try.
There's limits to how much sweetness and light
One person can take, let me testify,
A limit to all the *Gemütlichkeit*
Because now and then you just want to fly
Off the damn handle and start a big fight,
Like with Lili or Nora or that other
Dame I'm accustomed to calling "Mother."

53   A fish swims by, not Flynn's grouper, too small—
      But of the genus, both chunky and round,
      With goggle eyes like old Cuddles Sakall,[204]
      Errol not tempted to shoot but just found
      Himself reaching out to the critter in all
      Earnestness to pinch its cheeks, a profound
      Feeling of love stored in our hero's heart away,
      But now just causing the grouper to dart away.

54   Don't go Cuddles, don't leave me all alone—
      With Patrice . . . she with *me* . . . I'm not cut out
      For stolid monogamy, too monotone,
      It's futile for me to play the devout
      Husband with all of this testosterone
      Determining that I go walkabout.
      Should I feel guilty? About getting laid?
      Well, that's just the way this fellow is made.

55   Deep down it's not about sex, not really
      (Granted there might be certain exceptions,
      Most notably in the case of Lili)
      And yet one more of those misconceptions
      They have of me: that I can't keep my willy
      Under control—but my self-perception's
      One of a man who is driven far less
      By sex than by sheer inquisitiveness.

56   That is the urge, inherited from Dad,
      Which has been always my life's driving force,
      Especially if the thing is *forbad*,
      Getting me into this fix here of course;
      But in truth it's really not all that bad
      Because it's now proving to be the source
      Of untold insight, however queerly—
      I can't recall when I've thought so clearly.

57   This happens when I'm intoxicated,
Which is indeed the case now, I swear—
Drunk, yes, but my musings stimulated.
So let's stick around, I've got enough air,
And if somehow I've miscalculated,
If it turns out I've been too *laissez-faire,*
That'll be just hunky dory with me:
I've always wanted a burial at sea.

58   Now more than ever seems it rich to die,
Said Johnny Keats, and the bit about half
In love with easeful death would also apply . . .
And what is a suitable epitaph?
How about: *He had bigger fish to fry.*
Not good, but on point, and droll, since the laugh
Is on yours truly—how the fates do conspire:
The *fish* from the skillet, *me* into the fire.

59   You know, old sport, you always had a knack
For generating a world more trouble
For you than others—a raging Cossack,
But leaving your own village in a rubble,
What you had wreaked on your neighbor come back
To take its vengeance on you yourself double—
Attribute it, though, to my curiosity
And abhorrence of mediocrity.

60   That's where the Flynn rubber meets the Errol road—
My carrot and stick, my yin and my yang,
My AC-DC, how I've ebbed and flowed
All of my days and why things boomerang
Back at me, this a textbook episode
In that I'm set to go out with a bang,
My two mainsprings putting me in this crypt,
But shaping up now like some corny film script!

ERROL FLYNN

61   How middling, how trite, how stale can you get—
ACTION STAR DIES IN UNDERSEA ACTION
Errol Flynn, as of late deeply in debt,
Having once been a great film attraction . . .
Suicide! Yikes! To the end Flynn all wet!
That'd be the press corps' instant reaction:
Flynn not dying at home with his slippers on
But under the waves with his frogman flippers on.

62   No, I'll not have it! Once more the laughingstock
Of the whole world and not "in like Flynn"
But "Flynn in the swim" when you sink like a rock,
Highly unlikely to save your own skin
(Far worse than being a rampaging cock)
And I'll be damned if I'll let *that* guy win,
I simply won't have him being my mourner—
I flatly refuse to predecease Jack Warner!

63   Errol got a grip on himself and backed
Out of the cave, wriggling just like a snake,
Ears loudly ringing and his poor head wracked,
But not forgetting his precious keepsake,
The bright painted pieces of artifact—
Then swimming hard, not applying the brake,
Not keen on drowning, preferring the bends,
And making the launch now his brush with death ends.[205]

64   From time to time Flynn would venture ashore
To make a film, make a girl, make a deal,
Having decided after all the afore-
Mentioned financial disasters that he'll
Learn to love business and even adore
All those dull numbers, no more dumb schlemiel,
The words on his briefcase now highlighting this
Resolve by proclaiming: FLYNN ENTERPRISES.

65   Let's take a gander inside this briefcase
At the documents and diverse papers
That Errol's transporting from place to place
And get a glimpse at his latest capers,
At what comprises his thought-database,
And 'fore our stanza finally tapers
Off I won't keep you in further suspense—
Vodka, tonic, glasses are the case's contents.

66   George Bernard Shaw called booze the anesthesia
We use to endure this life-operation,
And whenever Flynn felt ill at ease a
Move to the medical kit for libation
Helped to induce some short-term amnesia,
Providing that much needed consolation
For our sick-at-heart patient Errol Flynn,
Who's out, far out, while Doc Smirnoff is in.

67   Most other items in Flynn's life had palled
On him but not vodka—that was the one
Feature of his life which yet still enthralled,
The one single thing that in the long run
He kept returning to and which forestalled
His creeping despair, just short of a gun,
Which he could always employ if need be,
When booze ceased to act as his sole security.

68   For now, though, vodka was refuge enough,
Flynn comparing his kit to a bible,
His faith invested now in the hard stuff,
Ever at hand and so reliable,
Your pleas not earning a silent rebuff,
And its existence verifiable,
With you still gaining the heavenly sphere—it
Equally holy but a *distilled* spirit.

ERROL FLYNN

69 Indeed there might be worse things than to throw
   In with demon rum—for example God;
   Worse things than abjuring all that you know
   Of logic and not so much as a nod
   To pure common sense; nor making a show
   Of resistance, if only token, to the odd
   Notion of an unseen man in the sky
   Who takes you up bodily when you die.

70 Or he might send you to that other place,
   Somewhere deep down in the bowels of the earth
   Where Mephistopheles has his home base,
   Who'll agonize you for all that he's worth,
   Your just deserts for your fall from God's grace,
   Who might have simply forestalled your rebirth
   But was resolved that he'd resurrect you
   To exact vengeance and not to *correct* you.

71 Torments that are forever can have no
   Reformative or remedial aim,
   Thus morally skewed right from the word go.
   And how can an all-knowing loving God blame
   Someone for "sins" when he runs the whole show?
   And *why* resurrect? It seems such a shame
   That death be disturbed for all that hell stuff,
   For haven't we suffered in this life enough?

72 Flynn had no wish for eternal reward,
   For none of that hereafter folderol,
   The thing made no sense right across the board:
   For if we're to live, why perish at all?
   But Errol might also have spurned his Lord
   And Savior and opted for alcohol
   Since his own mother was now with God smitten,
   Or in Flynn's words she'd become "Christ-bitten."

73   It seems that Marelle, in her declining years,
Had tempered her taste for fun and frolic
With Christian fervor, now up to her ears
In churchly affairs and deeds apostolic,
So Flynn's (just see how his world-view coheres:)
Scrapping of faith was more than symbolic
Since I'm quite sure had she been an atheist,
Flynn wouldn't God have so lightly dismissed.

74   When made aware that his liver was shot
And his days numbered, Flynn didn't just slide
Into the arms of the Church as we're taught
To do with death nigh and simply confide
Your soul to the care of adepts who will not
Just spout all that mumbo-jumbo graveside
But hasten your trip to the Great Beyond—
And if you're just dead you won't *know* you've been conned.

75   'Stead of repenting and turning to Christ,
Errol remained on the path he had trod
Right from the start, which was very high-priced—
Leastwise however with no debt to God,
Who came more costly since you sacrificed
Your human worth as one *not* overawed
By pledges of heaven, warnings of hell,
And able to think for yourself very well.

76   Flynn had his honor—even on the sauce,
Drinking itself being emblematic
Of noble instincts, and firstly because
It was expressive of his emphatic
Distrust in much of the public applause
That he'd received (though now more sporadic)
Throughout his career, his standards quite high,
He left to brood now on what'd gone awry.

ERROL FLYNN

77   Errol's success had of course been resounding
(No need here to further elaborate)
But his artistic conscience kept hounding
Him to accomplish a thing truly great,
Which he *had*—but Errol-Flynn types like foregrounding
(And even are prone to exaggerate)
Their failures: all to the good, since the main
Spur to their art is emotional pain.

78   Pain is our essential reality,
And that goes double for the great artist,
Not only due to his sensitivity
But to the fact that his anguish is grist
For the mill of his creativity—
Whereas most humans attempt to enlist
Every ploy so as their pain to escape,
The artist attests it to give his life shape.

79   It shapes his life since his life is his art,
The artist lending the suffering form
Through *trans*formation of his purple heart
Via the process of aesthetic brainstorm—
It's existential à la Jean-Paul Sartre:
Defining yourself, oft against the norm,
Through the creation of something higher
After enduring your trial by fire.

80   Artists elevate the suffering while
Purging themselves of it, which in turn will,
With luck, purge your audience in the style
Of Aristotle's catharsis and kill
Fear and self-pity and flush all that bile
While at the same time able to instill
What Schopenhauer called attenuation
Of the illusion of our individuation.

81 Is this becoming a bit esoteric?
  What I was merely attempting to say,
  Before becoming just slightly hysteric,
  Was that a person like Errol Flynn may
  Have a success that is stratospheric,
  Its nimbus like that of the Milky Way,
  But none of it real or quite solid, he
  With standards of a yet higher quality.

82 Lord Byron's buddy Sir Walter Scott saw
  In him "the careless and negligent ease
  Of a *man* of quality"[206] —hip hip hurrah!
  A perfect description of Errol since he's
  Deceptive that way, oh so la-dee-dah,
  All that flippant charm, just light as a breeze
  And thus (less the ken of a Walter Scott)
  You could well judge him as something he's not.

83 Let's stay with Byron on this one here,
  Since Errol (if he was anything at all)
  Was a *romantic*, that much is clear,
  If solely by dint of the game of pinball
  Played by his own inner life—that sharp veer
  Just slingshotting you from one emotional
  Bumper to the next and an external jilt
  Often resulting in a mental TILT.

84 Errol's inner life was just the reverse
  Of what those well-meaning people describe
  As nervous disorder, they themselves averse
  To real excitement; instead they prescribe
  A course in tai chi or yoga or worse,
  Like chanting or drumming like some native tribe,
  They wishing for you to achieve "peace of mind,"
  But Flynn didn't want peace—of any kind.

ERROL FLYNN

85   He *claimed* to want peace and yet all the same
His own life was far less Buddha than Pater,
Forever burning with that hard gemlike flame,[207]
Repose not a life-accentuator
When it's at boredom that you're taking aim,
Tension the ennui-annihilator,
Sad thoughts of death and your final demise
Best banished when lost in some fevered enterprise.

86   Here the imperative word is "interest."
He'd already had mega-stardom, and so
How possibly could Errol be impressed
By seeing his movie-star status grow?—
He'd been there done that and therefore his zest
For simply maintaining all this was quite low:
His *interest* was not just to keep on scaling
The heights he'd already gained but in *failing*.

87   I know it sounds odd and even perverse,
But I believe that's a plausible way
Of grasping the psychological curse
That Errol lived under from day to day:
A low boredom-threshold—which well ensures
His talent for mischief would come into play,
Keeping things brisk, ranging from persiflage
To pranks and hijinks and *self*-sabotage.

88   The main thing was that his life had to quicken—
Which can occur, of course, with the heady
Delights of success but then you can sicken
Of one triumph after the next—a steady
Diet of glory can make the blood thicken
Until you reflect: *Enough already!*
How would it be for a nice change of pace
If our great hero falls flat on his face?

89 And so you do—it's involuntary—
  "It" being thanatos, the death instinct,
  Not meaning you commit hari-kari;
  In each of us, though, there dwells a distinct
  Impulse that howsoever contrary
  To eros, the life urge, the two are linked:
  Life brings less pleasure than pain (watch the stealthy
  Logic now:) so to *negate* life is healthy.

90 Here Schopenhauer is the logician,
  That guy again, but with moral support
  From Freud and Lacan and such champs of cognition,
  The notion being that we tend to thwart
  Ourselves and often do demolition
  On our own lives so as to abort
  Any aspect that will finally save
  Much trouble and strife, if it just means the grave.

91 This perhaps more *my* own version than that
  Which the aforementioned group represents.
  But it suits Errol since he was broke—flat—
  Working himself to death thus made small sense
  When his film paycheck would just go kersplat
  In squaring his debts—this his sole "recompense"
  In making pictures he mostly deplored,
  And that's what they call the artist's reward!

92 Then Flynn, still going to pot on his yacht,
  Received a visit that came in the guise
  Of agent Sam Jaffe who had a soft spot
  For Errol and still could visualize
  A future for him: "So why the hell not
  Just give it a go and revitalize
  Yourself in the bargain, you lousy beach bum,
  Since that's essentially what you've become."

93   "I haven't become a beach bum, old sport,"
Errol replies with studied nonchalance,
"I've *always* been one, please don't sell me short,
I'm deep down a guy who just gallivants
About, simply drifting from port to port,
And not the fortune and fame but romance
Of adventure is my siren call"—then he
Adding: "What first took me out to New Guinea."[208]

94   Sam shakes his head—but Errol Flynn's mention
Of his own youth in New Guinea is fitting
Since he in fact has every intention
Of getting back into filmwork and quitting
The sea-drifting life; that is, Flynn's contention
That he's enjoying himself and just sitting
Pretty and happy to stay on his duff,
Is straight from his New Guinea playbook of BLUFF.

95   Errol was playing for time and position.
After their talk there followed a flurry
Of cables back and forth, our shrewd tactician
Making this top-agent Jaffe curry
Favor with a less than mint-condition,
Even washed-up star, Errol in no hurry—
And he succeeded with his cock and bull
In signing at last for the film *Istanbul.*

96   This quite a coup after all the to and fro,
For not only would Errol finally be
Working again with a big studio,
Universal Pictures, but moreover he
Could ship with *Zaca*, his vodka in tow
While visiting Byron's Near East—these three
(Career, love of travel and ocean-sailing)
Coming together and nicely dovetailing.

97   But Flynn seemed not to have read the fine print,
Since they would *not* be filming on location,
The irony being that it is by dint
Of wanderlust that Flynn's next waystation
Is where he'd some time ago done his stint,
The place that had *spurred* his peregrination.
So it's not Errol who gets the last laugh, he
Ceding that honor to Mr. Sam Jaffe.

CANTO IX

Recessional

(1956-1959)

Well—well, the world must turn upon its axis,
And all mankind turn with it, heads or tails,
And live and die, make love and pay our taxes,
And as the veering wind shifts, shift our sails;
The king commands us, and the doctor quacks us,
The priest instructs, and so our life exhales,
A little breath, love, wine, ambition, fame,
Fighting, devotion, dust,—perhaps a name.

Don Juan, canto II, stanza 4

French Equatorial Africa, 1958, with Juliette Gréco,
producer Darryl Zanuck and director John Huston
to film *The Roots of Heaven*

CANTO IX

1   So in the spring of 1956,
     Flynn and Patrice made their way to movietown,
     Errol now once again back in the mix,
     Although at this stage a bit broken down,
     And of all places to reside he picks
     What'd once been as chic as that Derby Brown
     (And still by no means a hole in the wall) a
     Place by the name of Garden of Allah.

2   It wasn't that Errol had a wistful pang
     For days when he languished in obscurity
     Ere that stage-manager Destiny rang
     The curtain up on his celebrity—
     No, his deciding for the Allah sprang
     Not from rank sentimentality
     But that the much older Flynn was likewise
     Doing what he could to economize.

3   At Garden of Allah he and Patrice
     Stayed in a one-bedroom cottage and had
     No car, just cabs, our Alcibiades
     Living a Spartan existence though clad
     As elegantly as ever since he's
     Of the view there's never excuse for bad
     Style irrespective of your quandary
     (Including regular trips to the laundry).

4   There's the old boy now! Looking clean and smart
     In his blue blazer, white slacks and ascot,
     Striding from his lodge and getting late start
     On the day, as is Errol's wont, but not
     Devoid of method since a vital part
     Is played by the *sun* in Flynn's little plot—
     Having to attain its height, as a rule,
     'Fore you have all the girls out by the pool.

ERROL FLYNN

5   He heads for an empty chaise longue, right next
        To a small table where sits a champagne
        Bottle in ice with two glasses, objects
        That Flynn (Pat gone) had his secretary feign
        To place "perchance" near some girl she suspects
        Will strike Flynn's fancy, not much of a strain,
        He liking them high-breasted and slim-hipped,
        Specs easy to spot with all the girls stripped.

6   Errol addresses our sunbathing beauty:
        "My child, do you mind if I sit next to you?"
        And since there's small point in being snooty,
        She says, "Why, no," and brooks the impulse to
        Blurt out: *Why you bet your sweet patooty!*—
        Which Errol senses, so he asks anew:
        "My child, some champagne?"—and things just then go
        From there till they end up in Flynn's bungalow.

7   That seems to have been Flynn's motto: "When flat,
        Put on the old front"[209] —when on the downslide,
        When bad times arrive, simply cock your hat
        And a snook at fate, let that be your guide,
        Act always the polished aristocrat,[210]
        And this applying of course to poolside
        When chatting up a cute little cookie
        Since it might lead to your getting some nooky.

8   Which brings us back to the movie that he
        Was working on now, *Istanbul*, Flynn playing
        A worldly roué, with Errol still natty
        And face still handsome but now betraying
        A wastrel lifestyle—and though perhaps "tatty"
        Is too strong a word, it helps in conveying
        The public's shock at the way Flynn appears
        In his first Hollywood film in four years.

CANTO IX

9   The movie's not much, just a tired remake
    Of a motion picture called *Singapore,*
    About smuggled jewels, and it no mistake
    To cast a Flynn who was wise on that score;
    But Errol's portrait of the middle-aged rake
    Is equally tired as the picture, or,
    If being kind, you might call it "subdued"—
    In any event with no spark imbued.[211]

10   But this feature film, howsoever drab,
    Did in fact spark a small Flynn-renaissance,
    Hollywood seeing no case for rehab
    But instead a "type," which it always wants,
    Other producers now taking a stab
    At Errol as "charming drunk" par excellence,
    Exploiting this old fallibility,
    To afford his acting new credibility.

11   *The Sun Also Rises, Too Much Too Soon,*
    The Roots of Heaven all followed in quick
    Succession—respectively: Flynn as buffoon,
    Engaging here in a bit of slapstick;
    Then as John Barrymore, an opportune
    Role since Flynn knew just what made the man tick;[212]
    Then as an army deserter with lots
    He needs to forget . . . and all three are sots.

12   Flynn was singled out for critical praise,
    Notably in *The Sun Also Rises,*
    Playing Mike Campbell from Ernest Hemingway's
    Selfsame novel; and Mike agonizes,
    In book and film, over how his girl strays,
    Brett Ashley by name, who dehumanizes
    Men, like Circe, by turning them to swine—
    Or mules, if you like, since they act asinine.

ERROL FLYNN

13   When Brett falls for the bullfighter Romero,
Campbell's attempt to stay somewhat jolly
(Though shaken clear to his sodden marrow,
And finally yielding to melancholy)
Reaches its height (Brett now with torero)
In what for me is the grand finale,
Though not the movie's terminating scene,
And gamest one Flynn ever brought to the screen.

14   Errol Flynn's great movie moments till now
Had been on the strength of his matchless charm
—Custer, Captain Courtney, Jim Corbett (and how
Forget Geoffrey Vickers, and yet no harm—
Just read the endnote)[213] but let us allow
For one certain scene where Campbell can't smarm
His way through it quite and this sad-brave mixture
Stealing your heart and the whole bloody picture.

15   Errol as Mike is sitting on the bed—
Bottle on nightstand—of his hotel room,
And the Pamplona fiesta now fled
As well as Ashley, a shadowy gloom
Enshrouding the scene, Mike's hand to his head,
When Jake (Ty Power) walks in, man for whom
Brett too means the world—which makes sense, pardner,
When she is played by stunning Ava Gardner.

16   Mike informs Jake that Brett's finally gone
Off with her virile bullfighter and takes
A belt of the booze, still tying one on,
Then tries making light of the matter while Jake's
Standing there helpless with this woebegone
Figure who jokes even as his heart breaks,
Trying to ride the whole thing out in style
And mustering even the ghost of a smile.

17   Jake suggests Mike should at last get some sleep—
      Then as Jake leaves, Campbell raises his glass
      As if he's feeling just top of the heap
      And not in fact simply dragging his ass,
      And it is all you can do not to weep
      When Campbell grins, spurning all gravitas,
      And says to Jake, who's not reeling in joy
      And ecstasy himself: "Bung ho, old boy!"

18   Jake briefly pauses—then replies in kind,
      A bit skeptically, and goes out the door
      While Mike downs his drink, his grin undermined
      By a bleak aspect, that brave mien no more,
      The face turning helpless and then resigned,
      Nothing at all he can do but just pour
      One more hefty belt—though 'fore he decants,
      Both hands fly up to his fallen countenance.

19   It's in the space of not more than a few
      Seconds that Campbell goes through five distinct
      Attitudes ranging from jauntiness to
      Utter dejection, but all interlinked
      Quite naturally, each emotion true,
      Naught in the chain of affects getting kinked—
      No hint of "acting"—and you feel a twinge,
      Like witnessing *Errol* on some desperate binge.

20   Is it incumbent on me to dilate
      On how suggestive this one certain scene
      Was of Flynn's life and career? Need I state
      How the gay rascal and bon vivant seen
      By the public often didn't equate
      With the Errol within, he able to screen
      The fact of his feeling a bit less than gung ho
      With what you might call a metaphoric *Bung ho*?[214]

21   What in fact, though, makes Errol's performance
In *The Sun Also Rises* so profound
Is how despite Campbell's sickening torments,
Flynn's just as skillful at clowning around,
His talent for farce attaining fine form, hence
Errol attaining that acting high ground:
Making you laugh while wanting to vomit, he
Scaling the rare heights of tragicomedy.

22   How many actors can pull off that trick—
Sublime and ridiculous cheek by jowl?
First wringing your heart and then doing shtick
Without anyone ever crying *Foul!*
The secret's not laying things on too thick
—Refraining from use of that infamous trowel—
In either direction, this or that side,
And not coming off like some Jekyll and Hyde.

23   You might imagine that Flynn would have won
The supporting-actor award that year,
But Oscar balloters managed to shun
Him for a deathless performance which we're
Still talking about: they ignored Flynn's in *Sun*
For Red Buttons' in *Sayonara*—don't jeer!
Red *must've* been tops, this substantiated
By the fact that Flynn wasn't even nominated.

24   There'd been enough wins to one-hit-wonders
Or to whatever new flash-in-the-pan,
For Flynn to judge it one of those blunders
That was endemic to Hollywood's clan.
But truth be told, it's the *theme* that plunders
At Oscar time and this year was "Japan"—
With, among others, four wins for *Sayonara*
And a nomination for Sessue Hayakawa.[215]

25   But if initially you don't succeed—
Then reprise the role! This time in the guise
Of John Barrymore as he goes to seed:
Too Much, Too Soon. And Flynn didn't despise
To use the "Method" and thereby exceed
His usual vodka intake, wherein lies
Dedication to craft, though it undermines
A performer's talent for retaining his lines.

26   By this stage Errol couldn't even face
The camera until he had downed a few—
The problem being that booze would erase
His short-term memory and put askew
His elocution and cadence and pace.
But when the movie's director tried to
Tell Flynn the scene that he'd just played had stunk,
Flynn said: "You'd tell *me* how to play a drunk?"[216]

27   A man has his pride. And Flynn's was well served
By a performance truly heartbreaking,
Barrymore's foibles expertly observed,
Not reproduced in any painstaking
Fashion, just the tics of a man unnerved,
"Oscar" being Errol's for the taking
Had it not been for the fact it's hard to
Win when the film kills you off halfway through.[217]

28   So take your glamorous drunkard routine
Out to Africa, the Dark Continent,
A swarthy backdrop to help voters glean
Those strains of Flynn gold, not all of it spent,
And some would argue with a richer sheen
Than in prior years—in any event,
That would appear to have been the strong view
Of Mr. John Huston . . . and you say—John *who*?

29   Yes *that* John Huston. It seems that their fight
Twelve years before had successfully shed
The bad blood between them, spleen taking flight,
Each ending up in a hospital bed,
Flynn phoning from his not as to incite
Another exchange but all Errol said
Was that two crushed ribs proved Huston did land some,
Huston's response being equally handsome.[218]

30   Not that the two then became bosom friends—
Or friends at all. But a certain respect
For one another resulted, which tends
To happen (in sobering retrospect)
When each of two fellows ably defends
Himself and one gets up from being decked;
So Huston and Flynn were presently working
Together with no seeming enmity lurking.

31   Everything taken together the shoot
Was more compelling than the film, which told
Of a man (Trevor Howard) in pursuit
Of a dream where Flynn and crew are enrolled,
Errol in the part of a dissolute
Trying to efface and atone for an old
Shame from the war and so leaps at the chance
To join Howard's outfit and save the elephants.

32   That wasn't why they filmed on location
(The needed shots were easily gotten
Minus the cast in the operation)
But to this scheme Huston was pleased to cotton,
Desiring to get in *his* shots—translation:
To hunt big game, the film misbegotten,
Getting us all on the eco-bandwagon
While the director'd been out trying to bag one.

33   With John Huston out on safari a
Rash of conditions caused all to fall ill
—Dysentery, sunstroke, malaria—
Except for Flynn who continued to swill
Vodka, not otherwise salutary, a
Drink that in cases like Errol's though will
Keep microbes at bay since intake's confined
To 80-proof bottles, and then combined

34   With the fact that Flynn had already been through
This kind of trial and even much worse
In New Guinea's jungle (recall that whole slew
Of nastiness I committed to verse)
And so, consequently, none of it new
To Errol who took an almost perverse
Pleasure in the challenge of the ordeal,
The others just trying to keep an even keel.[219]

35   And Errol was also able to meet
The challenges of this particular role,
Playing a guy who was down but not beat,
A sad haunted drunk but one with a goal—
And not without guts, this man who would cheat
His dubious past by taking control
Of present and future through what he judges
To be right action to scrub moral smudges.

36   Still Flynn's performance was not good enough
To gain any Oscar consideration,
Joining those given a lifetime rebuff,
Not even getting a nomination—
Doug Sr., Ty Power, Bob Taylor and above
All John Barrymore—the seeming explanation
Not to win an Oscar is simply take care
To be handsome and dashing and debonair.[220]

37   But Flynn had indeed gained critical praise
While now also back in the public eye,
Moreover attracting the eager gaze
Of famed Putnam press, which wanted to buy
Errol's life story (and with no more Hays
Code to which Flynn would be forced to comply);[221]
An offer—and hefty advance—which delighted
Flynn, but the problem was he couldn't write it.

38   The ironies pile up fast, dear reader.
First we had Errol's attempt to desert
A fickle Hollywood to supersede her,
But this bid only serving to divert
Him back in the maw of that foul man-eater,
Destiny causing Flynn's plans to invert—
Istanbul not filming in Asia Minor
But where he'd once been a top headliner;

39   His comeback then owing to the imprint
Left by liquor, his drinking in large part
Engendered by Errol's previous stint
In this locale where they'd broken his heart
With roles allowing for miniscule hint
Of what he could bring to the thespian art—
And with the booze having taken its toll,
The parts he was offered finally having real "soul";

40   Of course his stifled writing ambition
Being the other main reason he drank,
But with the hooch bringing to fruition
This chance to emerge a writer of rank
And tell his story backed by a patrician
Publishing house—*now* the booze played its prank,
Flynn lacking the focused effort required
To pen that memoir to which he aspired . . .

41   *There once was a Baghdad merchant who sent*
His servant to mart, who when he came back
Was ashen with fear and asked to be lent
His master's best horse, bred for the racetrack,
Because he'd seen Death, who in the event
Had flung out a menacing gesture right smack
There in the bazaar: "So to flee my fate
I'll ride to Samarra where Death won't await."

42   *After the servant had galloped away*
The merchant hied down to the marketplace,
Spied Death in the crowd and approached him to say:
"What was that menacing gesture to the face
Of my manservant earlier today?
I prize him highly, he'll be hard to replace;
This is a troublesome situation,
I think you owe me an explanation."

43   *Though taken aback, Death calmly replies:*
"That 'menacing' gesture was nothing bad
But just a reflex, a start of surprise,
At seeing your manservant here in Baghdad,
I hardly able to trust my own eyes
And somewhat put out and even quite mad,
As I've tonight—though now here in the bazaar—a
Longstanding date with him up in Samarra.

44   Fate, so it seemed, had its own plans for Flynn—
Not death, quite yet, but demise of his *dream*
Just as it beckoned, now with mocking grin,
Demise of his hope to finally redeem
His life and no amnesty for the sin
Of having betrayed his own youthful scheme
Of being a writer and leaving behind
Just one masterpiece, his bequest to mankind.

45   But Fate, as we know, can be quite fickle,
Second-guessing itself and changing its mind:
One moment the Grim Reaper with his sickle—
Then all your stars have been realigned;
One moment your dream not worth a plugged nickel—
Then in the next being wined and dined;
And though his writing hopes now seemed to blacken, a
Bit of help came from a deus ex machina.

46   It came in the person of Earl Conrad,
A "ghost" brought on board to help Errol write
His biography; and the deal they had
Was Earl posed questions, Flynn's words going right
To the pages of a stenographic pad,
Recorded in shorthand as he'd recite,
A court-reporter playing transcriber
While Flynn swilled vodka—still playing the imbiber.

47   He drank and regaled and the book took shape
On a porch outside his second-floor room
In Titchfield Hotel with its ambient landscape:
Palm trees, a pool, tropic flowers in bloom,
This giving way to a dazzling seascape,
Nine miles of Atlantic, the ocean's perfume
Wafting on a breeze, all in harmony—O!
The charms of Jamaica and Port Antonio!

48   Errol had once in fact owned the Titchfield,
Buying the place since he so loved the bar,
The ocean view having greatly appealed,
But then emerging as Errol's *bête noire*,
He ruing the deal so soon it was sealed,
A financial loss, and our movie star
Was even denied—when his mother stepped in—
The pleasure of dubbing his roadhouse "Flynn's Inn."

49   Why, you may ask, did *Marelle* have a say
In just what name Errol gave to his lodge?
Well, he'd brought both of his parents to stay
Out in Jamaica, joining his entourage
So as to manage his lush hideaway:
Errol Flynn Estates, that sprawling acreage
Serving as home, citrus farm, cattle station
And last but not least: as copra plantation.

50   Marelle had refused to sit idly by
While Errol fanned the flames of his infamy
With the cognomen "Flynn's Inn," nor she shy
Imposing her will like a fait accompli
In other ways—such as making him buy
The bell for a church along with belfry;
And when his father attempted to build
An airstrip for him, she near got Errol killed.[222]

51   But mother and dad were no longer there
When writing team Errol & Earl came back
To fair Jamaica and Flynn's pied-à-terre
At the Titchfield, our dipsomaniac
Resolved to pursue the dogged warfare
Between him and Mom with a counterattack—
His *memoir* this time the instrument, a
Resounding slap to her face in absentia.

52   The stuff concerning the airstrip and bell
Are found in the pages of Errol's memoir,
And I'm persuaded that it is Marelle
Who's the book's great negatory lodestar,
Third presence with Errol and his Boswell,
A shadowy one yet there insofar
As the tone's one of a small boy to shock—
Who better than Mom if describing your cock?[223]

53   Should this be true, that to scandalize
Marelle was a leading motivation
In the way Flynn sought to characterize
Himself (as "wicked") what a consummation
Of his life's quest to best and otherwise
Consign his mother to earthly damnation!
And Flynn's compulsion may even have spurred
His death so he could get in the last word.

54   And the *first* words that Errol Flynn spoke
To Conrad regarding his life story
(He giving Errol a green light to poke
Around in his past, it not mandatory
To be sequential but just to unyoke
His thoughts in whatever category)—
The words he spoke from the start, right up front,
Weren't about "Mother" but rather "The Cunt."[224]

55   All the way through their collaboration,
According to Conrad, Flynn was obsessing
On mommy dearest and felt elation
At the fact that he was now possessing
Birth-certificate documentation
That mother and father had been messing
Around pre-wedlock, and so at long last
He had pious Marelle "nailed to the mast."[225]

56   And Errol did not even let up there.
As late as when the corrected galleys
Were at the printers, he couldn't forbear
Getting off just one more of his sallies
At her in sending a "will" to the care
Of Conrad for the book's end where he tallies
His heirs, mom too, giving generously,
Though the "bitch still annoys the hell out of me."[226]

57   This didn't make its way into the book—
The circumspect Conrad demurred. All the same,
It can't be said Errol lets her off the hook
Or fails to take very purposeful aim
At memoir's end, for it's great care he took
That she's the last person mentioned by name:
"My war with Mother," writes this child of abuse
"Drones on steadily, toward a silent truce."

58   Then comes a coda, Flynn waxing poetic
On the charms of his Jamaican estate,
Light-years removed from a world frenetic,
Allowing a man to rejuvenate
In a location downright hermetic
Where one can slough off the burdensome weight
Of stardom and image and such impositions
As squire a fame fueled by headlong ambitions.

59   This last passage is poetic in more
Than just one sense, as it tends to reflect
Errol's abiding desire to restore
His New Guinea idyll and resurrect
His pre-stardom youth, those brief years before
His dream of becoming a writer was wrecked—
Back now in the tropics, book going full blast,
He'd prove Gatsby right: you *could* repeat the past.

60   Part of that studied rejuvenation
Was a young lovely of course at his side—
Also in bed for some fornication,
Though the *first* time he seduced this long-thighed
(She being a dancer by vocation)
Teenie could very well be classified
As "statutory rape," that particular charge
Which in Flynn's life had loomed somewhat large.

ERROL FLYNN

61   Beverly Aadland was the nubile's name,
      Sixteen years old and just fifteen when Flynn
      Committed his rape (such was Aadland's claim),
      First ripping her dress and then thrusting in
      And consummating the sex-act with main
      Strength, hurriedly, not even skin to skin
      (She too a virgin, as had been Nora)
      All just this side of Sodom and Gomorrah.

62   If Bev and Nora found it in their heart
      To forgive Errol then so too can we;
      Furthermore, both of these two, for their part,
      Fell head over heels for our debauchee
      (And Errol for them) pretty much from the start;
      Hence it'd seem date-rape, though not exactly
      What we would wish for our daughters and sisters,
      Can sometimes make lovers of initial resisters.[227]

63   Here we have Flynn in his tropic outpost
      With underaged Bev, like Tupersalei,
      Jamaica however this time playing host,
      Its black pidgin-speakers no distant cry
      From New Guinea days when Flynn'd been topmost
      By being the foreign Caucasian guy,
      Jamaica still on the British Empire's list,
      So Flynn could still play white colonialist.[228]

64   It's no wonder that the most compelling
      Sections of Errol Flynn's memoir are those
      On that place where half his mind had been dwelling
      Since he had left, now able to disclose
      This part of his brain while also dispelling
      Notions like Irish-born and thus expose
      A past that offset all the PR buzz
      To show folks exactly the man that he was.

65   Conrad writes how it was Flynn's tendency
To speak in a whimsical light-hearted vein
About his own life. But the events that he
Approached with earnest again and again,
With an intentness and deep urgency,
Were from his New Guinea youth, the urbane
Raconteurship and stories told drolly
Ceding to a mood gripped by something holy.

66   Conrad pumped Errol for information
Over the course of ten weeks from August
Into mid-Fall '58, Flynn's oration
Not leaving much of his life undiscussed.
Then came the process of distillation,
Conrad returning to New York where he fussed
Over the transcript, Flynn off in direction
Of Cuba and Castro for more insurrection.

67   Though he'd disburdened himself of his tale,
Flynn wasn't loath to add chapters to it,
Once again hitting the adventure trail
In order that after having lived through it,
Errol might give a vivid word-portrayal
Of Castro's revolt, a prose conduit,
Working for the Hearst outfit as before
When a reporter in Spain's civil war.

68   Off on another romantic crusade!
Attaboy Errol! Don't throw in the towel
Just as of yet! Let us all see you wade
Into the melee, not some wise old owl
Choosing to inconspicuously fade
Into the background but set up a howl,
Not going gentle into that good night—
And since Conrad's there to do the ghostwrite.[229]

69   But it was Errol who did the legwork,
Meeting with Castro (who wasn't too clear
On who this "Flynn" was) nor did Errol shirk
The riskier stuff (with the souvenir
Of a wound to his shin, this the handiwork
Of a stray bullet)[230] and was scrutineer
At an execution by firing squad
(Puking in horror) thus hardly a fraud.

70   But our intrepid stringer's masterstroke
Was to be sole U.S. correspondent
With Fidel Castro when he at last broke
Batista's regime and the consequent
Taking of Havana, which doubtless spoke
For Flynn or at least was a compliment
To his wide fame or perhaps nothing but
Fidel viewing him as just some harmless nut.[231]

71   But Castro plainly had Flynn's sympathy.
And in the spring of 1959
Flynn made a semi-documentary
Based on the imaginative storyline
Of Flynn as a writer in Cuba to see
Castro and interview him and to shine
A light on his fight and trumpet the cause
Of righteous rebels maligned as outlaws.

72   Beverly Aadland was also not idle,
Here now assuming the female lead:
A U.S. girl who amidst fratricidal
Conflict falls hard for a man pledged to bleed
For the uprising, this so-called film's title:
Cuban Rebel Girls—with critics agreed
That it is Errol's trashiest production;
No surprise here since it was a tax deduction.[232]

73   Flynn was still troubled by financial woes,
Trying to relieve his situation
Through random television cameos
(And their attendant humiliation)[233]
Though these spots hardly sufficient, God knows,
In bringing about any restoration
Of Errol's cash-flow—of some urgency
Since he was awash in insolvency.

74   Finally forced to it, Errol Flynn had to sell
His beloved *Zaca*. Though he had refrained
For long as he could in bidding farewell
To this sleek vessel which he had retained
Through thick and thin, still that cold day in hell
Had now arrived and she all that remained,
Outlasting his Mulholland Farm and much more,
Such as three wives, she Flynn's true paramour.

75   Immediate occasion for its sale,
However, might well have been for the sake
Of yet another competing female:
Beverly Aadland, whom he wished to make
His wife, he needing cash for defrayal
Of the amount Patrice Wymore would take
Errol for in their upcoming divorce . . .
But let's not be putting the cart 'fore the horse.

76   For *Zaca*, Errol knew a likely buyer
Out in Vancouver who was willing to pay
One hundred grand, they having talked prior;
So Errol and Bev began on their way
To British Columbia . . . and as higher
They rise in the sky with their plane, what say
We visit an actress in Paris, France,
Once victim of a snake in her underpants.

ERROL FLYNN

77   Olivia de Havilland was now married,
For the second time, to Pierre Galante,
Paris Match editor, why she tarried
These days in the French capital and with scant
Time for her career, not quite dead and buried,
But five or six films in the last decade can't
Be termed as thriving—though hardly on the skids—
Mainly she was busy raising two kids.[234]

78   Last we left Livy she'd recently played
Elizabeth Custer to Errol's selfsame
Hero in *They Died With Their Boots On*, made
Eighteen years prior, at peak of Flynn's fame.
And more or less after that movie they'd
Gone separate ways and even became
Estranged from each other, hard to say why,
Neither of them seeing fit to specify.

79   And then soon after, in 1943,
Both of them underwent trial by fire
'Fore state tribunals—and as we did see,
The upshot for Errol was fairly dire,
Chained to an image, but Livy set free
From her debased servitude to his Sire
Jack L. Warner, Flynn staying in harness,
Their lives diverging to the point of bizarreness.

80   While Flynn's career started going downhill,
Excepting his little comeback near the end,
Olivia now was all set to fulfill
Her destiny and began to ascend
The acting ranks and moved in for the kill
By gaining that for which she'd dearly yenned
In garnering two Oscars from her peers
And nominated for a third—in three years!

81 And now we move further forward in time
   To the year '57: Errol Flynn
   Back in Hollywood and trying to climb
   From bed every day and show *some* discipline
   In filming *Too Much, Too Soon,* when a prime
   Item of party news comes his way in
   Form of a gala to which he's now privy—a
   Function where he might in fact see Olivia.

82 The party is for *The Proud Rebel* which
   Livy stars in, a Goldwyn creation,
   Many years elapsed since that baffling glitch
   Which somehow caused their alienation,
   Flynn thinking that it'd be classy to stitch
   Things up between them through a demonstration
   Of his good will and fondness by showing
   Up at the party—without her knowing.

83 He crashes the fête like a two-ton bomb,
   Never the shy and retiring type he,
   Charming the guests with his nervy aplomb,
   Everyone on pins and needles to see
   What will eventuate when our grande dame
   Makes her grand entrance, and fashionably
   Late of course, requisite when you're a star,
   And no faded one like our friend at the bar.

84 And she's resplendent! Never looked better!
   Still fresh and lovely as always that face
   But now her *body* the appetite-whetter,
   With womanly curves, each in the right place,
   Nice sex appeal though remaining well-bred, her
   Beauty only matched by that unique grace
   (Poised and sure-handed while lacking pretense)
   And Errol draws near to announce his presence.

85   Livy can't see him, he comes from behind,
Planting a kiss on the back of her neck,
She whirling in anger, hardly inclined
To gladly suffer this insolent peck,
Giving whomever a piece of her mind,
That he can't be playing with a full deck—
Yet seeing this old lech, she can't follow through,
But halts, though still mad, and says: "Do I *know* you?"

86   "It's Errol," he says, confused and abashed;
And later Olivia told how, "He had
Changed so much," and how this visitant clashed
With Flynn of the past, that spirited lad
Whose eyes had twinkled and glittered and flashed,
Those blazing portals to his soul now "so sad,"
And her shock real since she can't recognize
The individual "behind the eyes."[235]

87   Let's leap ahead two more years to the Fall
(Hope all this time-jumping's not unpleasant)
Of '59, back in Paris, to call
At long last on that ex-pat resident,
Olivia now with her kids, both small,
At what for *her* is a major event:
This matinee in a French movie house,
Not watching cartoons, nothing here mickey mouse,

88   Since what she's viewing with Benjy and Gisele
Is *The Adventures of Robin Hood*—not
So fateful, you'll say, since the film casts a spell
On both age and youth and has quite a lot
To offer a self-involved actress who's well
Into her forties, eyeing what she had wrought
As a young pretty, the effect sublime,
But how about for *the very first time*?

89   She'd sidestepped the film ever since its release,
Afraid she'd been bad, not wanting to view
A Maid Marian who would fail to please;
But this anxiety proving undue,
The film itself proving a masterpiece,
And it is not only one but then *two*
Times she views Errol Flynn gallivanting
Through a film she deems "classic" and "enchanting."[236]

90   Olivia sits there glued to her seat,
And after the second showing then she
Hastens back home with wings on her feet
And pens a letter to Flynn saying he
Was Robin Hood and imparts other sweet
Sentiments that Errol most certainly
Would have enshrined—but come letter's end, it
All seemed too maudlin so she didn't send it.

91   So it is now that Flynn's Vancouver-bound
Plane has arrived at its destination—
But his boat venture's not with success crowned,
Maybe the whole thing a mere flirtation
With the idea, pussyfooting around,
Connoting a self-repudiation
—The bold seafaring swashbuckler denied—
And maybe Flynn felt this before he died.[237]

92   Errol *had* felt discomfort in his back
During his return to the airport, the pain
Expanding to a fatal heart attack,
He making the trip to L.A. by train,
In the baggage car, heading down the track—
Washington, Oregon, Cali—a plain
Wood box his capsule, a mere packing crate,
He not lying *in* but instead *inter*state.

ERROL FLYNN

93   Against Flynn's wishes his cadaver was not
Sent to Jamaica but to loathed Forest Lawn—
Perhaps she couldn't or simply forgot,
But Pat, still his wife, made the call here, mon,
And that he not be permitted to rot
In style with cravat and blue blazer on
But gotten up in a gray business suit,
Just like some 9-to-5 corporate recruit.[238]

94   And thus Errol Flynn was to his rest laid
Out in the "Garden of Everlasting Peace."
Lili and Nora and Beverly stayed
Home but Flynn's three oldest kids and Patrice,
Raoul Walsh, Vince Sherman and Alexis Smith made
Appearances as too did Michael Curtiz
And a handful of studio execs—
But that's about all who paid their respects.[239]

95   The eulogy—Jack Warner gave it, he
Sharing his own well-informed summation
Of Errol's "electric personality,"
Namely that consummate combination
Of equal parts "charm" and "vitality."
And adding a poignant palpitation
Was a sung version of that lyric gem,
Robert Louis Stevenson's *Requiem*:

Under the wide and starry sky,
Dig the grave and let me lie.
Glad did I live and gladly die,
And I laid me down with a will.

This be the verse you grave for me:
Here he lies where he longed to be;
Home is the sailor, home from the sea,
And the hunter home from the hill.[240]

96   A much larger public turned out to buy
       Wicked when published just two months later,
       Likely not hurt by the fact he *did* die,
       A kind of risqué commemorator,
       To which the title could well testify,
       Fine tribute to the Hollywood satyr—
       Furthermore in a classic tradition
       Of confessionals sans act of contrition.[241]

97   I mean here those unapologetic
       Picaresque tell-alls whose loquacity
       Is just the opposite of homiletic,
       Fueled by a personal audacity,
       None of the narrative theoretic
       (Which doesn't mean perfect veracity)
       But life supplying the tales they wove, a
       Cellini, for instance, or a Casanova.

98   And though it's no memoir in the true sense,
       In the same breath we might mention Don Juan
       As Byron this storied rogue reinvents:
       In his own image, more than a soupçon
       Of his own character and its immense
       Anomalies in the portrait he's drawn
       And those of the world that Juan occupies, it
       Much too complex to neatly capsulize it.

99   It is far simpler to draw a schematic
       Picture of the world when you've only had
       A limited life; but a systematic
       View of existence, girt by ironclad
       Logic and laws, becomes problematic
       When you've been driven, over time, near mad
       By life's recalcitrance in such matters,
       Your own knowledge leaving that view in tatters.

ERROL FLYNN

100   You've had too much of life to comprehend
    What it all means and just how it coheres,
    Sole thing we know being that in the end
    —After the laughter and boredom and tears,
    After the whole masquerade of pretend,
    After a play that would rival Shakespeare's,
    After this journey, our short earthly jaunt—
    Is our life-instinct: the maxim "I want."

101   Flynn was this life-instinct personified.
    Thus I will end by citing the haughty
    Personage who had once *Don Juan* decried
    As vulgar and self-indulgently naughty—
    And Byron, defending his baby, replied
    That it might well be "profligate" and "bawdy,"
    Not the most virtuous of his offspring,
    "But is it not *life*, is it not *the thing*?"

102   So my dear reader, I bid you adieu.
    The stanzas I've written were done sincere,
    And now that Flynn's life has passed in review,
    Now that we've worked our way through the whole shmear,
    Let's take up a glass—and that means you too!—
    Brimming with wine from a fine vintage year
    And raise it up high and let us all toast
    A man, if no saint, who was better than most.

FINIS

ENDNOTES

Canto I: *Tasmanian Devil* (1909-1929)

1   This is the first time in this work, where quotation marks appear, that I have not given the words precisely as rendered from whatever written source—in this case from Flynn's 1959 autobiography *My Wicked, Wicked Ways*. (I am using the 2003 edition issued by Cooper Square Press.) Not that Flynn's own version is an exact rendering thirty years later either. But as a rule I have given the passages of dialogue in the book exactly as they appear in the original sources; any changes are only slight adjustments to the exigencies of meter and rhyme, these comprising maybe ten or twenty percent of cases. Otherwise, unless obviously being used in the sense of "so-called" or in other minor ways, everything within quotation marks, particularly quotes from Flynn's own writings, is slavishly verbatim.

2   New Ireland is a smaller isle northeast of the main New Guinea island, part of the Bismarck Archipelago, Kavieng being its main port and administrative center.

3   *Beam Ends* (1937) and *Showdown* (1946).

4   Rabaul is on the isle New Britain, largest of the islands to the northeast of New Guinea proper, and was capital of the Australian mandated territory until 1937 when it was destroyed by a volcano. It was rebuilt and repopulated, only to again be destroyed by a volcanic eruption in 1994.

5   In *Wicked* Flynn says that it was "usually ten days to Rabaul" and that for "two weeks we went off course." (p. 77) Even the ten days seem like an inordinate amount of time to cover something like 250 kilometers. Flynn may have been just throwing numbers around—but the point is that with him at the helm it took considerably longer to make the trip.

6   Flynn recounts this jungle clash in *Wicked*, just as I have elaborated, but there is no corroborating evidence that it actually happened. What we do have is a letter to his father some years later where he says: "A friend Jack Ryan, is 50 years old and it is he who was mainly instrumental in having a charge of murder squashed against me in the other Territory when I shot a native there in 1929." Not only does he bring a third party into the episode—Jack Ryan—but he refers to it almost casually, as if he had already disclosed the murder to his father who was now quite familiar with it. This smacks of truth. Particularly as he may have fudged the truth on occasion with his father, as he did with many people, but was unlikely to freely perpetuate a lie with that man whom he held in the highest esteem. For the quotation from the letter, dated May 1932, see Thomas McNulty, *Errol Flynn: The Life and Career* (Jefferson NC and London 2004) 16.

Canto II: *Flynnanigans* (1929-1932)

7   Marelle wrote a check for 120 pounds after she, Theo and Errol paid a couple visits to the shipyard. Errol's gold-claim/windfall/drunken-purchase account can be found in *Wicked* (p. 98) and *Beam Ends* (New York 1975) 11-12; the corrected account is in John Hammond Moore, *The Young Errol: Flynn Before Hollywood* (Sydney 1975) 54-58.

8   The novel was apparently begun in 1935 but didn't appear until 1937. Knowing how eager the publishing world is to issue books authored by a celebrity while he or she is (still) hot, I think it's a fair surmise that the bulk of work on the novel was done in the intervening year of 1936.

9   Published in 1844, whereby the letter in question is "hidden" in such a plain and open place that it escapes initial detection.

10   There is debate as to whether the jewel-stealing incident took place precisely as described—or whether it took place at all. Flynn may have been gilding the lily in this tale, but it certainly can't be disproved. Some authors have expressed skepticism regarding the story, but none pretends to have any information outright contradicting it. And John Hammond Moore—a Flynn-skeptic himself whose entire research was devoted to separating fact from fiction as it concerned Errol's early life—does indeed confirm the tale's broad outlines: a love affair with an older socialite, stolen jewels, and Flynn's precipitate flight from Sydney. Of the Madge Parkes jewelry caper he writes that "like dismissal from Dalgety's [a Sydney shipping concern where 18-year-old Flynn briefly clerked] for plundering the stamp account and other embarrassing twists in his career, the basic elements are all there." (Moore, *The Young Errol*, 98-103)

Canto III: *A Heroic Inheritance* (1932-1934)

11   And this was precisely why the MGM publicity department, also in the mid-1930s, perpetrated the fiction that Merle Oberon came from Tasmania, thinking that the U.S. public would know scarce little about the place. Miss Oberon had the requisite exotic looks, but as the "illegitimate" issue of a British father and Indian mother, she had in fact been born in Bombay. She wished to keep this quiet, as did the studio, and the Tasmania fib came back to haunt her in 1978 when she was invited to Hobart for the dedication of a theater in her honor. Somehow she didn't know how to say no. She traveled down for the ceremony but immediately afterward the truth came out. She died the next year at age 68.

12   Flynn may or may not have invented this tale of a detour through the Australian Outback; but if he did then it is a richly imagined interlude as related in *Wicked*, including the infamous "dagging the hogget" episode where he was employed to bite the testicles off of young sheep in preparation for their shearing.

13   According to Flynn's as-told-to collaborator Earl Conrad, their publisher Putnam couldn't locate Erben for permission to use his name, so they insisted that Flynn and Conrad change it in *Wicked* ("Dr. Gerrit H. Koets") to forestall a potential lawsuit. Apparently Flynn, or Conrad, then took it a step further by fiddling with certain key identifiers of Erben's person, for instance making him not only Dutch but a "big man" when he was no more than average height and build, and calling him "fifteen or twenty years older" when he wasn't quite twelve years older than Flynn.

14   In June 1940, while Flynn was on a six-week flying tour through South America, he was interviewed in Buenos Aires by the American embassy regarding Erben, who the FBI thought might be a Nazi spy. Why a

Jew would be working for the National Socialists is difficult to say, though it does seem that Erben was involved in Nazi espionage at two or three points in his career. But the allegation leveled by Charles Higham in his *Errol Flynn: The Untold Story* (New York 1980) that Flynn himself was a Nazi spy is completely false—as conclusively proven by William Donati in "The Flynn Controversy," his appendix to Buster Wiles' *My Days with Errol Flynn* (Santa Monica 1988) and as elegantly argued by Tony Thomas in his book-length rebuttal *Errol Flynn: The Spy Who Never Was* (New York 1990); on pages 110-112 of his book, Thomas reprints Ambassador Norman Armour's report of the 1940 interview with Flynn. For the rest of his long life Erben fought to regain the citizenship he lost in 1941, even having two bills introduced to the U.S. Congress to reinstate that citizenship, but to no avail. Several attempts to enter the United States on a visa likewise failed.

15   The physicist Ernst Mach (1838-1916) was attempting to chart a monistic methodological path between Newtonian materialism and Kantian idealism, thus liberating modern science from useless metaphysical disputes between the two poles. There were no "right" or "wrong" theories but only useful ones. A theory's job was to describe sensory data—not pass judgment on it—and thereby helping to solve practical problems. Mach's epistemology not only cleared the way for Einstein's Theory of Relativity but in our Viennese context it impacted Freud as well as the logical positivism and literary expressionism which pervaded the intellectual atmosphere of the city and more particularly the University of Vienna. Erben studied science at this institution and would have been directly exposed to Mach's ideas. From what Flynn tells us of Erben's weltanschauung, and knowing Flynn's own opinions, I am here positing an ideational link between Mach's "critical positivism" and Flynn's world-view—a world-view mediated, whether consciously or not, by that "great influence" in Flynn's life, Hermann Erben.

16   In 1984, Josef Fegerl induced Erben to show him his diaries and then he put together a book with black-and-white photos taken by Erben that recorded the doctor's meetings with Flynn over seven years. See Josef Fegerl (ed.) *Errol Flynn, Dr. Hermann F. Erben: A Friendship of Two Adventurers 1933-1940* (Vienna 1985).

17   His 1959 autopsy report cited "an old healed scar in the right lower quadrant of the abdomen"—which is a perfect candidate for having been a mundane appendix operation.

18   In other words, I'm skipping that port of call. They were only there for two days anyway, from 7-9 May 1933, a period when Flynn claims to have had sundry adventures with "Ting Ling O'Connor" and have enlisted in the "Royal Hong Kong Volunteers" with whom he remained for three weeks—which is a great deal to do in 48 hours. See Fegerl, *A Friendship of Two Adventurers,* 5.

19   In Erben's journal of the 1933 trip (at least that portion of it which has been published) he makes but one explicit mention of a visit by himself and Flynn to a brothel, in Indian Egmore, whereas to hear Flynn tell it in his autobiography, they copulated their way across Asia; though Saigon and then Marseilles, their last stop, may have been two other cities where they whored, as these places arise in a conversation with John Barrymore that Flynn recalls in *Wicked* (p. 204).

20   The British Actors' Equity Association, a trade union for actors and stage managers formed in 1930.

21   By 1935 the quota had been raised to the extent that at least twenty percent of all films shown in the United Kingdom were required to be British productions. A British picture was defined as one that had a British writer, was filmed somewhere in the British Empire by a British or British-controlled company, and where 75 percent of the salaries were paid to British subjects. Ultimate ownership of the production seems to have been irrelevant—as was its quality.

22   British film wouldn't recover until the Second World War when the supply of American pictures substantially dwindled.

23   In 1952 Flynn was in England starring in *The Master of Ballantrae* and was invited to open the Northampton Repertory Theatre's garden party. He accepted but was worried about being served writs for all the money he owed when he'd blown town those many years back. He needn't have, since the statute of limitations on debt-recovery proceedings was six years. See Gerry Connelly, *Errol Flynn in Northampton* (Corby, UK 1995) 89.

24   Chapter two of Oscar Wilde's novel.

25   Jack Warner had a history of trying to upstage Wallis. At the 1944 Academy Awards when *Casablanca* won for best picture, studio head Warner rushed the stage to accept the award ahead of Wallis, who had personally shepherded the project from unproduced play to eternal screen glory and been officially credited as producer on the picture. In a huff, Wallis severed his ties with Warner and became an independent producer, two years later putting Burt Lancaster under contract, who might be seen as Flynn's real swashbuckling successor in at least two films—*The Flame and the Arrow* (1950) and *The Crimson Pirate* (1952). In the first of these Lancaster does some breathtaking acrobatics, most notably at end of the film, reprising his old circus act in performing giant swings and flyovers from one horizontal bar to the next—the bars mocked up to look like supports for a row of torches jutting out from a castle wall high above the ground. No star has ever done such stunts, which combined consummate skill and daring, not even Douglas Fairbanks Sr. The castle sets were from two Flynn films, *The Adventures of Robin Hood* (1938) and *Adventures of Don Juan* (1948).

26   *Murder at Monte Carlo* has gone missing and it's not entirely clear whether Asher was more impressed with Flynn's performance or with his person. By all accounts his acting was hardly earth-shattering. So Jack Warner's verdict of "she stinks," assuming he even *saw* the film, might be closer to the truth than one would care to credit; in which case, Asher was a real "seer"—though, as I make the argument, seeing through the eyes of another.

27   At a banquet given in January 1927 at L.A.'s Ambassador Hotel by MGM's Louis B. Mayer, Fairbanks was one of three dozen who became official co-founders of the Academy—and if the original idea for the Academy wasn't perhaps his, he was the motive force behind it. In recognition of this fact he was elected the Academy's first president, one of his first acts being to establish "awards of merit for distinctive achievement,"

of which he was the first host in May 1929 in the Blossom Room of the newly opened Roosevelt Hotel, whose partial owner he was and which lay across the street from Grauman's Chinese Theater, in which he also held part-ownership and where he and his wife Mary Pickford ("First Lady of Hollywood") were the first to place their footprints in the Forecourt of the Stars at the theater's opening in April 1927. There were lots of firsts for this pioneering action-adventure star—not least his sponsorship, as Academy president, of the nation's first film school at the University of Southern California and his founding (with Mary Pickford, Charlie Chaplin and D. W. Griffith) of United Artists in 1919, the first large-scale attempt by "the talent" to exercise creative control over their films and the revenues generated by them—on the occasion of which Richard Rowland, head of Metro Pictures, famously remarked that "the inmates are taking over the asylum."

28   The Hollywood Forever Cemetery composes sixty acres of prime Tinseltown real estate wedged between Santa Monica Boulevard and the back of Paramount Studios. Cecil B. DeMille and a cast of thousands call it home.

29   Namely as commander of the "Beach Jumpers," a diversionary unit whose job was to simulate amphibious landings, thus drawing off enemy troops from the main invasion force. Among other medals, he was awarded the Silver Star by the United States, the Croix de Guerre by France, and the Distinguished Service Cross by the British.

30   Asher seems to have nowhere mentioned the Fairbanks factor—which meant it was probably decisive.

31   The exact way that Asher quotes her is: "There's one fella I'll just bet will never go Hollywood."

32   And where drums make an appearance—i.e. garramut-like—these ever and always haunting the Flynn imagination. This "satire," according to Flynn, had "two pukka sahibs over their 'chorta pegs' saying interminably, 'Drums, old chap, I say, mustn't let the ladies know.'" (*Wicked*, 184)

33   Among other colorful aspects he speaks of ten native policemen accompanying them "with three months stores and enough rifles and ammunition to start a small war." The consensus among Flynn scholars is that the trip never happened—at least not with Hermann Erben, who is mentioned by name in the article as the producer who persuades Errol to take him up the Sepik River to film cannibals. Erben first met Flynn in New Guinea in 1933 at precisely that moment when the latter was departing its shores. Flynn probably tossed in Erben's name as a private joke; but the tall tale formed the basis for his novel *Showdown* a decade later. For a synopsis of the article, see Connelly, *Errol Flynn in Northhampton*, 55-57.

Canto IV: *Tiger Lil and Captain Blood* (1934-1937)

34   About two months after arriving in Hollywood, in January 1935, Flynn was given his first part in *The Case of the Curious Bride*—playing a corpse. Though reminiscent of his inaugural role at Northampton when he also played a murder victim, in this instance he had a short flashback scene

with leading lady Margaret Lindsay where he slaps her around and where it is alleged that Flynn accidentally knocked her out during its filming.

35   And it is the last rendition as told by Flynn in *My Wicked, Wicked Ways*. He apparently recounted another variant to a Hollywood magazine shortly after becoming famous: that he and Lili had first met in London . . . or maybe it was Paris, this latter being Lili's version according to Gerry Connelly's 1998 edition of his *Flynn in Northampton*. Who or what to believe? The fact is they met *sometime* before Flynn's arrival in Hollywood (this alleged meeting while crossing the Atlantic on the SS *Paris*—yes, to complicate matters, that was its name—might well have happened but was perhaps not their initial encounter); and whether it was Lili's tennis-court greeting which got things rolling, or back on track, it didn't take long for the two of them to get up a full head of steam.

36   Flynn later wrote in a letter that he'd never been able to share Lili's fondness for cunnilingus, which repulsed him and "left a scar which took some years to heal." But heal it did. Earl Conrad reports how Flynn told him of orally satisfying one woman in gratitude for the wild sex ride she'd given him—this in Jamaica with a beautiful mulatto who worked the front desk of the Titchfield Hotel where Flynn was living at the time. In her memoir *The Stars in My Eyes, the Stars in My Bed* (New York 1975) the Hollywood journalist Nancy Bacon likewise detailed the oral sex that Flynn performed on her when she was a contract player at Universal Studios in the mid-1950s. In the late 1960s she also had a year-and-a-half affair with Paul Newman who, apropos extramarital affairs and his marriage to Joanne Woodward, had once famously quipped: "I have steak at home, so why should I go out for a hamburger?" The affair was the worst kept secret in Hollywood, people joking: "Paul may not go out for hamburger but he sure goes for Bacon."

37   In the summer of 1934, at the Malvern Festival, Flynn confided to Elspeth March (later wife of Flynn's swashbuckling epigone Stewart Granger): "I promise you, within a year I shall be in Hollywood and I'll marry a film star and then be on my way." By the summer of 1935 Flynn had married Lili Damita and was starring in *Captain Blood* (1935) his breakthrough role. See Jeffrey Meyers, *Inherited Risk: Errol and Sean Flynn in Hollywood and Vietnam* (New York 2002) 103.

38   Flynn may or may not have been aware of this fact. On the marriage certificate, dated 19 June 1935, Lili stated her age as twenty-six, the same age Flynn would be the next day, June 20th, the date of his birth. In fact she was born 10 July 1904. It might be opportune to mention here that in marrying an older woman named Lili who was "a dead ringer" for Flynn's mother (Robert Matzen, *Errol & Olivia: Ego and Obsession in Golden Era Hollywood* [Pittsburgh 2010] 1) a certain Oedipal urge may have been in play, particularly since Flynn's mother's first name had originally been Lily Mary, she eventually changing it to what she perceived as the less dowdy "Marelle."

39   She starred opposite Gary Cooper in *Fighting Caravans*, a lavish 1931 Western; another decent-looking guy she appeared with was Cary Grant in his feature debut *This is the Night* (1932).

40   Jack Warner's fiancée was the actress Ann Page Alvarado, for whom Warner left his wife of twenty years and then married in January 1936, the two staying wed until Warner's death in 1978. Lili had known Curtiz from Europe since at least 1925 when she played her first leading role in *Das Spielzeug von Paris* under Curtiz's direction. He went on to direct her in two more films, *Fiaker Nr. 13* and *Der Goldene Schmetterling*, both from 1926. Curtiz and Damita would make their separate ways to Hollywood not long after.

41   Robert Donat, who had starred the year before in the swashbuckler *The Count of Monte Cristo* (1934) was followed by Leslie Howard, Ronald Colman, Clark Gable and Frederic March in their rejection of the Captain Blood role; then George Brent and Brian Aherne tested and were themselves rejected. Robert Donat later went on to win the Academy Award for best actor in *Goodbye, Mr. Chips*, beating out some great nominees in that immortal movie year of 1939—Clark Gable in *Gone with the Wind*, James Stewart in *Mr. Smith Goes to Washington*, and Laurence Olivier in *Wuthering Heights*. In short, Flynn was being called on to fill some very big shoes.

42   Despite Flynn's rough edges, Warner was duly impressed and later wrote: "I asked Mike Curtiz, who would be directing the picture, to make a test of Flynn in the Captain Blood costume. Mike and I sat in the projection room later, listening to Flynn reading lines, and seeing him whip a sword against an imaginary foe. I knew we had grabbed the brass ring in our thousand-to-one shot spin with Flynn. When you see a meteor stab the sky, or a bomb explode, or a fire sweep across a dry hillside, the picture is vivid and remains alive in your mind. So it was with Errol Flynn." From Jack Warner with Dean Jennings, *My First Hundred Years in Hollywood* (New York 1965) 235, as cited in McNulty, *The Life and Career,* 32.

43   Given voice in this film were mostly the Jolson songs and two minutes of accompanying dialogue along with sound effects and a synchronized music score. Previous "sound" films featured audio of one sort or another, four of which were Warners productions from 1926 and early 1927, but a year later in 1928 the studio came out with "The First 100% All-Talking Picture"—*Lights of New York.* Hollywood's other major studios tried to impede the growth of talkies but Warner Brothers defiantly produced a dozen of these films in 1928. At the first Academy Awards presentation in May 1929 the industry then gratefully conceded defeat by presenting Warners with an honorary award for revolutionizing the industry through sound. By late 1929 and the stockmarket crash, and except for the odd Chaplin picture in the years to come, silent films were for all intents and purposes extinct in Hollywood.

44   Warners presented *On with the Show* in 1929, the first all-color and all-talking feature film. This was followed that same year by *Gold Diggers of Broadway*, whose success opened the floodgates for color films in the next few years, most of these being musicals. When the public got sick of musicals, which they associated with color, the studios returned to black and white, this also being a cost-cutting measure dictated by onset of the Great Depression.

45   Technically speaking, the classic Looney Tunes and Merrie Melodies cartoons were created by Warners' animation division, Leon

Schlesinger Productions, which was established as an independent company in 1933, the cartoons then released and distributed by Warner Brothers. But Jack Warner bought Schlesinger's studio outright in 1944, at which point it became Warner Bros. Cartoons, Inc., and by which time their cartoon shorts had long surpassed those of Walt Disney in popularity within the United States. Warner Brothers' 1953 film *House of Wax* was the second 3-D color feature issued by a major studio, whose premiere was preempted by just 48 hours with the opening of Columbia's *Man in the Dark*, which was rushed into production and completed in eleven days so as to be first on the market. But it is *House of Wax*—also offering stereophonic sound, or, as the studio would have it, "Warnerphonic" sound, another innovative riposte to the television threat—which is generally credited as kicking off the short-lived 3-D craze of the mid-1950s.

46   A typical Warner Brothers "rewrite" would consist of someone like Bryan Foy, a Warners producer, noting a screenplay's total number of pages, ripping out a chunk in the middle, handing the script back to the writer and saying: "Bridge it." From Cass Warner Sperling and Cork Millner with Jack Warner Jr., *Hollywood Be Thy Name* (Lexington, Kentucky 1998) 160.

47   Other sterling efforts are *Angels with Dirty Faces*, *Yankee Doodle Dandy* and *Mildred Pierce*, not to mention five classic Flynn films: *Captain Blood*, *The Charge of the Light Brigade*, *The Adventures of Robin Hood*, *The Private Lives of Elizabeth and Essex* and *The Sea Hawk*. Curtiz is the greatest director in Hollywood history who the general public has never heard of—and he more than any other single artist helped to establish the Warner Brothers style. Hal Wallis, production chief at Warners, said in his memoir *Starmaker* that Curtiz was "my favorite director, then and always." (As cited in Matzen, *Errol & Olivia*, 26.) Curtiz's forte was not only the breakneck pace of his films but their composition, with intriguing props in the foreground, giant shadows cast on walls, and shooting at wild angles.

48   In his *Errol & Olivia*, Robert Matzen writes: "Conventional Hollywood history will imply decades later that Lili Damita wields her influence to secure for Errol the title role in *Captain Blood*, but two facts contradict this notion: First, an impressive string of memos circulating within the front office chronicle the dyspeptic casting process and the desperate feeling of Warner and Wallis, who believe that Flynn is the least offensive of the options at hand. Second, Damita is a fading star at this point who has gambled on Flynn to revive her own career—her position is so tenuous that she can't even find roles for herself, let alone for her husband." (p. 18) I have two rejoinders. First, by Matzen's own account, Warner was not at all persuaded by Flynn's performance in the screen tests that he repeatedly viewed, and Curtiz frankly thought he stunk; so a little whispering in the studio chief's ear by Ann Page, Lili's close friend, the woman for whom Warner was leaving his family, might well have turned the trick—the behind-the-scenes of the behind-the-scenes. As for Damita being a fading star, quite true, but even fading stars can still shine brightly, and while Flynn was making *Captain Blood* she was doing *Frisco Kid* across the lot with Warners' top star James Cagney. Damita wasn't without pull—and again, the key factor in this respect was Ann Page. Another major ingredient in Flynn's rise was the Wallis family—namely Minna Wallis, who was Flynn's first agent (Flynn in *Wicked* attributed

his gaining the *Captain Blood* role to her); along with her brother and Warners production chief Hal Wallis, who not only had Flynn brought over from England but, "well aware of Curtiz's bullying and brutality, kept a close rein on him and helped advance Flynn's career at Warner Bros." (Meyers, *Inherited Risk*, 26) But regardless of the exact configuration of personalities, Flynn had a powerful "team" backing him.

49   The Monmouth Rebellion was precipitated by the 1st Duke of Monmouth upon the death of Charles II in 1685. Monmouth was Charles' illegitimate son and he hoped that Protestant England would rally behind his bid for the throne, which had been assumed by the Catholic James II, Charles' younger brother. The rebellion failed, Monmouth and hundreds of his followers were executed, and hundreds more were transported to the West Indies. Flynn's Dr. Blood suffers this latter fate after having kept his Hippocratic oath and tended to the wounds of one of the Monmouth rebels. *Captain Blood* was based on Rafael Sabatini's eponymous novel of 1922.

50   Olivia de Havilland appeared in a total of eight feature films with Flynn from 1935 to 1942, all but one of these headed by Curtiz, who directed Flynn in a total of twelve movies.

51   Korngold scored seven and Steiner fifteen of Flynn's pictures. The respective Steiner and Korngold scores may not be interchangeable but they do have great consanguinity, not least the wash of sound and those long melodic lines as heard in traditional Viennese opera. Korngold would seem to have recognized their kinship. There is the anecdote that Steiner once chided him by asking why it was, after ten years together at Warner Brothers, that Korngold's music was decreasing and Steiner's increasing in quality. Korngold replied that Steiner was stealing from him and that he, Korngold, was stealing from Steiner. The story is likely apocryphal, particularly as Korngold's scores are on the whole more distinguished, especially *The Adventures of Robin Hood* and *The Sea Hawk*. Korngold's ambitions also went beyond Hollywood—he had a clause in his Warners contract that allowed him to take material from his scores for later use in his own free-standing compositions. Most notable of these is his violin concerto (dedicated to Alma Mahler, widow of his Viennese mentor Gustav Mahler) which cannibalizes themes from four of his Hollywood scores, two of these Flynn films, *Another Dawn* and *The Prince and the Pauper*, the other two being *Juarez* and *Anthony Adverse* (for which Korngold also won an Oscar). What I call the "classic" Warners formula of Flynn, Curtiz, de Havilland and Steiner/Korngold was wholly intact in six films: *Captain Blood*, *The Charge of the Light Brigade*, *The Adventures of Robin Hood*, *Dodge City*, *The Private Lives of Elizabeth and Essex*, and *Santa Fe Trail*.

52   *Gentleman Jim* is the ultimate Flynn vehicle. If you want some idea of the charm, mettle, caginess, opportunism and literal two-fisted toughness that were Flynn's essential attributes and which he employed liberally in getting to the top, then see this film about Jim Corbett's rise to heavyweight champion of the world. Offhand I can think of no more perfect pairing of historical personage and an actor's persona than Corbett/Flynn.

53   The screenwriter was Delmar Daves, who later went on to direct such films as *Destination Tokyo* (1943), *Dark Passage* (1947) and *Broken Arrow* (1950).

348

54   Byron himself put it this way in discussing the instant fame which came his way upon publication of the first two cantos of *Childe Harold's Pilgrimage* in March 1812 when in three days it sold out the first large format quarto edition (what Byron termed "a cursed unsaleable size"). The first edition was only 500 copies but was priced at a costly 50 shillings, equivalent to half the weekly income of a gentleman. Nine more octavo editions (smaller in size and half the price) were issued over the next six years, some 20,000 copies being sold. See Fiona MacCarthy, *Byron: Life and Legend* (London 2003) 159.

55   He entered a complaint with the Society for the Prevention of Cruelty to Animals. He had been disturbed by use of the "Running W," a method where one end of a set of wires was fastened to a stake in the ground and the other end to a horse's front legs; upon reaching the end of the wire the horse's forelegs were pulled out from under it with the animal crashing headlong as if being shot out from under its rider. This cruel device resulted in many outright deaths among the horses as well as serious injuries that necessitated their subsequent termination, though likely not so many as in the real charge where 335 horses were killed in action or had to afterward be destroyed.

56   In his autobiography Flynn grants these four films no more than a few lines.

57   Occasion for the fracas was Flynn's having been an hour late for their anniversary party. "It wasn't our wedding anniversary," wrote Flynn, "but it was the anniversary of the beginning of our romance. That was far more important in her logical French reasoning than a date on an Arizona wedding license." (*Wicked,* 205)

58   Flynn's character dies in *The Charge of the Light Brigade.*

59   *Cosmopolitan* had a circulation of 1,700,000 in the 1930s. During the period when it serialized Flynn's novel, the magazine was still specializing in fiction and not yet catering to a specifically female market.

60   This urge would raise its head again during the Second World War and once more in the course of the Cuban Revolution.

61   I don't think too much should be made of this but it underscores how Erben, like Flynn, could always be found where the action was.

62   Errol's second wife Nora Eddington said he confided to her that he had once caught Lili and Margaret Lindsay, a second-string Warners actress with whom Flynn appeared in two pictures, *in flagrante*. Lili was most assuredly bisexual. See Meyers, *Inherited Risk*, 111-112.

63   8152 Sunset Boulevard, at its eastern end, Flynn and Damita with adjoining abodes. The Garden of Allah had Moorish-style bungalows surrounding a pool in the shape of the Black Sea, its original owner having been the stage and screen actress Alla Nazimova who hailed from Yalta. The name "Garden of Allah" likely derived from Nazimova's pseudonymic first name "Alla" (her birth name was Miriam Edez Adelaida Leventon) and she having appeared in a play called *Garden of Allah*

in New York in 1913. In 1936 a film of the same name was made from the original book and starred Marlene Dietrich and Charles Boyer.

64   8946 Appian Way, in the Hollywood Hills.

65   601 North Linden Drive in Beverly Hills, a Tudor-style house that he and Niven rented from Rosalind Russell for the next two years.

66   These pictures, eight in number, are published in Fegerl, *A Friendship of Two Adventurers*. Erben seems to have been an accomplished photographer—though having Flynn in your shot would make any photographer look good.

67   Errol might not have been completely innocent in this fabrication, if only wishing to shake up Jack Warner and Lili (as well as discomfit Mike Curtiz when he returned from the dead) and this lie cushioned "with a fall-back claim that Flynn wasn't responsible for the unfounded story," in the words of Flynn expert Robert Florczak. Our brave correspondent may not even have been struck on the head by falling plaster, perhaps that too an invention, since there is no mention of it in the journal he was keeping at the time.

68   Erben joined the British Red Cross and worked on the Republican side as a field surgeon, possibly staying on a month longer after Flynn had already left Spain.

69   He made things easy for the Gestapo by obtaining the names and addresses of these family members—perhaps cajoled from those Germans serving the Loyalist forces with the promise to inform their families as to how they were faring in Iberia. Erben also took pictures of Loyalist gun installations and Fascist military objectives in Republican territory, some 2,500 pictures total, his camera shutter ceaselessly clicking.

70   See McNulty, *The Life and Career*, 54; and Thomas, *The Spy Who Never Was*, 91. Flynn's Spanish diary is surely sincere in every regard since it was to serve as material for the articles he wished to write upon his return; though he later only published a single piece entitled "What Really Happened to Me in Spain" with *Photoplay* in July 1937, where he mainly elaborates on his head wound.

71   See endnote 14 of Canto III. What I should like to add here is that Charles Higham in his *Errol Flynn: The Untold Story*, which is apparently still being read and believed by uninitiates, attempts to prove that Flynn was a Nazi spy by deliberately falsifying three FBI documents where Flynn and Erben are mentioned and—through crafty changes in wording that Higham terms "slightly condensed" versions—Flynn is implicated in Erben's spying for the Nazis in Spain. This is character assassination in its lowest form. Erben himself, still alive and residing in Vienna at the time of the book's release, called the spying claims "utterly preposterous," and the FBI exonerated Flynn as well. See William Donati's "The Flynn Controversy" in the appendix to his and Buster Wiles' *My Days with Errol Flynn*.

Canto V: *Apotheosis* (1937-1942)

72   The author having grown up in this part of the San Fernando Valley, he should know. The Errol Flynn connection to Reseda is the song "Errol Flynn" written by Amanda McBroom in which she refers to it as the town where she lives with a poster on the wall of Errol Flynn and her actor-father David Bruce, who appeared in two or three pictures with Flynn, and how proud she was of her father despite his low billing. It's a touching song, with a fine melody and nicely unadorned lyrics, and the miracle it performs is that she can mention Errol Flynn and Reseda in almost the same breath and there's no emotional disjuncture. (Last I looked there were versions of it by both McBroom and Barbara Cook to be heard on YouTube.)

73   Witness the recent version by Ridley Scott and Russell Crowe, two of the film industry's most self-serious artists. They have a kind of Midas touch manqué—the moment they get their hands on something it turns leaden.

74   Pyle's illustrated novel *The Merry Adventures of Robin Hood* first appeared in 1883 and has never been out of print. The lyric tone is set from the start: "It was at the dawn of day in the merry Maytime, when hedgerows are green and flowers bedeck the meadows . . ."

75   Through one of their music publishing firms. The opera premiered in Chicago in 1890 and opened in New York in 1900.

76   The most conspicuous of these being the stunt where he flew down a thirty-foot curtain to escape the clutches of his foemen. Fairbanks Sr.'s version was originally titled *Douglas Fairbanks in Robin Hood*. It was the first picture to have a Hollywood premiere, at Grauman's Egyptian Theatre on 18 October 1922.

77   These gold flecks are not really captured by the camera, particularly in black-and-white pictures, but I would argue that they are like subliminal frames inserted into a length of film—you don't consciously see but rather sense them. An unprovable conjecture, of course, but something has to explain that preternatural sparkle in Flynn's eyes.

78   Ira Grossel was the original name of Jeff Chandler, popular he-man star of the 1950s; Spangler Arlington Brugh was Robert Taylor's given name; and Archibald Leach was of course Cary Grant.

79   *The Adventures of Robin Hood* was one of the first films to use the three-color Technicolor process, the splashy hues allowing the forest scenes and medieval costumes and pageantry to blossom forth like a springtime welter of flowers. Fairbanks' first talkie was *The Taming of the Shrew* (1929) where he appeared with wife Mary Pickford. He starred in a few more sound films but none were successful with audiences. He didn't have a *terrible* speaking voice, but it was high-pitched and nasal and had no music in it.

80   Elinor Glyn's *It* appeared in 1927 and Clara Bow starred in the selfsame film based on Glyn's novella. Henceforth she was dubbed the "It Girl." In her review of the book for *The New Yorker*, Dorothy Parker wrote:

"It, hell; she had Those." This remark might have also applied to Bow, whose physical assets were a large part of her appeal.

81   On occasion of the New York World's Fair at high noon on 23 September 1938 (the precise moment of the Autumnal Equinox) the capsule was buried fifty feet below Flushing Meadows. It was filled with small everyday items—a fountain pen, a pack of Camel cigarettes, a kewpie doll, a dollar in change, a dictionary, a Sears Roebuck catalogue—and all selected on the basis of their potential for chronicling American life in the twentieth century. There is no greater testament to Flynn's status as a household name in the late 1930s than the fact that his *Life*-cover issue was included in this cache for the ages.

82   See David Niven, *Bring on the Empty Horses* (London 1975) 112. This memoir is a superbly entertaining and psychologically insightful account, mostly accurate, of Niven's Hollywood years. His chapter "Errol" is the best capsule portrait of Flynn that I have ever read, seizing the man better than entire books do.

83   Flynn had been preoccupied with what eventually became Mulholland Farm ever since 1935 when he was still living at Appian Way with Lili. He put a downpayment on the acreage in May 1936, and for the next several years the landscaping, planting and construction would absorb his free hours. Apart from the spectacular view it afforded of the San Fernando Valley and San Gabriel Mountains, this parcel of mesquite and chapparal lay adjacent to where they signed the Treaty of Cahuenga (1847) which had resulted in Los Angeles being ceded by the Mexicans to the Americans—rather apt, since Flynn himself had now taken the town by storm. And it should be noted that no matter how casual Flynn seemed about the whole Hollywood movie business, no matter his claim to not give a damn and his pretended willingness to chuck it all and go back to the life of a drifting bum, his early and substantial investment in the Mulholland property indicates that he was dead serious about making a success of this latest venture—and for once staying put.

84   Here again the connection with Byron, who had a fondness for fauna. In addition to the horses, dogs, cats, monkeys, peacocks, geese and guinea hens that Flynn likewise owned, in the course of his life Byron kept a fox, parrot, eagle, crow, falcon, heron, crocodile, badger and a bear—this latter while a student at Trinity College, Cambridge, supposedly out of resentment for the rules prohibiting pet dogs on the premises.

85   Sundays was also the day for tennis matches, and it wasn't just Hollywood types who were the guests but tennis greats Bill Tilden, Fred Perry, Pancho Segura and Pancho Gonzales. It's small wonder that Flynn was such an outstanding player if he always honed his game against the world's best.

86   The jealous and abusive Mike Curtiz called Errol "a beautiful puppet"—an opinion that could only have been shared by those who didn't know Flynn personally.

87   Flynn dedicated his second novel *Showdown* (1946) to Decker who had similarities with Flynn's other influential friend Hermann F. Erben.

Not only born in central Europe (Berlin) and a substantially older Scorpio (8 November 1895), Decker's personality seems to have also been that interesting mixture of sophisticate and scoundrel.

88   Rachmaninoff lived in Beverly Hills from 1942 to his death the next year in 1943. Although Flynn enjoyed going to clubs, he pretended to hate contemporary popular music, calling it "the offal of civilization . . . the excrement of idiots." More specifically he termed the swing music of his day "unearthly, hideous, cacophonic." For an intimate and revealing look at Flynn in his self-assigned role as Master of Mulholland, see the memoir of his second wife Nora Eddington Flynn Haymes as told to Cy Rice, *Errol and Me* (New York 1960).

89   This Marie "prepared him his favorite foods, reportedly roast chicken, cold cracked lobster in the summer, the finest cuts of steak, and omelets, fresh fruit and tea in the morning." (McNulty, *The Life and Career,* 132) According to Nora Flynn: "He enjoyed all sea foods—anything that swam, and adored French cooking. Cooking was just cooking to me before I met him. Now cooking became important—a culinary art—to be admired like a painting. He hated 'meat-and-potato men' and considered it bourgeois. 'They eat too rapidly in this country,' he said, and went on, 'Americans think it necessary to have music with their meals. Music can ruin the digestive tract. A chef in this land of ours is anybody who's a fry cook and has a high white hat.' If he ate roast beef it had to be seasoned a certain way and always sliced very thin; the only way he enjoyed it was rare. He knew all the sauces from Escoffier down to chili, and once when he saw me using the latter he wrinkled his nose in disgust and claimed that I had 'turned the plate into a bloody battlefield.' He was a wine connoisseur and had different kinds with each course . . . . For breakfast he refused to eat bacon and eggs. 'Two eggs staring up at me from a plate remind me of a basset hound's eyes after a hangover,' he said. He did like eggs, however, with certain sausage or as Spanish, cheese, or mushroom omelets. Kippers were a favorite. His appetite in the mornings was positively wolfish, sharpened by a swim before breakfast. Errol was a chain-smoker and a glass-carrier. Once he started drinking he never had two free hands. A glass was as common to his hand as a ring to the finger." (Nora Eddington Flynn Haymes, *Errol and Me*, 70-71)

90   The greatest archer of his day, Hill won 196 straight field-archery tournaments and was then forced to retire because no one was willing to face him and endure certain defeat. He also played Captain of Archers in *The Adventures of Robin Hood*. Flynn later wrote the foreword to Hill's *Wild Adventure* (1954) where he remarked that, "The charging wild boar calls to some deep inner response within us both."

91   Two and a half years after Errol's death, in an article published in Hobart's *Saturday Evening Express* (21 April 1962) his father tried to set the record straight about his son. He mostly deplored the fact that Errol's good name had been brought into disrepute through his autobiography, which Theodore Flynn felt was unnecessarily scandalous—i.e. casting Errol in a "wicked" light. He ascribed the book's sensationalist tone to the circumstance that Errol "needed publicity badly at that time" and that his great weakness was in fact an exaggerated desire for such, Professor Flynn adding: "Another of his weaknesses was that he was

courteous to women, no matter what they were . . . . Women would never leave him alone. The way they pestered him was enough to make you lose all your faith in womanhood. I know, I have stayed with him many times. Women would swim out to his yacht naked—dreadful, embarrassing, and insolent." As cited in Moore, *The Young Errol*, 140-141.

92   A Flynn-like character named Shamus O'Thames leads an antic cast of Hollywood characters up New Guinea's spooky Sepik River. Flynn biographer Charles Higham claimed to have read the now lost typescript of the novel and he reported that there were brutal caricatures of director Michael Curtiz, studio boss Jack Warner and Flynn's first wife Lili Damita. These were chopped from *Showdown* because they were considered libelous but were then recycled into *My Wicked, Wicked Ways*. After the memoir's appearance there were cries of protest and the libelous material was expunged in paperback editions. Now that all three are dead, you can read Flynn's warts-and-all version of them once again in more recent editions of *Wicked*.

93   Flynn supervised the building of both his house near the Laloki River and that off Mulholland Drive, and he uses similar language in describing them. For example the New Guinea lodge "went up swiftly . . . a place roomy enough for me to move about in"; the Mulholland house "went up fast, like the sails of a boat . . . and there was plenty of room." See *Wicked*, 102, 274.

94   People like Hedy Lamarr report such revels as "a nude water ballet done with multi-colored lights," and Veronica Lake wrote of a Flynn party in which there was "the usual evening swim with a few of the guests nude. Errol had stocked the house with an assortment of young and luscious starlets and they were available for any of his male guests who felt a sudden urge. It was all typical Errol Flynn; his clippings were not exaggerated." See McNulty, *The Life and Career*, 311-312.

95   The court judgment against Erben was that he had gained his U.S. citizenship under false pretenses, namely with untrue declarations that he had lived in the country continuously for five years before submitting his petition for citizenship (see Canto III, stanzas 36-38, endnote 14); it had nothing to do with espionage—in which Erben had not been engaged since start of the war anyway. But after saying goodbye to Flynn, Erben slipped across the Mexican border in November 1940 and shortly thereafter went calling on the German consul in Mexico City, Baron von Wallenberg, who offered him a salaried job with the *Abwehr*, the German military intelligence organization, an offer which Erben accepted. He was first shipped to Japan then transferred to Shanghai where he remained for the rest of the war and was instructed by his German superiors to pose as an American communist and report back on British and American movements. Just how helpful he was to the German cause and how harmful to the Allies is hard to say, but he seems to have been dropped by the Germans in 1943 and was then interned by the Japanese for whom he likely turned informant. When the Americans entered Shanghai in August 1945 he told them that he had become a German spy so as to secretly aid the American cause as a double agent—his aid so secret that U.S. intelligence had no knowledge of it—and he now spilled all he knew about German and Japanese activities during the war as well as their

espionage networks, which gave him a reprieve and job as doctor for the U.S. Army in early 1946. But a year later he was arrested once more due to complaints of the Chinese government regarding his wartime espionage; and Erben's having posed as a communist did him no good either. He was shipped to the U.S. Army Repatriation Center in Ludwigsburg, Germany, where he was interrogated over a period of months and then finally released in 1948. As Tony Thomas writes: "Trying to nail Hermann Erben with specific charges was like trying to swat a fruit fly." During these years he and Flynn had sporadic epistolary contact. Erben would then continue to travel about as a doctor in the Middle East, the Far East and the South Pacific, finally returning in 1979 to his native Vienna where he would die six years later at the age of 87 in a musty apartment filled with trunks and suitcases and cardboard boxes stacked to the ceiling with materials collected in a long, peripatetic and highly idiosyncratic not to say amoral life. See Thomas, *The Spy Who Never Was*, 113-119; and William Donati's appendix to Buster Wiles' *My Days with Errol Flynn*, "The Flynn Controversy," where he describes a series of interviews he conducted with Hermann Erben in Vienna.

96   Flynn was likely paraphrasing the first line of Robert Herrick's 1648 poem *To the Virgins, to Make Much of Time*: "Gather ye rosebuds while ye may, / Old time is still a-flying: / And this same flower that smiles to-day / To-morrow will be dying."

97   This term is bandied about so frequently that it needs to be defined. A "classic" for me is any film that epitomizes and simultaneously exhausts the form. In my estimation there has never been a better WWI-flyer film than Flynn's *The Dawn Patrol* (1938), never a better pirate movie than his *The Sea Hawk* (1940), and if you believe ex-heavyweight champ Mike Tyson then *Gentleman Jim Corbett* (1942) is the best boxing film ever. Even if you don't believe him, it's the most exuberant and winsome one that you're bound to run across.

98   Olivia de Havilland and Patric Knowles rounded out the foursome. Showing there wasn't anything he couldn't do, Mike Curtiz was at the directorial helm.

99   For *Jezebel* (1938), her first Oscar coming for *Dangerous* (1935).

100   To director Vincent Sherman on the set of their picture *Adventures of Don Juan* (1948).

101   This was probably one of the reasons he felt compelled to leave England and never return, as homosexuality was still a crime that could be punished with death; and the kind of boys he liked were more readily available outside of Great Britain—namely Mediterranean types.

102   In a scene in *Dodge City,* after Olivia de Havilland rebukes Flynn's character, he says: "Miss Abbey has a more biting tongue than my mother ever had." This piece of dialogue seems like a Flynn interpolation, enjoying the thought of Marelle's reaction when she eventually saw the film.

103   But alas the whole film, as Robert Matzen puts it, "sinks of its own considerable weight." Matzen details how the movie was a victim of

star tantrums, studio politics and a farrago of other problems, not least of which were a half-baked subplot and an awful title. (Matzen, *Errol & Olivia*, 110-129) In *Wicked* Flynn lavishes much ink on his competition with Bette Davis on the set of *Elizabeth and Essex*—a competition that was not good-natured. Noteworthy is the story he tells of his jaw going out after a rehearsal where she gave him "that dainty little hand, laden with about a pound of costume jewelry, right across the ear"—and he then preparing to deck her if she repeated the procedure in the next rehearsal, which she didn't, seeing the look in his eyes, instead delivering herself of a stage-slap that "came just delicately to the side of my nose, missing by a fraction of an inch. I don't even believe she touched me, but I could feel the wind go by my face, and it looked technically perfect." This anecdote—in its seven-page entirety—is a gem of the raconteur art and reveals what it must have been like to hear Flynn tell tales in a bar. For the Bette Davis passages, see *Wicked*, 258-265.

104   Bogart was playing a half-breed outlaw and that's how his accent sounded—half faux-Mexican and half Rick Blaine.

105   Flynn's Geoffrey Thorpe was likely modeled on Sir Francis Drake. The whole film was an object lesson to America that she should enter the Second World War on the side of England. It was filmed in 1940 during the Battle of Britain, and the parallels between the megalomaniac King Philip II and the tyrannical Adolf are pretty clear. Substitute the Luftwaffe for the Spanish Armada and you've got a perfect historical allegory—for instance the English ships are powered by the free-roaming wind while the Spanish vessels resort to chained galley slaves. In terms of sheer male beauty, Flynn is at his peak in this film; Korngold's music is glorious, with stirring fanfares and a dulcet love theme; and Curtiz's pacing and energy permeate the whole. Flynn, Curtiz, Korngold—the only thing missing from this winning combination is Olivia de Havilland. Brenda Marshall as Flynn's leading lady is merely passable. She certainly looks the part of a Spanish princess, with her dark hair and eyes, but her face falls apart when she starts to cry and there isn't the chemistry with Flynn that de Havilland had—although Marshall and Flynn did play one sublime scene together, in a rose garden, accompanied by Korngold's love theme. As in all those Warner Brothers films, you have a stellar cast: Claude Rains exuding oleaginous evil, Donald Crisp as the stalwart adviser, Gilbert Roland looking good as the Spanish captain. But stealing the show is Flora Robson as Queen Elizabeth—in which role she is far more charming, natural and believable than Bette Davis' affected star turn with Flynn the previous year. Everyone speaks of Davis and Blanchett and Dench as Elizabeth—but what about Robson, the best of the lot?

106   Logically the Wilshire Warner was down on Wilshire Boulevard; and the Hollywood Warner, which was Warner Brothers' flagship theater, was on Hollywood Boulevard.

107   Granted my father hadn't been on the scene when Douglas Fairbanks Sr. was at his peak, as he was born in 1928.

108   The contract also provided for nine pictures in the next three years at $90,000 per film; Flynn's new contract was signed in May 1942, the same month that his divorce was finalized.

356

109   It appears that Errol and Lili attempted every permutation in the book to reach some kind of modus vivendi. They tried staying together while living apart; sharing a house while calling it quits; remaining a couple but taking a breather from each other; no longer a pair but still having sex; having no sex but still somehow in love. It was a case of two antagonistic personalities perversely finding their gyroscopic center in the other.

110   After a short period of playing undistinguished swashbuckler roles in Europe in the early 1960s, Sean Flynn chucked it all for Vietnam to perform with valor and distinction as a war photographer. In 1970 he went missing and presumed dead in Cambodia after a suicidal foray into enemy territory. See Meyers, *Inherited Risk*.

111   In *Wicked* Flynn implied that Lili had tricked him. After her announcement of the pregnancy, he has her saying: "Fleen, you think you've screwed every dame in Hollywood, but now I've screwed you, my friend. You will have a child!" (p. 277)

112   They also have Marie Joseph Eugène Sue who wrote the novel *Mathilde* (1841) where a form of this French proverb first saw print: "la vengeance se mange très-bien froide." Choderlos de Laclos wrote the book that is often credited with this phrase, *Les liaisons dangereuses* (1782), but where it never actually appears; and Alexandre Dumas, père, was author of the greatest novel of calculated comeuppance ever penned, *Le Comte de Monte-Cristo* (1844-45).

113   *The Thief of Baghdad* (1924).

114   Notably in *The Birth of a Nation* (1915) playing John Wilkes Booth. Walsh served his film apprenticeship under D. W. Griffith, also functioning as assistant director and editor on that movie.

115   Bette Davis had tried and failed to buck the contract system in 1936. Her complaint was that she didn't care for the second-rate scripts she was being sent, and it was similar discontent which impelled Olivia de Havilland to bring suit against Warner Brothers. She'd had six suspensions for rejecting scripts, and since these suspensions kept being added to her standard seven-year contract, it became a vicious circle—particularly so since her unloved younger sister, Joan Fontaine, was starring opposite such distinguished actors as Laurence Olivier in *Rebecca* (1941), Cary Grant in *Suspicion* (1941) for which Fontaine won an Academy Award, and Orson Welles in *Jane Eyre* (1944). De Havilland's suit made the case that the practice of suspending actors and adding the time to their contracts was in fact illegal, contravening an old California law against peonage. While her case dragged through the courts, Jack Warner made sure she wouldn't get work at other studios, Warner Brothers retaining the rights to her services until the case was finally settled, which it was by the California Court of Appeal in 1944, ruling that de Havilland was not compelled to perform services beyond seven years from the date at which her contract started. The case was enshrined in state law (Labor Code Section 2855) and shifted negotiating power from the studios to the artistic talent and their agents. Now released from her Warners contract, de Havilland quickly made up for lost time, receiving her first Academy Award in 1946 for Paramount's *To Each His Own*, receiving

an Oscar nomination and the New York Film Critics Award in 1948 for Twentieth Century-Fox's *The Snake Pit*, and winning both the New York Film Critics Award and the Academy Award in 1949 for Paramount's *The Heiress* with Montgomery Clift. Regarding the studios' penchant for putting talented actors into second-rate vehicles, Otto Friedrich writes: "There were various explanations for this Hollywood tradition of miscasting. One was that the studios had to produce a good deal of fodder to satisfy their theater chains; another was that they believed a star could carry an inferior film; another was that they sometimes assigned a star to a bad script as a form of discipline; and yet another was that they didn't know the difference between good and bad, and didn't much care . . . . Still, holdouts and suspensions were more of a problem at Warners than anywhere else. They were relatively rare at MGM and almost unknown at Paramount. Perhaps Warners' problem lay in Jack Warner's fondness for typecasting, or perhaps simply in the feistiness of his repeatedly suspended stars—Bette Davis, Errol Flynn, Jimmy Cagney, Humphrey Bogart, John Garfield." See Friedrich's splendid *City of Nets: A Portrait of Hollywood in the 1940s* (London 1986) 194-195.

116   There was apparently some dust-up on *Santa Fe Trail* (1940), she later recalling that Flynn "had taken a passionate dislike for me. I don't know why. He refused to look at me during any of our scenes together. He stared at my forehead instead or pulled any number of tricks to upstage me. It was infuriating." For this quote see Meyers, *Inherited Risk*, 123; and for further discussion of Errol's scene-stealing during this picture, see Matzen, *Errol & Olivia,* 98-101.

117   I'll confine myself to stating that de Havilland herself has gone on record that she was in love with Flynn at various stages in their work together, which spanned seven years, and Errol was not one to leave a situation like that unexploited.

118   This was in May 1936 on the set of *The Charge of the Light Brigade*. It was either a rubber snake from the props department or a four-foot dead snake—accounts vary—but what is clear is that the panties weren't being worn by Olivia at the time.

119   *Desperate Journey* (1942) is the first film where Flynn's real nationality was disclosed, as it were, and this right from the opening scene, which ends with him striding off singing *Waltzing Matilda*.

120   John L. Sullivan himself was a friend of Walsh's family in New York when the young director (b. 1887) was growing up.

121   The real-life bout portrayed in the movie took place on a barge off the coast of Benicia, California, on 1 June 1889, Corbett winning the fight by KO in the twenty-seventh round.

Canto VI: *Errol's War* (1942-1945)

122   This according to Jeffrey Meyers' *Inherited Risk*, 80. In *The Loves of Errol Flynn* (Derby, Connecticut 1962) Tedd Thomey writes that the next day, after consulting police, Peggy and her mother left Los Angeles

but "before leaving, Mrs. Satterlee purchased a complete and very expensive new wardrobe for Peggy. Where did Mrs. Satterlee, who was not well off financially, get the money for that wardrobe? And why did she and Peggy suddenly drop out of sight? Even the jury in Superior Court discovered that the answers to those questions were extremely elusive." (pp. 32-33) An issue was made of this by Flynn's defense attorney during his trial but it was finally disallowed by the judge. It should also perhaps be mentioned that the fateful outing on the *Sirocco,* which included diverse crew members and Flynn's stunt-double Buster Wiles, was likewise occasion for Peter Stackpole—the fellow who took the photograph of Flynn for the cover of *Life* in 1938—to obtain some more shots for the magazine. (For one of Stackpole's photos see the back cover of this book.) Peggy Satterlee, together with one or two other girls, was brought along as window dressing, but it wasn't as if Peggy's assenting to the trip was tacit assent for Flynn to bed her; this wasn't the context at all—and presumably not even the subtext.

123   In any event it was a tangled skein. Adding to the complexity and behind-the-scenes machinations, Flynn claimed to have received a phone call the evening of his clearance by the grand jury, a tough-guy voice at the other end telling him he'd gotten lucky and that if he knew what was good for him he'd inform Jack Warner that "Joe" had called and relay to Warner that he should drop $10,000 at the corner of Melrose and La Cienega that night or the next. Flynn asked him if he wanted it in nickels or dimes. The day after the second night with no money paid, the DA's office brought in Peggy Satterlee and declared they were going ahead with the case. (*Wicked*, 317-318)

124   On the witness stand Lynne Boyer, a singer who accompanied Hansen to the party, said she went upstairs looking for a telephone and knocked on the locked bedroom door where Flynn and Hansen were sequestered, Flynn giving some flip answer, and then she heard a giggle which Boyer identified as Betty Hansen's. (I made free with the term "bedsprings" in stanza 27 of Canto VI, because if you're a willing female in a locked bedroom with Errol Flynn, you're probably not having a casual chat in the vertical position.) Boyer also testified that in bidding farewell—both Flynn and Hansen now having exited the bedroom—Flynn kissed Hansen "on the lips." Chi-Chi Toupes, a dancer who'd also been present, confirmed the kiss and added that Flynn had promised he would phone Hansen the next day— which sounds precisely like the line you'd feed a girl after determining that your brief interlude would have no reprise. With no next-day call forthcoming, Hansen said that she later got Flynn's private number from Freddie McEvoy (fellow Australian playboy whose Bel Air house had been the scene of the alleged rape) simply by calling and asking for it. McEvoy on the witness stand, sweating profusely, professed ignorance of any sexual encounter between Flynn and Hansen, but it seems unlikely that he would have relinquished Flynn's private number to Hansen had he not been aware of some intimacy between the two. He might also have been involved in some monkey business with regard to the lock on the door of the room where Hansen said Flynn bedded her. In *Wicked* Flynn wrote: "Betty Hansen said I had locked the door before getting undressed. Giesler set out to prove that there was no lock on this door, or that it wouldn't work. The prosecution sent sleuths around and they found evidence of steel scrapings on the floor, proving somebody had tampered with the lock. Actually I am pretty sure somebody had. It was none of my doing. But it caused a great outcry when

they brought in these steel scrapings and swore they found them under this supposed lock that wouldn't lock. That was a dark day. It looked as if my legal help had somebody go out there and frame this thing." (pp. 331-332)

125 Among Giesler's other famous clients were director Busby Berkely (manslaughter), producer Walter Wanger (murder), Robert Mitchum (marijuana possession), Lana Turner's daughter Cheryl Crane (murder), Bugsy Siegel (murder) and Charlie Chaplin (violation of the Mann Act), all of whom he exonerated or for whom he managed a much reduced sentence. He also successfully defended DA Fitts in a trial relating to bribes that he allegedly took to drop the statutory rape charge against a wealthy real-estate promoter. Raymond Chandler's fictional L.A. of the 1930s and 1940s, where venality and moral corruption run rampant, had nothing on the real place.

126 Giesler's insinuation was that Joseph Kennedy, father of the future U.S. president and himself owner of RKO Studios at the time, was attempting to gain control over film distribution and had framed Pantages in revenge for not accepting Kennedy's offer to buy his profitable theater chain. Kennedy had tendered $8 million, which elicited no response from Pantages, then he stopped showing his movies in Pantages' theaters, and when that failed to induce the theater mogul to sell, Kennedy used seventeen-year-old Eunice Pringle (ergo this likewise a "statutory" rape charge) to set him up. With Pantages' reputation in tatters due to the rape trial, Kennedy once more offered to buy his theater chain but this time for $3.5 million, less than half his original offer. Pantages relented. Whether or not one believes that Kennedy was pulling strings behind the scene, the whole series of surface events does look suspicious. Giesler appealed the first trial's guilty verdict and Pantages was found innocent by the California Supreme Court in a second trial that hung on the admissibility of evidence with regard to Eunice Pringle's less than chaste private life. This was the first time that the morals of a minor had some bearing on deciding a case of statutory rape. In more recent years the state courts have been reluctant to admit evidence as to the past sexual behavior of alleged rape victims, and in 1978 such evidence was completely barred from federal courts by the U.S. Congress (Federal Rules of Evidence 412).

127 This again sounds like classic Flynn, something that the girl—at least on her own—would have been hard pressed to devise from whole cloth.

128 The first time was when she'd bedded down for the night and he entered her cabin and joined her in the sack. In her testimony regarding this first instance of rape, Peggy Satterlee said she told Flynn to stop but did not resist physically, while Betty Hansen seems not to have resisted at all.

129 Flynn said that Satterlee's "upholstery was sensational" (*Wicked*, 325) and Hansen testified that during their 30-50 minute sex session—admirable stamina on the part of our stud—"He said I had a nice pair of breasts." Giesler: "Did he say anything else?" Hansen: "He said I had a nice fanny." Hence not bad upholstery in her case either, and all this by way of saying that neither Hansen nor Satterlee were what you would call late-bloomers when it came to *womanly* contours.

130   Peggy Satterlee testified that when she first boarded the *Sirocco* Flynn began calling her "J.B." ("Jail Bait") and "S.Q.Q." ("San Quentin Quail"). Later in his own testimony Flynn denied any such thing. But Satterlee's assertions ring true. In *Bring on the Empty Horses* David Niven describes Flynn parking his car on Sunset Boulevard opposite Hollywood High when the school was getting out so as to show Niven "the best looking girls in L.A." Before a cop finally told them to scram, they had gotten an eyeful, Flynn shaking his head regretfully: "'Jail bait,' he said, 'San Quentin Quail, what a waste.'" (p. 123) This was in the 1930s and if Flynn's future behavior is any guide then his regret was not so much that these girls were hands-off as it was for the risks you ran in trying to get your own hands *on* them. But one thing is certain—a comment like this meant he knew the difference between legal and underage sex.

131   Post-trial the jury member Nellie S. Minear said: "We knew Flynn was not guilty all the time, but we didn't want to come out too soon because we wondered what the public might think if we did." (McNulty, *The Life and Career*, 162) This was doing no kindness to Flynn, who probably aged a comparable number of months in those 24 hours.

132   Niven is again witness for the prosecution insofar as he once arranged to play a practical joke on Flynn in revenge for a nasty prank his friend had perpetrated. (Flynn departed with his speedboat and abandoned Niven after towing him on water skis half a mile out to sea; Niven claims to have swum back to shore with a shark on his trail for much of the way.) It was an elaborately scripted gag but the upshot for our purposes was that Flynn, when he thought no one was looking, forced his attentions on "a real stunner of seventeen." (Niven, *Bring on the Empty Horses*, 118-120)

133   The full quote (p. 315): "If you meet a young lady who, in fact, invites herself for a trip on your yacht [untrue: Flynn likely extended the invitation—and if not he personally then it was Peter Stackpole the photographer or stuntman Buster Wiles who was Flynn's housemate and sometime procurer of women for the star; Peggy did not initiate things]—'I'd love to cru,' she said, in the vernacular unknown to yachtsmen—knowing in advance full well *what the risks are* [my italics], who the hell asks her for her birth certificate, especially when she is built like Venus? And if afterward she tells you she has had the most wonderful time in her life, *who has been hurt?* [my italics] What is all the fuss about? Why international headlines? Who approaches a prospective sweetheart by asking her to whip out her birth certificate, or driver's license, or show a letter from her mother? Naturally I had no knowledge of how old she was [very likely untrue: Flynn knew her sister, through whom contact with Peggy was made, and if he called her "Jail Bait" and "S.Q.Q." then he was well aware of her precarious age], nor did I know the difference between rape and statutory rape [also untrue if David Niven's anecdote (see endnote 130) is to be believed]."

134   Two small ironies to finish off: With a week to go in Flynn's rape trial the man behind it all, DA John Dockweiler, who had sought to destroy Flynn's life, dropped dead of a heart attack; and the next year 1944 the father of the alleged molestee, Peggy Satterlee, pled guilty to being a child molester.

135   In fact Flynn's sitting out the war was no clear-cut deal; that is, he was 4-F in America, but since he was still a subject of the British crown in February 1942, when he attempted to enlist in the U.S. military, theoretically he might have tried to join the British forces. He had taken out U.S. citizenship in late 1938 or early 1939, perhaps owing to problems with the U.S. government engendered by purchase of his yacht *Sirocco*. According to Thomas McNulty (*The Life and Career*, 90): "The *Sirocco* came under scrutiny by the federal government because it exceeded the maximum length allowed under alien ownership. To settle the matter, Flynn negotiated an agreement where he was allowed to sell the vessel to a corporation of which he was a stockholder. Lili Damita and Flynn's business partner, Al Blum, also held stock in the corporation. Flynn filed for citizenship, a process that would take three years, at which time he would be able to purchase the *Sirocco* back from his stockholders. In the meantime, of course, Flynn could borrow the boat and use it for his pleasure." Flynn finally received his citizenship papers in August 1942. He likely felt no exceeding patriotic fervor for America and even less loyalty toward the British Empire, so his efforts to enlist in the U.S. armed forces is admirable; and his failure in joining the British forces (to which David Niven—a Sandhurst graduate who returned to England to serve when the war broke out in 1939—unchivalrously alludes) should not be held against him. Super-patriot John Wayne also didn't serve in the Second World War and he theoretically could have, being only 3-A (with a wife and four children) and not Flynn's prohibitory 4-F.

136   In terms of espionage, Flynn summarized his argument as follows: "[I]f I were to go there openly, as a Hollywood figure in an American Army uniform, I would be far less suspected of gathering information than the usual sort of agent. A Hollywood movie star, behaving innocuously, tritely like a Hollywood movie star, would not, I am sure, excite suspicion of the above kind of activity." Once more riding his father's coattails, but understandably so, Errol cited the fact that Theodore Flynn was the Dean of the Faculty of Science at Queen's University, Belfast, "and since he has made a life-long practice of disassociating himself with all forms of politics, the result is that he is persona grata, and, I might add, pretty highly regarded in Eire also. The Faculty of Trinity College, Dublin, has invited him to lecture there many times, so I think it will be apparent to you that when a Northern Irish professor is extended invitations of this sort he must not only be in good standing with intellectual circles but official as well—this is important to remember. And if before the war he was a prominent figure in Northern Ireland I think it can safely be said that he is now also a beloved one, since for these past two years he has been the head of the A.R.P. (Air Raid Precautions) for the entire North, and is generally credited with having secured for the unfortunates there a greater measure of war relief from England than they would otherwise have received." In adducing his own credentials, Flynn was more ironic: "Now quite apart from my father's situation there, perhaps you know that the Irish, both North and South, are great movie goers. When last there it was a constant source of astonishment to me that while Bridget O'Toole had only the foggiest notion whether the Panama Canal divides America or Africa, she did know without a shadow of a doubt that Clark Gable cherishes a marked antipathy for striped underwear and that Hedy Lamarr wears a false bust." (Letter from Flynn to Colonel William J. Dono-

van, 4 February 1942, as cited in Thomas, *The Spy Who Never Was*, 137-139) Flynn penned the missive just two days after being rejected by the U.S. military, so he wasted no time in seeking alternative ways of doing his part—however farfetched they might have seemed.

137   This line is uttered by Flight Lieutenant Flynn as he and his crew make their escape from Germany in a stolen bomber that is bound for England, he pronouncing "Australia" like an Aussie: Australyer. It's rather touching, as if reflective of some real feeling for his homeland, which hadn't been greatly evidenced hitherto and particularly during his early Hollywood years when he more or less went along with the fiction that he was an Irish national. Even more touching is the film *Montana*, from 1950, where he portrays an Australian sheepherder (an occupation with which he was somewhat familiar if *My Wicked, Wicked Ways* is to be believed) in the American Wild West. Again, right from the start, we are apprised that Flynn's figure is from Down Under. Responding to the question, "Where ya from?"—he replies: "Originally Australia, recently California." Cute. And later when his co-star Alexis Smith asks, "You said you came from Australia, didn't you?"—Flynn answers: "Yeah. Say, there's a lovely country," and this uttered a bit wistfully. It had been seventeen years since Flynn had seen that "lovely country" and he would never see it again.

138   In a letter dated 30 September 1942, Flynn reported "some great news, finally got the spot I wanted, war correspondent for I.N.S.," which stood for International News Service, the Hearst wire service. It was eleven days later on 11 October that two policeman arrived at Flynn's Mulholland Farm to notify him of the rape charge leveled by Betty Hansen.

139   The Hollywood Canteen was open to all Allied servicemen and servicewomen. Everything was free—admission, food, dancing, entertainment. The Canteen was operated and staffed exclusively by volunteers from Hollywood showbiz, and glamorous stars could frequently be seen waiting tables and performing other decidedly unglamorous KP-related tasks. From 1942 to 1945 almost three million uniformed individuals passed through the Canteen's doors. Not only were the stars' salaries for the film ($50,000 each) donated to the Canteen but ticket sales as well—though the studio still profited since the movie showed in Warner Brothers theaters. As Flynn put it, "they were getting a big chunk out of the bottom drawer—through distribution." (*Wicked*, 332)

140   The idea for the piece was also apparently Flynn's. See McNulty, *The Life and Career*, 175-176.

141   The prosecuting attorney Thomas Cochran had concluded his closing arguments with: "This man is a sex criminal! One of the lowest forms of criminal the courts ever come in contact with! A man who preys on young girls!" (Thomey, *The Loves of Errol Flynn*, 113) Flynn wrote: "I knew I would never escape this brand that was now upon me: that I would always be associated in the public mind with an internationally followed rape case . . . . I now knew that everything in my life dated from before that event and after it." (*Wicked*, 335, 349)

142   In October 1931 from his Laloki plantation he wrote Theodore Flynn that he had recently built a furnace and concrete firebox for cur-

ing tobacco: "This one is all right though and should still be here in two hundred years time, barring earthquakes. It is a depressing thought to consider that at the end of that period of time I shall most probably not be here to enjoy the fruits of this labor." (*Wicked*, 335)

143   This by Errol's own account, in an expression of humility vis-à-vis the old man. (Apparently *Who's Who* had rather snooty standards back then.) Later on in *Wicked*, in another revealing passage, Errol writes: "My father has not been Theodore Flynn, exactly, but a will-o'-the-wisp just beyond, whom I have chased and hunted to see him smile upon me, and I shall never find my true father, for the father I wanted to find was what I might become, but this shall never be, because inside of me there is a man of New Guinea, who had other things in mind for himself besides achieving phallic symbolism in human form." (p. 436)

144   The piece was entitled "Let's Hunt for Treasure" and appeared in the April 1939 issue of *Photoplay*. Here Flynn says that in treasure hunts the cache itself is secondary; what matters is beating the odds, or at least engaging in an extraordinary enterprise. In short, Flynn touts the virtues of the glorious failure, i.e. whatever you undertake just do it on a grand scale, which he summarizes as: "Right royal robes or sackcloth. One end or the other." The piece is reproduced in *From a Life of Adventure: The Writings of Errol Flynn*, ed. Tony Thomas (Seacaucus, New Jersey 1980) 191-198.

145   After a scoreless tie with Duke University in 1953.

146   Flynn made six pictures during the Second World War where he directly or indirectly defied the Axis powers—*Dive Bomber* (1941), *Desperate Journey* (1942), *Edge of Darkness* and *Northern Pursuit* (1943), *Uncertain Glory* (1944) and *Objective, Burma!* (1945).

147   Not only is Shamus O'Thames' external life similar to that of his creator—both captaining schooners, both managing copra plantations, both prospecting for gold, etc.—but there are large chunks and shards of Errol's real personality in the psychological makeup of O'Thames. Flynn speaks of Shamus' "desperate loneliness for his mother, his secret sense of guilt for never having loved her"; describes him, upon first landing in New Guinea, as, "Especially fitted for nothing but ready for anything"; tells of him having subsequently learned "a certain wisdom in the art of living eagerly, of sailing a ship to strange places and making a living at it, of how to appraise men, the kind of men who would be living in this kind of land, and, above all, the priceless lore of how to out-maneuver and control them"; speaks of O'Thames' boat the *Maski*, "which he had come to love as he was sure he would never love any woman," of the "strange two-sidedness of his nature, the oddly proportioned mixture of disciplined intellectuality with the sensuality," and of his having finally gotten a "bellyful of the South Seas. He was going . . . to London, where he would make out somehow, begin again, and find out what it was for which he was fitted"—to cite some of the more obvious overlaps.

148   The film was *Across the Pacific* (1942) and the way Huston tells it: "Actually, I was at the end of the picture. The story involved a Japanese plan to pull a 'Pearl Harbor' on the Panama Canal. Bogart had been cap-

tured by the Japanese—led by master spy Sydney Greenstreet—and was being held prisoner in a house near the Canal. I proceeded to make things as difficult as possible for my successor. I had Bogie tied to a chair, and installed about three times as many Japanese soldiers as were needed to keep him prisoner. There were guards at every window brandishing machine guns. I made it so that there was no way in God's green world that Bogart could logically escape. I shot the scene, then called Jack Warner and said, 'Jack, I'm on my way. I'm in the Army. Bogie will know how to get out.' They put Vincent Sherman on the picture. Warners wasn't about to go the expense of re-doing anything I had already shot, so it was up to Vince to figure out a way to get Bogie out of that house. His impossible solution was to have one of the Japanese soldiers in the room go berserk. Bogie escaped in the confusion, with the comment, 'I'm not easily trapped, you know!'" See John Huston, *An Open Book* (Boston 1994) 87-88.

149   Though Flynn was skilled enough to make a good showing in the 1927 New South Wales amateur boxing championship (Moore, *The Young Errol*, 30) his formal pugilistic experience had been largely confined to school competitions. Huston was a swashbuckling adventurer like Flynn and their lives were parallel in many ways—multiple wives, living in Europe, collecting art, possessing menageries (both had a pet monkey), a love of Mexico, an aversion to Hollywood, both of them authors of fascinating autobiographies as well as being extremely hard drinkers. But it was just as Huston's star was ascending that Flynn's began to dip. And in terms of real accomplishments, Huston probably had the edge. For instance both men designed their own houses but it was Huston who received kudos from Frank Lloyd Wright; both men wrote, but it was Huston who got his screenplays filmed and his prose published in *Esquire* and the prestigious *American Mercury*, while Flynn's contributions in this latter vein were generally relegated to the movie magazines; Flynn played cavalrymen in his films but Huston had an honorary commission with the Mexican cavalry in the 1920s; Flynn played up his Irish connection but Huston eventually lived there, at his St. Clerans manor home in Galway and riding to the hounds as a fox hunter. All in all it might be said that Huston out-Flynned Flynn.

150   Huston made three documentaries for the U.S. military: *Report from the Aleutians* (1943), *The Battle of San Pietro* (1944) and *Let There Be Light* (1945). All three unflinchingly show both the real heroism and appalling waste of battle.

151   Japanese-held Attu was some five-hundred miles from Adak, while Kiska, another island in enemy hands and the target of U.S. bombing, was 250 miles distant, which made Adak closer to the Japanese than any other U.S. territory. Flynn was in Alaska for six weeks in late 1943. He'd been nervous about his reception by the servicemen but then turned out to be a hit, making himself the butt of his jokes and lampooning his recent troubles with lawyers and young nubiles. Olivia de Havilland visited the Aleutians a few months after Flynn on another USO tour. As Robert Matzen cogently states: "The Aleutians became a fashionable place to go see the war without really seeing the war." (Matzen, *Errol & Olivia*, 182)

152   According to Huston, his precise words were: "That's a lie! Even if it weren't a lie, only a sonofabitch would repeat it." The verbal exchange

prior to these words, in lieu of any explicit Huston description, has been re-imagined by me. But forming my point of entry into trying to recapture their dialogue is the sentence: "Errol must have been spoiling for trouble, or maybe he sensed my mood and picked up on it, for he very quickly got around to saying something wretched about someone—a woman in whom I'd once been very interested and still regarded with deep affection." (*An Open Book*, 96-97) Interestingly, though Flynn wasn't shy about recounting his many dustups in *Wicked*, he doesn't even mention this Huston encounter—perhaps for the very reason that it touched on Olivia and cast himself in the role of cad. Their scrap took place on 29 April 1945 (Matzen, *Errol & Olivia*, 183).

Canto VII: *Descent from Olympus* (1945-1950)

153   Even during the rape-trial proceedings Flynn continued to play it fast and loose. For at least part of the time he had a beautiful 19-year-old named Blanca Rosa Welter stashed at his Mulholland retreat. He had met her in Mexico shortly before the rape charges were leveled, taking her back with him to Hollywood and promising to start her in the movie business. His good offices were apparently effective because it wasn't long till she landed both a contract with MGM and Tyrone Power as her husband, the marriage lasting from 1949-1956 and producing two children. Flynn paid to have her teeth fixed and also bestowed upon her the stage name "Linda Christian," the second part an allusion to his first film role as Fletcher Christian. Her stint in movies was unremarkable. Christian's best-known role was with Johnny Weismuller in 1948's *Tarzan and the Mermaids*—but not as Jane, played by Brenda Joyce, who had succeeded Maureen O'Sullivan in the role, so Linda didn't even make it to Jane. But Flynn had at least kept his promise to get her career started. And she could have marked the end of *his* career had the prosecution in his trial made anything of the fact that a sexy teenage mistress was keeping his bed warm. At one point Flynn's lawyer Jerry Giesler had Buster Wiles, Flynn's stuntman friend who lived at Mulholland Farm, go missing for awhile since Giesler feared that the prosecution might call Wiles to testify, who would then, short of perjuring himself, have to come clean about Blanca/Linda. She wasn't technically jailbait, but it wouldn't have looked very good. One entity that was fully aware of her existence was the FBI, which had been tapping Flynn's phone and recorded at least one of their conversations. See Meyers, *Inherited Risk*, 188-190.

154   See Eddington Flynn Haymes, *Errol and Me*: "I was beginning to care more and more for him. It wasn't love with any of the recognizable symptoms. It wasn't fascination. It wasn't hero worship. He was simply a wonderful guy plus the fact that he was an attractive man. You couldn't be around a man of his qualities very long without having a warm feeling for him, and often there was an exhilaration that sent me tingling—like I'd stepped into a cold-needle shower on a red-hot day." (p. 37) This type of description was par for the course in recounting the invigorating effect Flynn had on people of both sexes.

155   Nora wrote that, directly after the incident, "My feelings toward him were changed. I loathed him. It was as if a knife had cut away all the love. Home was where I wanted to go. And fast. I had to take a hot tub

bath first, though. My thighs were stiff and I was so sore inside." (Eddington Flynn Haymes, *Errol and Me*, 53)

156   The marital alliance with Haymes lasted from 1949-1953, then she went on to wed Beverly Hills businessman Richard Black. Mr. Haymes was married six times, Nora wedged between some pretty fair company in the glamorous figures of Joanne Dru (1941-1949) and Rita Hayworth (1953-1955).

157   The suicide attempts were with pills. All of this can be found in her frank and revealing book *Errol and Me*. After Flynn kneed her in the belly, she pregnant with their second child, Nora tells how she "sank to the floor, dizzy, hurt, gasping . . . . I started bleeding internally. For three days I stayed in bed." There seem to have been no complications with the pregnancy, however, and on 12 March 1947 Rory was born—"pretty, blond, and nine pounds." (pp. 107, 119)

158   See Eddington Flynn Haymes, *Errol and Me*, 66. He was even more cavalier outside the confines of Mulholland Farm. They eventually reached an agreement whereby he would refrain from coition with other women on his yacht, where Nora also spent much time, but when she once voiced suspicion that he had done precisely that, Errol quipped: "Not on this boat. I banged her on the one tied up next to us." Nora's reaction: "I didn't know whether to laugh, cry, or murder him." (*Errol and Me*, 96) On such occasions she tended to laugh, or try to, good sport that she was, and being in love with him of course.

159   Flynn built at Mulholland Farm a nursery-annex where Nora and daughters Deirdre and newborn Rory moved in, by which time both Nora's sense of humor and her love for Errol were fading fast. Well before her divorce from him she moved out again, taking Deirdre with her but Rory staying at Mulholland Farm and minded by Nora's step-mother Marge, who Flynn had installed as his housekeeper some years before.

160   Flynn wrote in *Wicked*: "It was growing on me that I had had a hard time with ladies—to employ the term in a liberal sense—all my life. There had been no consolation from or with my mother. Lili had nearly destroyed me. Two women, pawns in a big political game, had been used to try to destroy me. Women I never knew accused me of siring their children. I was candidly disillusioned with the opposite sex, much as I needed the female of our species, biologically speaking." (pp. 346-347)

161   Flynn was aware of this fact. As he was to write: "Candidly, life with the Eddingtons, Nora and her stepmother, provided no pattern for the human race on which to model itself in any effort toward fashioning the perfect home." (*Wicked*, 345)

162   The novel evidently went through several editions, but Flynn's feeling was that he had failed to make any real impression on the literary world—which was right—the novel being competent but undistinguished. This has to do with the language, which is conventionally "literary," as well as the attitude, which is high-romantic, and the plot is fairly contrived. I rate *Beam Ends* the far better work because it's not as ambitious as *Showdown*. In trying to compose a NOVEL, i.e. writ large, Flynn tight-

ens up. The semi-autobiographical *Beam Ends*, on the other hand, is a breezy picaresque romp and more accurately reflects Flynn's personality with all its raffish charm.

163   Flynn to Stephen Longstreet (co-writer on Flynn's film *Silver River*): "Hell, it's inelegant, a life here in fast motion . . . . It's unbearable, the sentimentality here, combined with the greasy hunt for the big dollar that makes this picture business a disembodied presence." See Stephen Longstreet, "Errol Flynn: Gentlemanly Rogue," *Close-Ups: Intimate Profiles of Movie Stars by Their Co-Stars, Directors, Screenwriters, and Friends*, ed. Danny Peary (New York 1978) 157-160.

164   But there should be no mistaking—Flynn's body was hardly just a shell for his soul. He was such a sensual man, such a physical being, that it's impossible to imagine some Flynn "soul" divorced from that Flynn form and floating disembodied in the ether. He pretended that his face had been an impediment to his becoming whom he truly was, but more to the point is when he mused in *Wicked* as to whether he would have had the same spirit had he been born an ugly dwarf—the implicit assumption being that he wouldn't have. How can we begin to conceive of a repulsive Errol Flynn? If his face and form defeated his ultimate ambition of becoming a full-time writer, then that's who he essentially was—his face and form. It dominated his character. As it should have. We mere mortals like to think that body and soul are separate entities, that our character or spirit is superior to our outward form, even the good-looking among us, but with Flynn they were so intertwined as to be inseparable.

165   These might either be the supposed offspring of Flynn's island dalliances or men named in his honor, perhaps not always one and the same. I have never been to Jamaica, but I have met two black Jamaican Errols, the first an English professor in graduate school, and the second one a fellow on the Berlin U-Bahn in 2010. He was a tall genteel chap who asked if we might exchange places with our bikes—that is, he asked where I might be "disembarking" since it would be easier if he had his own bike against the wall and mine against the pole—from a purely logistical standpoint one ought to be prepared. I thought it a tad fastidious, but he was polite and had a certain elegance, so we switched. And fell into conversation. He was a Shakespearean-trained actor, originally from Jamaica, and I asked his name and he said "Errol." A Jamaican actor named Errol. I seized on this and he told me that his mother had indeed named him after you-know-who. He said that Flynn had first discovered Jamaica by being blown off course with his boat, which wasn't entirely true, but who was I to contradict this namesake of the great man. He proceeded to explain that the name Errol derived from the Latin meaning "to wander." Well, it's a long way from Jamaica, I said, so I guess you're living up to your name; that I am, he said, ha ha. I asked him if he was also living up to his name by playing any swashbuckling roles; no, unfortunately he hadn't. Then came my stop and I said goodbye.

166   Flynn did eventually accumulate much land in Jamaica, starting in 1948 when he returned to that country, and amounting to some two miles running along the coast near Port Antonio on the island's northeast side. He also acquired Navy Island in Port Antonio's harbor, consisting of some sixty acres. As Flynn himself said, "Once I arrived there I lapsed into

a completely different life. It was a reversion to my New Guinea days." (*Wicked*, 384) Jeffrey Meyers elaborates: "Flynn's Jamaica was an idealized version of his youthful days in New Guinea, when he rode around his plantation and watched his copra grow. In Jamaica the people were friendly, not savage, the tropical climate benign, not lethal. The island reminded him of the South Seas, but had no unpleasant associations. He liked the uninhibited Jamaicans, their patois and their music, as well as the lush foliage, the privacy and the baronial freedom of his personal domain. Flynn loved to create his own hedonistic microcosm and control the people in it: in Mulholland House, on the Zaca and on his Jamaican estate. He even built a racetrack and a runway." (Myers, *Inherited Risk*, 228-229) Providing even deeper insight into Errol's relationship to Jamaica is Earl Conrad's memoir of his collaboration with Flynn on *My Wicked, Wicked Ways*, a collaboration that took place largely on the island nation. See Earl Conrad, *Errol Flynn: A Memoir* (London 1978) and particularly pages 43-44.

167   In *Wicked* Flynn asserts that *zaca* is a Samoan word meaning "peace." There appears to be no such word in the Samoan language, which does have a word for "peace" but it is *filemu* (Meyers, *Inherited Risk*, 343). Flynn was likely misquoting Templeton Crocker, the boat's original owner, who wrote in the *The Cruise of the Zaca* that "*Zaca* is an Indian word meaning 'peace'." Thomas McNulty also opines that "Crocker was probably right. *Zaca* almost certainly derives from Chumash Indian, but unfortunately Chumash is a dead language and the etymology cannot be conclusively verified." (McNulty, *The Life and Career*, 194) But whether *zaca* in whatever language means "peace," at least Flynn thought it did, which is the crucial point. As he wrote, his previous boat the *Sirocco*, where the Satterlee dalliance took place, "had an evil memory for me and I decided to get rid of her." Nonetheless, Flynn put the likeness of a crowing cock on the new boat's house flag and said to himself: "Let her be a symbol of what I have come to represent." (*Wicked*, 353-354) Why he should want to make a fresh start with the boat while having it symbolize precisely what he was trying to put behind him with that fresh start, is just one more token of the paradox that was Flynn. The *Zaca* was a 118-foot, wooden-hulled, two-masted schooner, first launched in 1930, and only Flynn's death would do them part in 1959.

168   According to Robert Matzen, Flynn did indeed pitch this project to production head Hal Wallis and Jack Warner, but to no avail. (Matzen, *Errol & Olivia*, 78)

169   Film posters advertised it as "Warner's Adventure of the Century!!!"

170   Co-star Ann Sheridan was also drinking. According to the movie's screenwriter Stephen Longstreet: "The stars' behavior resulted in delays, which led to cost overruns, which forced the studio heads to declare *Silver River* finished. It is the only major studio film I know of for which there is no ending; the picture ends in midair, but no one, as far as I know, ever bothered to ask why." See Longstreet, "Errol Flynn: Gentlemanly Rogue," 159.

171   In a written communiqué to Earl Conrad, Flynn said, "Anyone who comes to my funeral is automatically cut out of my will . . . and I mean it. I absolutely hate the idea of well loved people being subjected

to the maudlin, sloppy, bullshit Lov ya, Flynn of some priest or minister spouting off hurriedly over my grave and wanting to get home to lunch." (Conrad, *A Memoir*, 210)

172   Not only Forest Lawn, but from Mulholland Farm he also had a view of Warner Brothers Studio in Burbank. Between the two of these places, Flynn was often given to ruminate on the life he had chosen and how posterity would regard him.

173   Flynn writes of how, during this period in his life, "I was placing figurative bullets into my soul and it was only a matter of time before I'd try real ones . . . . My smile got broader and broader, so broad that one night I went to a dresser in my bedroom at Mulholland and took out a gun." (*Wicked*, 351, 352) The rest I imagined for myself.

174   I'm thinking of embarrassments such as *The Adventures of Captain Fabian* (1951) and *Cuban Rebel Girls* (1959)—to name the worst of the lot.

175   It was in *The Prince* where Machiavelli famously wrote that to retain his grip on power a ruler should be both loved and feared—but never hated, for hate engenders discontent among one's subjects and can lead to revolt.

176   The light satirical tone is set from the opening scene when Flynn climbs the balcony of a young beauty whom he takes in his arms. "I have loved you since the beginning of time," he says, and she replying: "But you only met me yesterday." Flynn: "That was when time began."

177   Like George Cukor, Sherman had a reputation in Hollywood for being good with "women's pictures." Whatever that meant, he was certainly good with the *women* in those pictures (among his love affairs were Rita Hayworth, Bette Davis and Joan Crawford) and was a solid man for whatever type of film, sort of a junior-grade William Wyler—or Mike Curtiz for that matter.

178   The trips included sailing away on the *Zaca* or having a helicopter take him down the coast to film gray whales migrating to their spawning grounds in Baja. His drinking was incessant, usually starting in the late afternoon and continuing on through the night and making for a very groggy Flynn the next day when the pattern would repeat itself. He snuck the alcohol into his dressing room in a variety of ways, for instance replacing the containers in his makeup case with liquor bottles and putting the makeup labels on them; and, most ingeniously, by injecting oranges with vodka using a syringe. Until the syringe ploy was discovered, the film crew thought Errol was turning over a new leaf and living quite healthily—all that vitamin C!

179   The film's director Vincent Sherman later implied that Flynn's drinking was triggered by bad reviews of *Escape Me Never*. "At the beginning of the picture, he told me he knew I had heard about his drinking, and he wanted to assure me he wouldn't drink on this picture. He said he'd give me all the cooperation he could in making *Don Juan* a great film. I found him charming and sincere, and I think he was serious. The first ten days

he was marvelous, he was never late and he knew his lines. One day, he called me into his dressing room: he had a bunch of clippings on the table. He said, 'Have you seen these?' He had just opened in New York in his previous picture and the critics were very unkind to him. In essence, they said that if Flynn wasn't on a horse and shooting in a Western or a costume picture, he was pathetic as an actor. I read these things and it was embarrassing to do so in front of him. He sort of made fun of them, kidding, but inside I could see he was terribly hurt by these reviews. He was covering up. Two days later, he came on the set completely drunk, and for the rest of the time, he was drinking on the picture." (Thomas, *The Spy Who Never Was*, 40-41) I don't doubt the story, but the truth is that if it hadn't been the bad reviews then any number of things might have set him off since he was a habitual drunkard by that point.

180   Flynn tried valiantly to ward off the creeping "mother" in him by hooking up with his real-life father on a scientific-research expedition aboard the *Zaca* in 1946, from which a twenty-minute film *Cruise of the Zaca* was made by Flynn and distributed by Warner Brothers in 1952. As Jeffrey Meyers puts it, "their cruise reenacted on a grand scale their matey scientific trips in the Tasmanian bush." (Myers, *Inherited Risk*, 212) But the voyage ended in farce—the "mother" in Flynn finally gaining the upper hand. For a detailed rundown of the trip, see McNulty, *The Life and Career*, 193-206.

181   He touches upon it in *Wicked* (as did we in Canto III, stanza 158)—"I had chosen to be an actor, to make big money, to become famous, and I had put by a deeper yearning to write"—but his general stance, particularly in this extended passage which treats the rape trial, is one of being victimized if only by circumstance: "My principal emotion was that I was hoaxed by life, that I had become something other than what I set out to be . . . . I felt used. Used by the studio. Used to make money. Used by the press for fun. Used by society as a piece of chalk to provide the world with a dab of color." For the entire passage, see pages 348-353.

182   His drinking impacted both his acting and writing. He had been hoping to pen his autobiography for some time but found he was unable to muster the concentrated effort required due to his alcoholism. When he finally took Earl Conrad on board as collaborator, he needed booze to prime the narrative pump. Conrad writes: "He tried talking about himself when he was sober, with no liquor in him. That method failed. He couldn't seem to talk, he was tongue-tied, his mind wouldn't go, his hands trembled, his voice chattered, his memory wouldn't function. We tried that only a few times. Once or twice a week when he had a drug in him his thoughts flowed, he talked freely and recalled extensively." (Conrad, *A Memoir*, 96-97)

183   As mentioned—*The Sun Also Rises* (1957), *Too Much Too Soon* and *The Roots of Heaven* (both 1958). These were far from being Flynn's best films but they were arguably his three best roles and performances of the 1950s.

184   As opposed to the smaller and newer one. In 1947, two years before general release of *Adventures of Don Juan*, full-scale commercial television broadcasting had begun in the United States and had the Hollywood studios running scared; by 1955, half of all U.S. homes owned television sets.

185   Flynn was originally slated to play either the romantic lover of Soames' wife or the bohemian artist she leaves him for (the lover eventually played by Robert Young and the artist by Walter Pidgeon) but Flynn wanted to attempt a role that went against type. This is completely justifiable from the artist's perspective, but it doesn't mean the public has to enjoy it. Flynn's co-star Greer Garson underscored this point when she wrote that they had done "a picture that wasn't much, I am afraid, for the audience, but was a ball for the cast and crew that made it." See her foreword to The Films of Errol Flynn, Tony Thomas, Rudy Behlmer and Clifford McCarty (New York 1969). She also made a fine observation regarding Flynn and his contradictions: "The paradox of the actor is always an intriguing study. Those in the audience who stop to think about it at all must wonder how often is the laughing Pagliacci hiding a broken heart? And is it possible that our swashbuckling screen hero in real life is an insecure, lonely and unhappy man . . . ? Personally, I believe the contrast is seldom that absolute. Actors, like other people, are not usually sharply schizophrenic so much as a complex of overlapping and interrelated qualities, both active and latent. Consider this book for example . . . it could well have been titled 'The Mask and the Man,' for while Errol Flynn will be remembered by movie fans as the handsome, confident cavalier, the romantic conqueror in boudoir and battlefield, his friends and companions also will remember facets totally at variance with the heroic illusion. But they will remember, too, his wit and charm, his lifelong love of ocean and sailing ships, his fascination with sagas of buccaneers and soldiers of fortune, and his desire to live life fully as a gay, daring adventure—and these were characteristics which reconciled the man and his image." (pp. 8-9)

186   Though quite understandable that a world-famous movie star wouldn't care to put his genitalia on public display, Flynn's reaction to Ghika's own willingness to bare all was tinged with a surprising primness: "Once we sailed near the Isle de Levant, visiting a nudist colony. I couldn't be a nudist, but astonishingly, the reserved, holding-out Princess Irene could." She'd already had sex with him before visiting the island, presumably with her clothes off, so it wasn't as if there was some weird disconnect between her not disrobing for him but in front of him. (Wicked, 374)

187   With respect to Irene Ghika's suicidal tendencies, Flynn writes in Wicked (p. 375): "One night one of my sailors saw a trickle of blood coming from under her cabin door. He called me and we pushed our way inside. She had so many razor cuts on her wrist, it looked like a washboard. We revived her, tried to get an explanation. It was not easy. I was reminded of Lili." To be perfectly accurate, although Lili was always threatening suicide, she may never have actually attempted it—as opposed to Nora, for example, who never threatened but did try it twice.

188   Rocky Mountain, appearing in 1950, the same year as another ho-hum Flynn Western with the title Montana. Both were obligatory Warner Brothers productions. The one thing we can be thankful to Rocky Mountain for is that it marked the last feature-film Western which Flynn would ever make. Flynn himself asserted that, at least post-rape trial, his Westerns were "mediocre vehicles. I walked through them and reviewers remarked that I walked through them." (Conrad, A Memoir, 168)

Canto VIII: *Sea Drift* (1950-1956)

189   The civil ceremony had been performed earlier that morning in Monte Carlo at the invitation of Flynn's friend Prince Rainier. Errol and Patrice were of one accord in their desire for a traditional wedding and it was a grand public event complete with paparazzi—this in marked contrast to Flynn's spur-of-the-moment elopement with Lili to Yuma, Arizona, and his secret marriage by proxy with Nora in Cuernavaca, Mexico. There was even a wedding cake of the multi-tiered variety. Shortly after the ceremony, that very same day, Flynn was presented with a summons which accused him of the statutory rape of an underage French girl. Flynn thought it a practical joke by one of his crowd, perhaps Freddie McEvoy, who had served as Best Man, but it turned out to be real—and ultimately groundless. The girl and her parents simply thought Flynn, based on his reputation, would be an easy mark.

190   It is reproduced in Thomas, *From a Life of Adventure*, 207-210.

191   This is the online *Oxford English Dictionary* definition: "2. the state of being whole and undivided." The *OED*'s first definition wouldn't have quite applied to Flynn either: "1. the quality of being honest and having strong moral principles: *a gentleman of complete integrity.*"

192   Both pictures were released in 1950, *King Solomon's Mines* making Granger a Hollywood star, he then going on to films like *Scaramouche* and *The Prisoner of Zenda* (both 1952) which would bestow upon him the dubious mantle of an aspirant Flynn.

193   As Tony Thomas writes of Flynn: "Sometime in his later years he remarked to a group of friends, 'I think I'm going to have to give up something I've always had a passion for.' They laughed because they naturally assumed he was talking about women. He then explained that what he was referring to was writing, which had become too difficult for him." (Thomas, *From a Life of Adventure*, 12)

194   The relevant passage reads: "I am going to China because I wish to live deliberately. New Guinea offers me, it is true, satisfaction for the tastes I have acquired which only leisure can satisfy. I am leaving economic security and I am leaving it deliberately. By going off to China with a paltry few pounds and no knowledge of what life has in store for me there I believe that I am going to front the essentials of life to see if I can learn what it has to teach and above all not to discover when I come to die, that I have not lived." (Moore, *The Young Errol*, 118) The attentive reader will note that in 1932/1933, when the journal was kept, Flynn was intent on England, not China, and had more than "a few paltry pounds" on his person. This entry, though unmistakably Flynn in terms of its sentiment, was likely a red herring to put the Australian authorities off his trail ever since the "Madge Parkes" incident of the stolen jewels. He had placed the journal in a trunk and left it at a well-known inn at the goldfield's trailhead—one of the first places the cops would look for clues as to his whereabouts—and the trunk boldly lettered with the name ERROL FLYNN. Why leave the journal behind? It was small and would have been the one thing he'd have taken with him, filled as it was with Errol's recruiting adventures and other material that might later prove invaluable to an aspiring writer.

195   *The Roots of Heaven* (1958) was filmed in French Equatorial Africa. The film's director John Huston knew that the screenplay was shoddy and the picture dead in the water, but he needed the money, as did Flynn, who received $90,000 for his pains. See Meyers, *Inherited Risk*, 270-271.

196   Tony Thomas writes: "When Flynn finished work on *Kim*'s Indian location shots in early 1950, he came back to Hollywood for the remainder of shooting by way of Italy, where he stopped off to appear in a picture under a partnership deal with ex-actor turned producer-writer-director, William Marshall . . . . The resulting sixty-four minute semidocumentary plea for pacifism concerns an 'unknown soldier' (Flynn) who tells of the thoughts, hopes, and aspirations of four young soldiers who were shot down in their attempt to reach Anzio Beach during World War II. As they approach heaven, the soldiers ask to be accepted, though they have arrived long before they were permitted to complete their lives on earth. *Apparently Flynn wanted to break his Warners contract at the time (which stipulated that his outside films must be first-class, major studio productions)* [my emphasis], but later, after negotiating a revised contract, Flynn decided that the release of *Hello God* would be detrimental to his career. While working on another film with Marshall in France (*Captain Fabian*), he allegedly arranged to have the negative of *Hello God* picked up at the laboratory in Hollywood by a friend, Charles Gross. Marshall retaliated by suing and by reconstructing the film, using out-takes and additional material shot in Santa Barbara and Hollywood. Flynn filed a cross-complaint to block the release, stating that Marshall had fraudulently represented details regarding the production. He also claimed that he did not realize that the subject of the film would be detrimental to the public welfare, in that it was of a pacifist nature and contrary to the foreign policy of the United States. Finally, he contended that the film was of a poor quality and couldn't be improved. The suits were never completely settled, and *Hello God* drifted into obscurity." According to Thomas, in Flynn's next Warner Brothers film *Maru Maru* (1952) "it was apparent that Warners had little regard for Flynn or his vehicles at this stage of the game." (Thomas, *The Films of Errol Flynn*, 173, 177)

197   Though Errol didn't bring quite the same gusto to his derring-do as in earlier efforts, Tony Thomas writes that *The Master of Ballantrae* (1953) "was Flynn's best all-round film since *Don Juan*." (*The Films of Errol Flynn*, 193) Not bad for a guy who, during the picture's making, registered in London as a morphine addict. (Meyers, *Inherited Risk*, 245)

198   According to Tom McNulty, "over two dozen reels of footage from William Tell, including tests and outtakes, lie in storage in the Special Collections department at Boston University." (*The Life and Career*, 256)

199   Flynn wanted people to believe that he was dead broke, but Lili was perfectly aware of his assets—not only Mulholland Farm but his valuable paintings and thousands of acres in Jamaica as well as the *Zaca* where he had gold bars stashed if worse came to worst; though it isn't clear she knew about the gold bars.

200   As Geoffrey Meyers explains: "Lili Damita—still bitter about Flynn's rejection and her own decline from Hollywood star to Florida celebrity—now reentered his life and completed his ruin. The ill-advised Flynn

had originally agreed to pay Lili $12,000 a year tax-free alimony, which meant he had to provide an additional $6,000 for the IRS. Since he paid the entire amount directly to Lili, the IRS maintained that her alimony was actually $18,000. They then made him pay an additional tax of $12,000 on the original alimony-plus-tax ($18,000), which raised the amount from $12,000 to $30,000 a year . . . . The court could not change the terms of the private settlement, Lili kept suing and winning, and Flynn's debt kept increasing." (Myers, *Inherited Risk*, 250-251) Throughout this period Nora was also constantly seeking recompense for delinquent child-support payments.

201   Patrice Wymore gave birth to Flynn's third daughter Arnella on Christmas Day 1953. According to Jeffrey Myers, "Flynn, who'd seen too many historical movies, wanted to name her after William the Conqueror's mother, Arletta, but he made a mistake and called her Arnella." (Myers, *Inherited Risk*, 237) She hardly knew her father, who died when she was five. Arnella went on to become a fashion model, have a son, retired to her mother's estate in Jamaica (inherited from Flynn) where she then drank and drugged herself to death at the age of 44, not unlike her father, in whose life she'd never figured as more than a footnote.

202   Allen Loomis was his name and they wed in 1962. They spent their winters in Palm Beach, Florida, Lili's post-Hollywood home, and summers in Loomis' hometown of Fort Dodge, Iowa. They divorced in the 1980s. In her later years she suffered from Alzheimer's and died in 1994. To the onlooker it would seem that the second half of Lili's life was filled largely by two obsessions—retaliating against Flynn and doting over their son Sean. After Sean went missing in action, presumed dead, in Vietnam in 1970, she hired soldiers of fortune to find him (or what was left of him) but nothing was ever recovered. Lili spent her remaining years mourning this loss. Despite Errol's epithet of "Tiger Lil," she seems to have been quite the vulnerable soul and an all-around sad figure.

203   Flynn could have made things easy on himself by declaring bankruptcy, but his pride and sense of honor saw it as "a form of welching." The notion of paying back his debts at ten cents on the dollar called his super ego down upon him: "Somehow the thought of what my father would think entered my mind." (*Wicked*, 16) Flynn had no problem, however, paying fifty cents on the dollar for the back taxes he owed the IRS—like most people, he probably felt that the government was getting a large enough cut as it was.

204   Flynn was in four films with Jewish-Hungarian actor S. Z. "Cuddles" Sakall, the go-to-man at Warners for comic relief in the 1940s and early 1950s. He is probably best remembered as Carl the sentimental head waiter in *Casablanca* (1942), the role which first brought him to public attention. Jack Warner bestowed the sobriquet "Cuddles" because he was so sweet-tempered and adorable, with chubby cheeks that all but invited you to pinch them. In *Wicked* Flynn writes: "Sakall was a funny old guy. I always liked him for his screwy, mushy personality, but most actors hated him. He messed up the English language so much that they couldn't get their cues. I let him run on. It was fun to see the effect of him on the other character players. He ran off with many scenes, and that was enough to make him despised by the others. [Alan] Hale couldn't stand him. They hated each other and refused to work with each other. To see them to-

gether was like a meeting of two prima donnas at a tea party. Naturally I brought them together as often as I could, and on this night Hale hollered, 'For Chrissakes, Zakall, ain't it time you learned to speak English? You been here long enough!' [Sakall replied:] 'And for vy I should spik Englich better, ven mitt dis Englisch I em makin more vot is you!'" (p. 300)

205   This episode happened, Flynn recounting it in *Wicked* (pp. 404-405) and I've rendered it more or less faithfully, with some poetic license, mainly the thoughts I've attributed to him while floating in the cave, these musings largely culled from journal entries he made during the period 1953-1955 when he was at loose ends professionally and otherwise, selections from that journal being reproduced in *Wicked* and elsewhere. Flynn recounts no specific instance where he seriously contemplated suicide while scuba diving but he does relate thinking at the time: "Maybe if I'm lucky I'll go down a hundred feet some day and not come up. I was full up with the whole act of living." (*Wicked*, 19) Commenting on Flynn's scuba diving, Earl Conrad said: "He seemed at home with the sport. He had told me of a dozen narrow escapes. It seemed as though this was what he wanted, the narrow escape, the risk, the danger, punching death in the face—but surfacing once more." (Conrad, *A Memoir*, 92)

206   As cited by Camille Paglia, *Sexual Personae: Art and Decadence from Nefertiti to Emily Dickinson* (New Haven 1990) 356, with me italicizing *man* in the quote. What Paglia herself says about *Don Juan*, and by extension Byron, can also apply to Flynn—in fact it's a wonder that she doesn't bring Flynn or his films into her discussion, so obvious are the parallels and so learned is she when it comes to not only historical but modern pop-cultural references and particularly Hollywood ones: "Don Juan the character and *Don Juan* the poem are world skimmers. The skimming is in both style and content. Byron's poetry is not 'finished,' that is, finely crafted and polished . . . I call *Don Juan*'s lightness and quickness *breeziness* . . . the freshness of a spring breeze, a new spirit entering and aerating history. The breeze emanating from Byron—literally, his emanation—is the spirit of youth, which was to have enormous impact upon European and American culture. Rousseau invented the modern cult of childhood; Goethe popularized Rousseau's moody adolescent. But Byron created the glamorous sexy youth of brash, defiant energy, *the new* embodied in a charismatic sexual persona. Hence Byron senses the dawn of the age of speed. Youth is swiftness in emotionally *transient* form. Transience from the Latin *transeo*, contains the ideas both of travel and of the short-lived." (pp. 356-358) And compare this with Earl Conrad's experience of Flynn: "One day when we were looking over the galleys of [*My Wicked, Wicked Ways*] he pencilled in three words at the end of a certain sentence: go go go. I had never heard the triple expression. I wasn't that hip. 'Errol,' I said, 'three go's?' 'Yes, three go's. Go go go.' 'Aren't two enough?' 'No.' He looked at me as if there was something I didn't know, as if I were ignorant. Which I was. This was 1959 and I had never heard the expression 'go go go,' but it was known in the Hollywood set; the go-go set had become the go-go-go set. I don't remember how that was finally set up in *Wicked Ways*, whether with two go's or three, but Errol was himself go go go. He had to go and to keep going. It dawned on me that he never stayed still very long, not for more than a few minutes or a few hours. Then he had to go to his boat, or go below water, or go to the bar, or go see a friend, or go to Cuba, or go to New York, or go to Hollywood, or go to England, or go to his estate, or go

to the pool, or go ride a horse, or go to a party, or go in a plane, or go in a sailboat, or go in a motorboat, or go in a limousine, or go to a whorehouse, or go somewhere and go do something." (Conrad, *A Memoir*, 204-205)

207   The germane passage, which influenced an entire generation together with Oscar Wilde, and which can be found in Walter Horatio Pater's conclusion to his *Studies in the History of the Renaissance*, is as follows: "To burn always with this hard, gemlike flame, to maintain this ecstasy, is success in life . . . . With this sense of the splendours of our experience and its awful brevity, gathering all we are into one desperate effort to see and touch, we shall hardly have time to make theories about the things we see and touch. What we have to do is to be for ever curiously testing new opinions and courting new impressions, never acquiescing in a facile orthodoxy of Comte or of Hegel, or of our own. Philosophical theories or ideas, as points of view, instruments of criticism, may help us to gather up what might otherwise pass unregarded by us [but t]he theory or idea or system which requires of us the sacrifice of any part of this experience, in consideration of some interest into which we cannot enter, or some abstract theory we have not identified with ourselves, or of what is only conventional, has no real claim upon us." This is the aesthetic complement to Ernst Mach's epistemology as conveyed in vulgarized existential form by Dr. Herman Erben (see Canto III, stanzas 44-47 as well as endnote 15). What comes immediately to mind in terms of Flynn himself is his New Guinea diary where he writes: "Time, for example, just one hour of time is far more important than money for time is life. Whenever you waste your time over printed words that neither enlighten nor amuse you, you are, in a sense, committing suicide. The value, the intrinsic value, of our actions, emotions, thoughts, possessions, way of life, occupations, of the manner in which we are living—this is the first thing to be determined; for unless we are *satisfied* that any of these things have a true value, even if only relative, our lives are futile, and there is no more hopeless realization than this." (As cited in Moore, *The Young Errol*, 118-119) Even the cadences smack of Pater. And in *Wicked* he wrote what might be termed his manifesto in albeit plainer and lustier language than Pater's but nevertheless it's hedonistic equivalent: "I was thirty-four, in my prime; women liked me, I liked them; nobody got hurt. I thought, Let's have fun, let's live by the sunshine, let's swim and play; let's make love, let's cruise in the Pacific, let's have pleasant parties, let's entertain the people, let's be artists, if we can. This was my balls, my way of living, breathing and exulting in this short swift act called Creation." (p. 321) In that same conclusion to his Renaissance book, Pater wrote: "Well! we are all *condamnés* as Victor Hugo says: we are all under sentence of death but with a sort of indefinite reprieve—*les hommes sont tous condamnés à mort avec des sursis indéfinis*: we have an interval, and then our place knows us no more. Some spend this interval in listlessness, some in high passions, the wisest, at least among 'the children of this world,' in art and song."

208   Though I have imagined this response of Flynn's, the thrust of his tactic in the interview was to play for time and bluff his way to a favorable deal. See *Wicked*, 20-21.

Canto IX: *Recessional* (1956-1959)

209   *Wicked*, p. 16; and on p. 11: "Following an early policy, when broke, put on your best clothes, if you have any and if you haven't—borrow them, make the tie neater, and go around hoping you never looked more prosperous."

210   I believe this was Flynn's pride. In a New Year's card addressed to screenwriter Stephen Longstreet, Flynn quoted Shakespeare: "All the wealth I had ran in my veins. I was a gentleman." See Longstreet, "Errol Flynn: Gentlemanly Rogue," 160.

211   In his survey of *The Films of Errol Flynn*, Tony Thomas calls Errol's turn in *Istanbul* "merely an adequate and subdued performance." (p. 208) *Singapore*, which *Istanbul* derived from, was a 1947 film starring Fred MacMurray and Ava Gardner and apparently no better than the remake, the *New York Times* critic Bosley Crowther writing that "*Singapore* is a pretty poor excuse for an entertainment, even as minor league jewel smuggling fare."

212   Flynn was a crony of John Barrymore in his final years. In his waning days Barrymore lived at Mulholland Farm where among other things he drove Flynn nuts by urinating out the window of his bedroom, where Flynn was putting him up. As he wrote in *Wicked*, these were the "most frightening three weeks I had since I was in the New Guinea jungle . . . . Somehow the three weeks passed and Jack left. I could work again. But it was the opportunity to see Jack in these declining days that made it possible for me, fifteen years later, to play as authentically as I could feel it, the role of Barrymore in *Too Much Too Soon*." (pp. 278, 281) David Niven was not so easily impressed: "I never quite understood Errol's hero worship of John Barrymore . . . . He seemed to go out of his way to shock and be coarse: he was also conspicuously unclean and often smelled highly." (Niven, *Bring on the Empty Horses*, 121)

213   Name of the character that Flynn played in *The Charge of the Light Brigade* (1936). There's a wonderful scene where Flynn's character Geoffrey Vickers is off for the Crimean War and his eventual death, when the woman he loves, played by Olivia de Havilland, enters his quarters while he's packing and pleads for him to arrange that his brother, played by Patric Knowles, with whom *she* is in love, be withheld from the Crimean action. Errol gives her his promise and she replies that he, Errol, is the finest man she's ever known. It sounds corny but rises to great art through the subtle yet visible tension felt by Flynn in his wish to do the noble thing—both promising and later carrying it out—and his hurt that Olivia should care for his brother over him. Flynn achieves a delicate balance between wounded self-abnegation and highborn solicitude, his poise and beauty doing the rest in handsomely conveying the inner conflict of a great spirit suffering greatly.

214   Flynn himself put it succinctly: "I laugh a lot, and I weep secretly more often than most men." (*Wicked*, 417) Patrice Wymore also shed light on Flynn's dichotomous personality: "I found generally that when he was at his lowest ebb or most frightened he would appear to be at his gayest. I had to know him quite some time before I was able to recognize his low ebbs." See Thomas, *The Films of Errol Flynn*, 188.

215   Sessue Hayakawa was nominated as best supporting actor for *The Bridge on the River Kwai*, which takes place in a Japanese prisoner-of-war camp and won best picture along with six other Academy Awards—Hayakawa's was the only of the film's eight nominations which didn't win an Oscar. The reason might have been that the best supporting actress award went to Miyoshi Umeki for her role opposite Red Buttons in *Sayonara* (six nominations, four wins) and members of the Academy couldn't bring themselves to make history twice in one night by awarding the first ever Oscars to both an Asian actress and actor (if you don't count Yul Brynner, who had Buryat-Mongol blood, and had won for *The King and I* the year before). In any event by the mid-1950s, if Flynn wasn't in, at least with the Academy, the Far East was, and this perhaps the ironic reason why Hayakawa didn't turn the trick with his performance in *The Bridge on the River Kwai*. He really should have won—that is, in lieu of Flynn gaining the prize. To gauge Flynn's achievement in *The Sun Also Rises* we need go no further than that author of the source material for the movie, Ernest Hemingway. He and Errol knew each other, having crossed paths several times, and Hemingway had decided that he disliked Flynn. This was probably owing to jealousy of his earning power and success with women—the usual things—and the fact that Flynn was not only a war correspondent in the Spanish Civil War but in Cuba during its revolution, invading Hemingway's turf in both a professional and territorial sense and Papa not liking invasions of his turf. He also wrote books, this froufrou actor, and could likely have taken Hemingway in a fight. At least I'd have put my money on Flynn. Hemingway was a ponderous slugger and Flynn fast on his feet (just watch *Gentleman Jim*) as well as having a height and reach advantage and being every bit as mean as Hemingway when necessary. He was also ten years younger. Suffice it to say that Hemingway had many reasons, from his own alpha-male standpoint, to resent Errol Flynn, and would invariably cast him in a negative light. But his comment on the film version of *The Sun Also Rises*—"Any picture in which Errol Flynn is the best actor is its own worst enemy"—is still a backhanded recognition of Errol's prowess in the role of Mike Campbell. See Meyers, *Inherited Risk*, 138.

216   The exact words were: "Are you, Art Napoleon [the film's director], telling *me* how to play a drunk?" (Meyers, *Inherited Risk*, 264) Jack Warner later wrote: "When we talked about casting the role of John Barrymore, who had literally boozed himself into the grave, I immediately thought of Errol. Frankly, I missed his gaiety and taunting laughter and the excitement he generated on the set, and I sent him a letter offering him the part . . . . He came back to the lot, but I could not bear to watch him struggle through take after take. The once strong and handsome face was puffy and gray, the dancing shimmer was gone from his eyes . . . ." As cited in Thomas, *The Films of Errol Flynn*, 215-216.

217   The film is based on Diana Barrymore's confessional *Too Much, Too Soon* which chronicles her descent into sexual and alcoholic sordidness as the lovelorn daughter of two neglectful parents, so the main story was hers and not that of her father John Barrymore. But even if dying halfway through, Flynn ran away with the film, as confirmed by *The New York Times* (10 May 1958): "And Mr. Flynn, as the late John Barrymore, a moody, wild-drinking ruin of a great actor, steals the picture, lock, stock and keg. It is only in the scenes of his savage disintegration, as the horrified girl hangs on, that the picture approaches real tragedy."

218   Namely that he had "thoroughly enjoyed the fight and hoped we'd do it again sometime." All of this, including an account of the fisti-cuffs, which I used as basis for my description in Canto VI, is according to Huston's autobiography *An Open Book*, 96-98. In *Wicked* Flynn is very complimentary to Huston in those passages devoted to *The Roots of Heaven* and he never once refers to the fight. Why? As mentioned, I believe that Olivia was nub of the matter, Flynn having made some nasty remark about her, and it was all too indelicate for him to rehash in print years later (see endnote 152). But I also believe, because he had gotten the better of Huston in their fight (remember: Flynn had telephoned Hus-ton after the brawl, not vice versa, which almost always happens when you've bested the other man) and because after having gotten to know and like Huston in Africa (Flynn had just recently returned from *The Roots of Heaven* shoot when he embarked on the writing of *Wicked* with Earl Conrad) he didn't want to boast or make Huston look bad. Which wasn't his style in any case. In his storytelling he was usually self-deprecating to a fault and liked having the joke be on him—his ego robust and healthy that way.

219   In *Wicked* Flynn summed up the six months by writing: "French equatorial Africa is a place anybody can leave off their world itinerary when they take their next vacation." And adding: "Personally, I made it fun. I went there mentally determined whatever kind of hell it was going to be, I was going to make it merry for myself and for everybody else, if I could. Yet perhaps I had some preparation for all this. I had been through the New Guinea jungles, worse even than French Equatorial Africa, so probably I had a gearing for this that the others didn't." (pp. 428-429)

220   You also have to be in bad films. Flynn's three comeback pictures—*The Sun Also Rises*, *Too Much, Too Soon* and *The Roots of Heaven*—admittedly ranged from poor to awful. Partial testimony to this fact was that their cumulative number of Academy Award nominations was zero. The point being that "better" roles didn't make for better pic-tures—not by a long shot.

221   Popular name for the Motion Picture Production Code, which comprised the self-imposed moral guidelines governing the American film industry from 1930 to 1968.

222   Flynn was a licensed pilot and would now be flying his single-engine Navion from California straight onto his Jamaican property so as to have it out with his mother regarding the $5000 bell. He had commis-sioned his father with building an airstrip for the plane, but when Flynn came in for landing, low on fuel and no other runway in striking distance, he found the airstrip laid out in a dogleg: at one corner an enormous 100-foot tree and beyond the tree the strip skewed off at an angle. After landing the plane, within a few inches of his life, there was hell to pay for his father, who had acceded to Marelle's demand that he not cut down the tree: "She likes to see the little calves gambol under it of an evening." When Errol later brought up the subject of the bell with the Grand Em-press Dowager, she first cowed Theodore into silence, he not daring to take Errol's side, and then faced down her son by commanding him to take a walk "and come back when you make some sense." The $5000 was apparently not just for the bell or the belfry but restoration of the

entire *church*, which had previously been a dilapidated ruin. Her reasoning was that you didn't place a belfry with no church beneath. Did Errol expect "to see this belfry hanging up in the air just with a bell and with no church under it to support it?" Flynn writes: "My father beat it then, leaving me trying to envision a belfry defying gravity, sitting in mid-air, with a bell and no church underneath it. They'd have a helluva time with that one even in the special effects department of Warners." For the bell/airstrip anecdote see *Wicked*, 389-396.

223   This didn't make it into the book, but it was in speaking with Conrad that Flynn broached the topic, Conrad devoting four pages to Flynn's "good right arm" (as Flynn termed it). One day Flynn whipped this arm out to show that, despite the rumors, he wasn't built like King Kong: "He was agile about opening his fly, buttons or zipper no matter. Sheer speed: and his air was always one of fun, never salaciousness. His penis was indeed unremarkable. It was, if not short, certainly not much longer than that, and rather stout, I thought. That's all there was, there wasn't any more, except a terribly full, bulging scrotum." This is an idiotic description since what he's trying to say is that Flynn had a perfectly normal phallus—only made to look smaller by his "bulging scrotum"—as if one can even judge such things based on a flaccid schlong. For the sake of posterity Flynn suggested he might "press it into a bit of cement in front of Grauman's." (Conrad, *A Memoir*, 64-65)

224   Conrad recounted their first session working together, before they had employed a stenographer, when he encouraged Flynn to talk freely and eschew chronological order: "He sipped on vodka from time to time. I began to listen keenly as he seemed to be talking about someone very specifically. He was talking aloud but not exactly to me. He paced about the large room. 'The cunt gave me so much trouble when I was a kid.' I didn't know what he was talking about, whether he was talking about sex or something else. 'She made my life miserable. I hated the cunt.' I made notes. What the hell was he talking about? 'I ran away from her whenever I could. And while the old man was taking eighty-million-year-old fish out of the ocean she was running around with big shots in Paris—the cunt.'" And when they did get down to chronological telling: "'It must have been a hard birth,' he said of his appearance on June 20, 1909, 'because it's been difficult with my mother ever since. Hard for her, hard for me.'" (Conrad, *A Memoir*, 20-21, 28)

225   In gathering documentation for his autobiography, Flynn wrote Conrad: "Looked up my birth certificate, a Photostat of which I reproduce here, and at the age approaching fifty I find that I narrowly missed illegitimacy. Read it for yourself. I am quite sure that my mother will have a ready answer for the discrepancy between my birth and her marriage. I have written Mother a sort of congratulatory note, although we are hardly on speaking terms let alone writing terms for the last forty years. I just put her one mild question since she is rather old now, but still can swim better than me: 'Was I an incubator baby in 1909? I figured that they didn't have such things.' In other words I must have been desperately premature—by five months." (Conrad, *A Memoir*, 193)

226   The "will" is worth reading and starts out: "My friend and lawyer, a realist, just yesterday shocked me with the startling news that I

might one day die. I should draw up a will, he said. 'Draw Up'? You draw up a bucket from a well, don't you? Or draw up something from the ocean bottom, or draw a mug of beer." Then comes the body of the will, which is in the same frisky vein, and it winds down with Flynn wondering whether he might still have money left over: "The pretty secretary typing this just observed she could use some, so why don't we give her some? Especially as I just noticed her outspoken attractive tits lean over the typewriter at an engaging angle, but that's beside the point, or points." As indicated, the "will" did not make it into *My Wicked, Wicked Ways*, but when Conrad heard of Flynn's death he showed the thing to his attorney "who took one look at it, said it was not legally drawn, it was unsigned, the accompanying letter with [Flynn's] signature was insufficient, and I didn't have to enter it for probate." (Conrad, *A Memoir*, 208-209)

227   Flynn had initially approached her while on the Warner Brothers lot filming *Too Much, Too Soon*, she a dancer on the set of *Marjorie Morningstar*. Their relationship is detailed in the book *The Big Love* by Beverly's mother Florence Aadland, which William Styron called a work of "wild comic genius"; what he meant was that it's a masterpiece of high camp. After Flynn's rape of Beverly, according to Florence: "Errol saw her the next day at the studio and begged her forgiveness. He told her she was a very sweet girl, something very special to him, but after what had happened she didn't believe him. He phoned her at the studio every day after that, asking for forgiveness . . . . She kept getting these phone calls from Errol and even though she was still frightened and shocked about what he had done, his charm and sincerity got through to her. He was very straightforward about it, kept apologizing, but I don't think he said he was sorry because I don't think he was. From the very beginning he was in love with her, and when he talked to her on the phone I think she realized this and began to fall in love with him." (pp. 9-10) This sounds very Flynn, for Nora recounts similar displays of abject and sincere apology after his having behaved in a beastly fashion. See Florence Aadland as told to Tedd Thomey with a foreword by William Styron, *The Big Love* (New York 1961).

228   Jamaica finally gained its independence from Great Britain in 1962. Flynn played the white colonialist to the full, talking pidgin to Jamaicans (who were perfectly able to comprehend and even speak standard English) while strutting about on a cane (with a sword in it and a tiger's head for a grip) as he had in his New Guinea days. Earl Conrad wrote that Flynn treated blacks "very much in the tradition in which he had been reared in New Guinea—as serfs, as lesser species." (Conrad, *A Memoir*, 27)

229   When Flynn returned to New York from the revolution, he met with Conrad who later wrote: "In the next few days he recounted his adventures in Cuba and I put them into a series of articles that were published in this country and throughout Europe . . . . There was a surge of new spirit in him. The war correspondent role. He must go back to Cuba, be present as Castro took over, report the scene, send back correspondence. 'I will send it to you,' he said. 'You will put it in shape. Maybe I can get to do a column for a chain of newspapers.' He was reverting back to his origins, to the time in the late 1920s when he was a reporter for an Aussie paper, the Sydney *Bulletin*, from New Guinea; reliving his forsaken literary dream." (Conrad, *A Memoir*, 186-187)

230   The story of the flesh wound is difficult to verify, though Flynn's private journal entries from 5 and 8 January 1959 make the claim that he was nicked by a bullet; or a piece of masonry. He himself was apparently unsure—but blood seems to have been drawn.

231   Their relationship was goofy. Not only was Castro in the dark as to why he should view this Flynn guy seriously, but as Thomas Mc-Nulty writes: "Later reports quote Flynn as saying to Castro: 'Look, sport, do you mind if I take an occasional draft of the delicious wine of your land so as to make the revolution a little more viable?' Castro told Flynn to enjoy himself but he had an allergic reaction to wine. 'I have the same thing,' Flynn told Castro, 'but by dint of great discipline I have overcome it.'" (McNulty, *The Life and Career*, 286-287)

232   This wasn't Flynn's first movie in Cuba. Two years prior he had starred in the undistinguished film *The Big Boodle* (1957) playing a croupier in a Havana casino, and after a day's shooting he would hit the other side of the gaming table at the city's real-life gambling dens.

233   Jeffrey Meyers describes three lamentable outings—on Steve Allen's show where he was "'spaced-out on God-knows-what'"; in a TV Western comedy where "as usual, he needed vodka to keep going, but drank so much that he forgot his lines"; and on Red Skelton's show to perpetrate "a grotesque and humiliating self-parody." (Meyers, *Inherited Risk*, 292-293)

234   In 1946 she had married Marcus Goodrich, an author and navy man with whom she had a son; they divorced in 1952. In 1955 she married Pierre Galante, editor of *Paris Match*, with whom she had a daughter; they separated in 1962 and divorced in 1979.

235   *The Proud Rebel* was Olivia's first film role in two years and directed by Michael Curtiz, now in a wheelchair owing to cancer. The next day after the neck-kissing incident Olivia would meet with Flynn for lunch, of which to my knowledge no details have made it into print. See Matzen, *Errol & Olivia*, 189-190.

236   Matzen, *Errol & Olivia*, 190.

237   Buster Wiles was perhaps not the most reliable witness to the facts of Flynn's life (he claimed Flynn could not have had sexual relations with alleged rape-victim Peggy Satterlee due to "sinus troubles"—which, if the case, would more than likely have been cocaine-induced and have only heightened Flynn's sexual urges) but he did know Flynn intimately, living at Mulholland Farm for several years, and he felt that Errol never intended to sell the *Zaca*: "He loved that boat better than any woman and would never have parted with it." (Wiles, *My Days with Errol Flynn*, 183) Relatedly, Mickey Rooney, who was an incongruous pallbearer at Flynn's funeral, used to say that Errol woke up one day realizing he wasn't Robin Hood anymore and it killed him. This is overstated and Hollywoodesque in its glib rendering of what was surely a more complicated process—but there's truth in it: Errol realized he was aging and would never recapture his own preferred vision of himself. Most people can handle this, but Flynn had a hard time, likely because the image was so powerful and so universally acclaimed (and frozen in time through his filmwork) that it was

far more integral to his self-conception than the youthful images most of us have, which are shrugged off or at least modified over the years.

238   Though to be fair, the practicalities were stacked against Flynn's being transported to his elected burial ground. Having died in Canada, as a foreigner, his body had to undergo autopsy and then be shipped to Flynn's legal residence, which would seem to have been Los Angeles. The L.A. County Health Department subsequently filed an "immediate burial writ," which meant interment within 48 hours, ostensibly due to the threat of cholera or typhoid. At that point the exhumation and reburial in Jamaica would have been a legal and logistical ordeal since entailing yet another international transfer. On the Internet see *The Errol Flynn Blog*, "The Last Sad Rites of Errol Flynn," 6 February 2010.

239   Vincent Sherman wrote that "the vast public that Errol attracted in his heyday both to his films and in person, had not shown up. Inside, not even the chapel was filled." As cited in Meyers, *Inherited Risk*, 296.

240   It's not clear the exact tune, but Dennis Morgan's lyrical tenor carried it—Morgan a leading-man at Warners in the 1940s.

241   Jeffrey Meyers writes: "Though Flynn died broke, his estate eventually became solvent from the substantial royalties of his autobiography (paid to Pat) and the appreciation of his remaining property in Jamaica." (*Inherited Risk*, 298-299)

SELECTED BIBLIOGRAPHY OF PRINTED WORKS

Aadland, Florence. *The Big Love,* as told to Tedd Thomey, with an introduction by William Styron. New York: Warner Books, 1986 (originally published in 1961).

Connelly, Gerry. *Errol Flynn in Northampton.* Corby UK: Domra Publications, 1995.

Conrad, Earl. *Errol Flynn: A Memoir.* London: Robert Hale, 1978.

Eddington Flynn Haymes, Nora. *Errol and Me,* as told to Cy Rice. New York: Signet Books, 1960.

Fegerl, Joseph. *Errol Flynn, Dr. Hermann F. Erben: A Friendship of Two Adventurers* 1933-1940. Vienna: Joseph Fegerl, 1985.

Flynn, Errol. *Beam Ends.* Mattituck NY: Amereon House, 1975 (originally published in 1937).

_____. *Showdown.* New York: Buccaneer Books, 1976 (originally published in 1946).

_____. *From a Life of Adventure: The Writings of Errol Flynn*, ed. Tony Thomas. Seacacus NJ: Citadel Press, 1980.

_____. *My Wicked, Wicked Ways*, with a new introduction by Jeffrey Meyers. New York: Cooper Square Press, 2003 (originally published in 1959).

Friedrich, Otto. *City of Nets: A Portrait of Hollywood in the 1940s.* London: Headline Book Publishing, 1986.

Godfrey, Lionel. *The Life and Crimes of Errol Flynn.* New York: St. Martin's Press, 1977.

Huston, John. *An Open Book.* Boston: Da Capo Press, 1994 (originally published in 1980).

Longstreet, Stephen. "Errol Flynn: Gentlemanly Rogue," *Close-Ups: Intimate Profiles of Movie Stars by Their Co-Stars, Directors, Screenwriters, and Friends*, ed. Danny Peary. New York and London: Simon & Schuster, 1978.

Matzen, Robert and Michael Mazzone. *Errol Flynn Slept Here: The Flynns, the Hamblens, Ricky Nelson, and the Most Notorious House in Hollywood.* Pittsburgh PA: GoodKnight Books, 2009.

Matzen, Robert. *Errol & Olivia: Ego and Obsession in Golden Era Hollywood.* Pittsburgh PA: GoodKnight Books, 2010.

McNulty, Thomas. *The Life and Career of Errol Flynn.* Jefferson NC and London: McFarland & Company, 2004.

Meyers, Jeffrey. *Inherited Risk: Errol and Sean Flynn in Hollywood and Vietnam.* New York and London: Simon & Schuster, 2002.

Moore, John Hammond. *The Young Errol: Flynn Before Hollywood.* Sydney and London: Angus and Robertson, 1975.

Niven, David. *Bring on the Empty Horses.* London: Coronet Books, 1975.

Rathbone, Basil. *In and Out of Character.* New York: Limelight Editions, 1989 (originally published in 1962).

Thomas, Tony and Rudy Behlmer and Clifford McCarty. *The Films of Errol Flynn,* with a foreword by Greer Garson. New York: Citadel Press, 1969.

Thomas, Tony. *Errol Flynn: The Spy Who Never Was.* New York: Citadel Press, 1990.

Thomey, Tedd. *The Loves of Errol Flynn.* Derby CT: Monarch Books, 1962.

Wiles, Buster. *My Days with Errol Flynn,* with William Donati and his appendix "The Flynn Controversy." Santa Monica CA: Roundtable Publishing, 1988.

PHOTO CREDITS

ACKNOWLEDGMENTS

There are myriad reasons why Britta Gansebohm's name graces the dedication page, but in summary she brought unending love and humor and understanding to this throw of the dice.

Chris Moore, by way of Donegal, now deceased, is the book's other dedicatee. He was a fine friend here in Berlin and my great Flynn interlocutor. He knew as much about Errol as almost anyone, and his considered opinion was that Flynn had ultimately failed in life. I didn't take such a dim view and it made for some spirited exchanges. I can still hear his voice: *I hope you're not getting any romantic ideas about the scamp. When I was younger Flynn fooked me up but good. All that charming rogue bullshit. Him and his fookin sword and harem of trollops. The booze and the trollops will wreck ya every time!*

So of course he adored the guy.

I must thank Professor Carey Harrison of Brooklyn College. Not only for consenting to write the foreword but for giving the completed poem its first public presentation here in Berlin. A few more Carey Harrisons in this world would make it a far better place, but not a more boring place, au contraire, if only at the level of bizarre tattoos and exquisite literary inventions such as the incomparable Margot Brenner in Carey's novel *How to Push Through* (volume four of his opus *The Heart Beneath*) who utters the immortal phrase: "Got any luggage, mister?" If merely owing to that single locution, Carey, you have not lived in vain.

Thanks also to Robert Florczak, who is a trove of Flynniana and who read the poem in manuscript and gave pointers as to its factual accuracy; in addition he graciously supplied two of the photos in this volume and helped access a third. I made Robert's acquaintance through David DeWitt, who was the first man to make my poem welcome in a public forum, namely on his Errol Flynn Blog. It was also through David that I made contact with Thomas McNulty, author of the magisterial *Errol Flynn: The Life and Career*, who was a gentleman in suffering my pesky e-mails regarding salient points about our shared subject. Josef Fegerl placed at my disposal his collection of photographs pertaining to Flynn and Hermann Erben, whom Herr Fegerl knew personally, and thanks to Inga Klein for placing Herr Fegerl at my disposal, a man as mysterious as Erben himself . . .

My sister Mindy Saggiani shares my enthusiasm for old Hollywood and we have taken trips both celluloid and real through those storied environs, she always proving a savvy and delightful companion on these forays. My younger brother Timothy McAleer has supported my Flynn endeavor from the start; though he had his reservations about the poem's saucier passages, being the decorous man he is, I am grateful for his culture, taste and perspicacity in all things literary. My sister Jennifer Klein has had her own bouts to contest, but she has never ceased to be in my corner, and just knowing this fact has been a morale boost over the years.

I once asked my mother Doris McAleer (née Carlson) why she had married my father who, like all complex and fascinating characters, could be a tricky quantity on occasion. At which point she revealed that she had never set her cap at marriage. "So why do it," I insisted, "aside from the very real prospect of begetting a charismatic and eminently talented firstborn son, why marry the guy?" The answer of this sober-minded Nebraskan surprised me: "He was so good looking!" Though I shouldn't have been surprised, since by that time I had practically memorized *My Wicked, Wicked Ways*. ("Any notion that a woman's mind is nobler, purer, higher, more decent, cleaner, or anything else gentler or superior to a man's is pure delusion.") So I'm thankful that her mind wasn't higher or nobler and she got together with that movie-star handsome guy, Tom McAleer, who was a boy during the glory years of Hollywood and even lived there, at 832 North Orange Drive, and graduated with Hollywood High School's class of '46. Among numerous other things, my father imbued me with a love for the magic that motion pictures can evoke, and I shouldn't imagine that I would have spent twelve years of my life thinking and writing about Errol Flynn without that early influence. I only grew keen on Flynn in my early twenties after reading a biography on him—my interest piqued by the *man* and not his movies—but in the course of my life I have come to realize that the seeds of obsession are planted at a very tender age.

I would be delinquent in not mentioning the "Poetry Café" of which I was a habitué from 1995 to 1997. The Poetry Café is long defunct but was located in an even longer defunct factory building in Berlin's Moabit district. In those days it was next to a women's crisis center and had a hearse parked out front, for whatever reason, maybe to cart away the stiffs who often read at these open-mic events. You walked up a dank stairwell, old posters peeling from the walls, and on the second floor you jerked opened a heavy metal door, swept aside a blanket, then practically stumbled onto the stage. The furnishings were old ratty couches and easychairs, a couple kidney-shaped coffeetables, a chalkboard on an easel to the left of the proscenium, and cigarette smoke everywhere. My first time to the Poetry Café I came in the middle of someone's "reading." I made my way to the back, standing next to an improvised bar that had a few bottles of liquor and a small fridge filled with beer, and then beheld a girl on stage who was sporting a platinum-blond wig, a serious push-up bra, and declaiming *Son of a Preacher Man* from a scrap of paper. She didn't sing it, just talked the words, while moving her body in a way that Errol Flynn most certainly would have endorsed. She finished to hoots and whistles and then a guy in glasses and a string tie mounted the stage and read to us from journal entries he had made at a scholarly conference on the German philosopher Theodor Adorno. The entries were finely wrought, full of incisive observation, with great sensitivity to psychic undercurrents, and nothing happened. No one did anything. After he left the stage to relieved applause the bartender turned up the stereo which played some Della Reese, her cha-cha stuff, and I made space for the rush to the bar.

So this was the Poetry Café.

I recalled Voltaire's phrase that the Holy Roman Empire was neither holy nor Roman nor an empire.

But I mingled with the people at the bar, pal Claudius Hagemeister introduced me around, and two weeks afterward I took the stage myself and read some maiden attempts at fiction. The response was encouraging enough for me to return again a fortnight later to reel off some poetry and soon I was a regular, chalking my name on the board and doing what I could. At the time I was transitioning out of academia, so the Poetry Café was fine discipline for breaking down my unsupple expository prose and getting something readable on paper every two weeks to impress this audience of writers and would-be writers and other free spirits. When people ask if I've ever taken a creative-writing course, I will cite the Poetry Café.

Manja Müller has lived through the poem's second half, and in my mind I call her "Mathilde," after Heinrich Heine's young French wife during his Paris exile. Mathilde had no substantial grasp of German and said of her husband that he was always poeticizing but that his poetry was likely no great shakes since he was forever dissatisfied. I'm *fairly* certain that Manja never thought this kind of thing, and her English far surpasses Mathilde's German, but I liked entertaining the Heine comparison, and it holds true in a real way since Heine loved his sweetheart and would have been lost without her.

Finally I have the actor Steve McQueen to thank. As a 1960s anti-hero, McQueen was far removed from the classic Hollywood heroism embodied by the likes of Errol Flynn. But as I scribbled away at Flynn's life, McQueen was often in my thoughts—or rather his character from the movie *The Great Escape*, the unconquerable Virgil Hilts, aka "The Cooler King." These many years sitting in my German solitary confinement, i.e. my top-floor Berlin study, this American bouncing his rhymes off the unyielding walls of the *ottava rima* stanza, I could hear Hilts bouncing that baseball off the walls of his isolation cell and catching it in his mitt. Bounce-bounce-pop! Bounce-bounce-pop! Not exactly iambic pentameter, but I swear it heartened me in my less than dauntless hours.

"Coo-lah!"

"Right."

Kevin McAleer
December 2017
Berlin, Germany

Selected Books from PalmArtPress

Dennis McCort
A Kafkaesque Memoir - *Confessions from the Analytic Coach*
ISBN: 978-3-941524-94-1
474 Pages, English

Carmen-Francesca Banciu
Light Breeze in Paradise
ISBN: 978-3-941524-95-8
ca 360 Pages, English/Greek

Michael Keith
Perspective Drifts Like a Log on a River
ISBN: 978-3-941524-387-3 (EN) *
200 Pages, Pensees, Softcover, English

John Berger / Liane Birnberg
garden on my cheek
ISBN: 978-3-941524-77-4
60 Pages, Poetry/Art, Softcover/flaps, English

Carmen-Francesca Banciu
Berlin Is My Paris- *Stories from the Capital*
ISBN: 978-3-941524-66-8 *
204 Pages, English

Michael Lederer
In the Widdle Wat of Time
ISBN: 978-3-941524-70-5 *
150 Pages, poetry and very short stories, Hardcover, English

Manfred Giesler
The Yellow Wallpaper - *A Monologue*
ISBN: 978-3-941524-75-0 *
68 Pages, Theatre, open-thread cover, English/German

Dorothea Flechsig
NightSwim
ISBN: 978-3-941524-72-9
60 Pages, Poetry, Hardcover, English/German

Matéi Visniec
MIGRAAAAANTS!- *There's Too Many People on This Damn Boat*
ISBN: 978-3-96258-002-5
220 Pages, Theatre Play, English/German

Carmen-Francesca Banciu
Mother's Day - *Song of a Sad Mother*
ISBN: 978-3-941524-47-7 *
244 Pages, English

Jörg Rubbert
Paris-New York-Berlin - *Streetphotography 1978 - 2010*
ISBN: 978-3-941524-58-3
260 Pages, Photo Retrospective, Softcover/flaps, English/German

Runhild Wirth
Come Here, I Want to Ruin You!
Palast der Republik - Analysis of Dissolution
ISBN: 978-3-941524-52-1
120 Pages, Poetry/Art, Hardcover, English/German

Alexander de Cadenet
Afterbirth - *Poems & Inversions*
ISBN: 978-3-941524-59-0
64Pages, Poetry/Art, Softcover/flaps, English

Wolfgang Nieblich
Distant Yet so Near or **The Currywurst**
ISBN: 978-3-941524-49-1 (EN) *
64 Pages, 18 Coloured Fotos, Engliish

Michael Lederer
The Great Game - *Berlin-Warschau Express and Other Stories*
ISBN: 978-3-941524-12-5 (EN) *
242 Pages, 18 Short Stories, Softcover, English

Maria Reinecke
La Rambla - *Barcelona Story*
ISBN: 978-3-941524-20-0 (EN) *
91 Pages, Short Story, English

* Also available as E-Book